D0270899

SAGE has been part of the global academic community since 1965, supporting high quality research and learning that transforms society and our understanding of individuals, groups, and cultures. SAGE is the independent, innovative, natural home for authors, editors and societies who share our commitment and passion for the social sciences.

Find out more at: **www.sagepublications.com**

Intercultural Communication and Ideology

Adrian Holliday

Los Angeles | London | New Delhi
Singapore | Washington DC

SAGE Publications Ltd
1 Oliver's Yard
55 City Road
London EC1Y 1SP

SAGE Publications Inc.
2455 Teller Road
Thousand Oaks, California 91320

SAGE Publications India Pvt Ltd
B 1/I 1 Mohan Cooperative Industrial Area
Mathura Road, Post Bag 7
New Delhi 110 044

SAGE Publications Asia-Pacific Pte Ltd
33 Pekin Street #02-01
Far East Square
Singapore 048763

Library of Congress Control Number: 2010928263

British Library Cataloguing in Publication data

A catalogue record for this book is available from the
British Library

ISBN 978-1-84787-386-6
ISBN 978-1-84787-387-3 (pbk)

Typeset by C&M Digitals (P) Ltd, Chennai, India
Printed by CPI Antony Rowe, Chippenham, Wiltshire
Printed on paper from sustainable resources

MIX
Paper from
responsible sources
FSC
www.fsc.org   FSC® C013604

Contents

List of Figures

List of Tables

Preface and Methodology

This book will look at intercultural communication against the backdrop of an unequal global politics in which ideology plays a major role. It will consider the way in which popular narratives of 'culture' lead us easily and sometimes innocently to the reduction of the foreign Other as culturally deficient. Means for countering this cultural prejudice will be sought in an awareness of how culture and prejudice operate in everyday life. The aim will be the development of a sociological imagination which understands the politics of the 'us'–'them' of how culture works. It will critique a common, established idea that (a) intercultural communication is problematic because of the meeting of normally national cultures which have very different yet ostensibly equal psychological underpinnings, values and forms of communication, and that (b) the problem can be somehow solved by a close investigation of these characteristics and the subsequent education and training of the interactants. The alternative approach growing out of this critique will be that this perception of difference and its solutions is itself the product of a Centre, Western, chauvinistic ideology of superiority. This is not to deny cultural difference, nor the importance of nation, but to place it at a deeper level of complexity which transcends the fixity of a Centre-Western concept of nation.

Whether a particular chapter is about global or personal politics, the nature of culture or of communication, the discussion will be brought back to particular interpersonal instances. Examples of intercultural behaviour, based on reconstructed ethnographic observation, will provide a focus around which the discussion can be arranged and made accessible and generate suggestions for action in the investigation section at the end of each chapter. An empirical base will be provided by interviews with people caught at the intersection of cultural experience, description of intercultural events in everyday life, and the author's own personal narrative of an intercultural voyage through a series of international locations.

The book will aim to reach both academic and professional audiences. It will be suitable for undergraduates and postgraduates following degree courses in intercultural communication, and cultural studies, and a range of professionals undertaking training in intercultural communication.

It will also inform trainers, lecturers, theorists and researchers. Each chapter will attempt to satisfy the interests of this broad readership. Although firm outcomes will be presented, the overall tenor of the book will be to involve the reader in an exploration of issues that face us all in everyday life.

Chapter 2 presents a methodology for learning how to avoid prejudice in more effective intercultural understanding, which will be used throughout the book. While this is employed implicitly in the discussion of experiences and texts in each chapter, it is present in explicit form in the extended investigation section at the end of each chapter in which readers are invited to carry out intercultural investigations based on the principles discussed in the chapter in question. An important aspect of the tasks is a movement from discussion of intercultural issues at the more expected national level to what goes on between people generally, wherever they are and wherever they come from. This movement represents an important principle, promoted throughout the book, that intercultural issues and the connection with ideology and indeed race are all around us within every society. The investigatory tasks are thus intended to generate discussion and to introduce a sense of problem-solving throughout the book, and the application of a strong interpretive methodology for critical cultural awareness. Each investigatory section concludes with planning an intercultural orientation session.

Research Methodology

As well as presenting a methodology for critical cultural awareness, the book is also the product of social research. This does not pretend to be objective in the commonly understood scientific sense; indeed its significance is that it breaks from the established, largely linguistic methods of intercultural communication studies. I employ a postmodern, critical qualitative approach to the analysis of interview data, the details of which are described in Chapter 3. The interviewees are all middle class, often academics, expert users of English, and personally known to me. They were handpicked for their engagement with cultural boundaries in their lives. However, the remarkable commonality of the overall nature of cultural complexity which they expressed led me to suspect that there was an indication of universality that might be found in any group. Another important point is that, as is implicit in qualitative research, I do not claim representativeness of a larger population but intend simply to raise sufficient discussion to interrogate established views. In my treatment of interview data I not only select themes which seem to me to be significant, but also group them in one of a range of possible ways and then claim significance in that. The rigour is in the cautious self-consciousness with which I do this, and in the recognition of the way it makes sense within a broader thick description. The validity is also in the resounding fact that what these informants had to say deeply shook the assumptions with which I began the book. While I began with the intention of completely overthrowing the notion of national culture, they led me into unexpected areas of understanding and to acknowledge the cultural realism – the power of national influences which is nevertheless mediated by powerful personal cultural realities – which forms the basis of my approach. A difficult task was to steer a coherent line of discussion through the immense complexity of material which they produced. Readers will wonder why I did not pause more to talk about the broader issues of identity which they raise. Researchers will also be aware of the need to strike a balance between multiplying themes and a single agenda if they are ever going to finish what they have to say. There is therefore a richness emerging from my informants, and also from my other examples, which has a life of its own and from which readers will develop their own impressions and trajectories. The investigations at the end of each chapter are just the beginning of an invitation for such personal exploration.

The truth about culture is extremely difficult to get at. Running through my discussion is a mistrust of established methods and the illusions which they create. The task is therefore to find alternative, more creative methods which dig beneath the surface – to find the hidden and counter-cultures of the Periphery with which to shake the Centre image. To understand how complex, unrecognized identities negotiate dominant social and political orders, researchers need to use creative methodologies such as personal narratives, diaries, popular culture and media.

Central to this creativity is my use of reconstructed narratives and extracts from fictional literature. Fiction is particularly significant in that where it is good it represents acute observation of a complexity of social life (e.g. Goffman 1972: 79, 240). Indeed, the good novelist's intention to present a richness of experience from which readers can enter into their own explorations succeeds in working beyond the established imaginations about cultural description.

The reconstructed narratives are based on diverse prior experiences which are distilled into consolidated texts and enable the exploration of ethnographic realities which are difficult to capture by more established means. They are also simply stories, or allegories, which represent sets of personal experiences for the purpose of generating discussion. Like much qualitative data, none of which can escape subjectivity, the major purpose of each story is to make one think again about established truths. Within this sort of reflection a number of observations emerge. I take the writing style for each narrative from Kubota's (2003) deconstruction of cultural understanding through a reconstructed conversation between three friends. The act of writing these narratives was in itself a process of making sense of data. They were written with the same disciplines as other ethnographic writing – trying to be as faithful as possible to what I perceive to have happened – which are explored explicitly in Chapter 2. As with the statements of my informants, these narratives took on lives of their own. Each reconstructed narrative is analysed by means of what I term categories of cultural action. While it may be suspected that the narratives were constructed to suit the categories, in effect, the categories grew out of the narratives in dialogue with what emerged from my informants, and in turn helped me to make new sense out of prior research. The fuller description of the workings of culture in Chapter 6 had an early version in an elaboration of the categories and was then developed through further thinking about my 'small culture' idea from the late 1990s. From this emerged the idea of *underlying universal cultural processes*; but this idea did not take root as a major tenet of the book until what emerged as important in the process of writing the Qing and the seminar narrative, now in Chapter 8.

The book was not therefore written chapter by chapter, but tended to emerge as an unruly whole to be painfully organized and reorganized quite a number of times. A major task has been that which faces many research students – what to say before what and how to say something which cannot be said until after something else has been said. Unlike most doctoral theses, in a book of this nature substantive content needs to be present in every chapter. Because a major part of this content is suggestions for analysing cultural interaction, the categories of cultural action need to be presented early even though they do not emerge until late. The sacrifice is an appearance of circularity.

The majority of examples are very largely connected with the Middle East, often Iran, or China and the Far East. This is partly because of my personal familiarity and contact with these regions, but also because they represent major current preoccupations. Looking out from the Centre-West, concerned with what causes it to think about the foreign Other in the way that it does, the relationship with the Middle East, and more specifically with Islam, has become a 'symbolic battleground' of cultural identity (Delanty et al., 2008a: 10). Iran is a particularly important aspect of this because of the added politics of confrontation and the struggles for modernity within its own structures. At the same time China and the Far East are playing a particularly significant part in the internationalization of Western education and business (Reid et al., 2009). I nevertheless intend that principles gained from these examples can be generalized to other intercultural scenarios.

Notes on Presentation

For ease of reading I have placed most of my references to other research and literature in notes at the end of each chapter, leaving in the main text only the references which I make active use of. Throughout I use three dots (...) in citations to indicate missing text. Where these are enclosed in square brackets ([...]) the dots are in the citation itself.

Acknowledgements

An immense debt needs to go to the 32 informants who gave their time to respond to my questions by email and face-to-face interview. Most of them remain anonymous in how they appear in the text. While some of them do not appear in the text, they are all present in the thinking that helped to form the book. I am therefore grateful to Alba Miranda, Andrea Emara, Anne Swan, Ashleigh Stewart, Brieg Powel, Burkhard Scherer, Christopher Trillo, Emine Merdin, Farzad Sharifian, Fidel Cakmak, Geraldine Ward, Gu Qing, Haesoon Kim, Hazel Yilmazoğlu, Helen Potter, Jenny de Sonneville, Katharina Urbantat, Mario Saraceni, Peyvand Khorsandi, P.J. Coke, Priyali Ghosh, Rigas Goulimaris, Ritu Mahendru, Sadia Ali, Salah Troudi, Sarah Khan, Simon Gieve, Stefania Ciocia, Stephanie Vandrick, Duan Yuping, and Trish Flynn. I would also like to thank Alireza Janshidnejad, Ayesha Kamal, B. Kumaravadivelu, Bojana Petrić, Chris Anderson, Dikaia Chatziefstathiou, Elaheh Rostami-Povey, Irasema Mora, Jo Angouri, Linden West, Pamela Aboshiha, Robert Johnson, Sara Alavi, Shabnam Holliday, Shane Blackman, Viv Griffiths, and Zhu Hua for contributing in different ways, and in particular to Anne Swan, Paul Hudson, Bill Sughrua, Cathie Wallace, César Cisneros-Puebla and Richard Fay for comments that changed the direction of the text. A very large debt is to the immense inspiration from the work and eternal friendship of Mehri Honarbin-Holliday.

1

Key Discussions

In this book I will present culture and intercultural communication as movable concepts with fluid and negotiable boundaries. While national structures are important and influential in framing our lives, they do not confine or explain some very important aspects of our cultural behaviour. The book will explore the possibility of significant underlying universal processes which provide people from all cultural backgrounds with the potential to dialogue with and transcend national structures, to cross boundaries and contribute to and enrich cultural practices wherever they find them. This cosmopolitan potential may well have always been there; but it is becoming increasingly evident within a globalized world.

There is, however, another side. Theories of culture are also employed by social groups to construct ideological imaginations both of themselves and others. I will argue that this takes place in everyday life and in the academy, and that current common and established theories of culture are ideological in nature. This relationship with ideology is complex, for it may also be argued that constructing imagined theories of culture is an innate part of the way in which to be is at the same time an artefact of their cultural make-up. Investigating the relationship between culture and ideology is therefore not simply to untangle fact from fiction but also to understand more deeply the workings of culture itself.

The concept of discourse is used as an instrument of analysis throughout the book. It is at the level of discourse that individuals are able to negotiate, make sense of and practise culture; and it is within this process that imaginations about culture are generated and ideology is both experienced and manufactured. It is from an interrogation of the discourses of and about culture that the book builds a new 'grammar' of culture and suggests its implications for understanding a cosmopolitan world.

The relationship between ideology and culture cannot, however, be left as an aspect of how culture works. Ideological imaginations of culture very often lead to the demonization of a particular foreign Other. While it is very clear that this Othering happens at all levels of national and international life everywhere in the world, I shall focus on the Western imagination for three reasons. First, the majority of the established theories of culture within the academy derive from Western sources. Second, the West is the major driving force in current global politics, operating from a position of political, economic and cultural dominance in relation to the rest of the world, and these theories of culture impact on the desire to export 'democracy' and somehow 'improve' the imagined culturally deficient non-West. While people are Othered in all walks of life, the global politics which is dominated by the West permanently positions large parts of the world. Significant here is Kumaravadivelu's (2007b) statement that a major feature of the 20th century was the West defining the rest of the world – a state of affairs which I feel still continues, and which is (has been) embedded in history to the extent that it is very hard to undo.

Third, Western theories of culture also demonstrate a high degree of *denial* of ideology. In the academy there is a powerful emphasis on the scientific neutrality of theories of culture, and in recent years the sub-discipline of intercultural communication has claimed to move away from Othering. In society generally there is the major irony that the West claims a high degree of awareness and understanding. Hence the primary research question which the book seeks to answer – how is it possible that, in such a climate of sensitivity towards people from other cultural backgrounds, there is still such a lack of awareness and understanding?

To address these issues I will adopt a critical cosmopolitan approach in which common perceptions of culture are recognized as being ideological and constructed by political interest. While there will be a postmodern orientation, in appreciating that the many established 'truths' about culture are in fact socially constructed, there will also be an acknowledgement of cultural realism in that there *is* a cultural truth which is hidden by these ideological constructions. This will be supported by empirical investigation involving interviews with 32 informants from a wide range of national locations across the world and with reconstructed ethnographic accounts and evidence from the media and literary fiction. This fits with the critical cosmopolitan view that there are unrecognized cultural realities which have been pushed to the margins by Western definitions, and that it is therefore from the margins that we must learn the real nature of culture (Hall, 1991b).

At a practical level, the success of intercultural communication will not be modelled around awareness of and sensitivity to the essentially different behaviours and values of 'the other culture', but around the employment of the ability to read culture which derives from underlying universal cultural processes.

The discussion of culture and intercultural communication is difficult at all times. The approach taken in this book is further problematized by the insurmountable dangers of falling into the same trap of overgeneralization and Othering that is being addressed. The terminology – 'the West' and 'the non-West', 'Centre' and 'Periphery'– which any discussion of global Othering has to employ, is clumsy and creates a seductive ease which could paper over the complexity that I am trying to represent. It is hoped, however, that the necessary sense of complexity will be rectified in the breadth of examples and issues posed.

In this chapter I will rehearse some of the major themes which underpin a critical discussion of culture. The discussion of essentialism and non-essentialism will be traced back to established theories of national cultural difference and how they have been sustained in current views within the academy. The familiar themes of individualism and collectivism will be critiqued as basic icons of an idealized Self and a demonized Other, to be interrogated further throughout the book. The critical cosmopolitan approach, which recognizes the influence of ideology and the marginalization of non-Western cultural realities, will then be introduced to counter these discussions.

Chapter 2 will present the interpretivist methodology for a critical intercultural awareness which supports the critical cosmopolitan approach and enables a non-aligned reading of culture. The concept of critical reading and categories of cultural action will be introduced, to form the basis of cultural awareness tasks throughout the book. Chapter 3 will make the first reference to my major data set of interviews and use them to establish a cultural complexity which begins with the individual and presents a cross-cutting dialogue with national structures. This picture of culture will be aligned with the social action theory of Max Weber and set in contrast to the structural-functionalism of Emile Durkheim which has been the basis of established essentialist thinking.

Chapter 4 will look in detail at how the deep narratives of an idealized Western Self have penetrated everyday life and lead to a demonization of a non-Western Other. The strength and sustainability of these narratives as apparently positive, sensitive and 'helping' will be located in a liberal multiculturalist ideology which denies the chauvinism implicit in the individualism–collectivism divide and persists in a disbelief of non-Western cultural proficiency. Chapter 5 will present the alternative, Periphery narrative of the non-Western Other struggling to establish visibility against the dominant imagination of the Centre-West. The purpose here will not be to speak for the Periphery, whose arguments are well rehearsed in postcolonialist theory, but to unpick the common narratives of modernity and Westernization which continue to cast the foreign as only able to succeed through learning the values of the West. The basic tenet that one does not have to be Westernized to be modern will be established.

Chapter 6 will pull together observations regarding the nature of culture from previous chapters in order to construct an alternative grammar of culture which indicates the loose, negotiated relationship between the *particularities* of national structures and cultural resources and the *universality* of small culture formation at a discoursal level. Chapter 7 will continue with the notion of discourse in small culture formation and explore how within everyday and professional contexts it can also work to generate cultural disbelief in the foreign Other. The notion of an uncrossable line between Self and Other and the resulting concept of the third space will be critiqued as discoursal products of this disbelief.

Chapter 8 will explore the more positive, creative side of small culture formation in order to make sense of the behaviour of cultural newcomers. The discoursal strategies which they employ will be explored. The phenomena of silence and withdrawal will be framed as strategies of resistance; and the principle of transferring cultural experience from familiar to unfamiliar settings can enable newcomers to change and enrich the practices which they find. Chapter 9 will conclude with a discussion of the relationship between the imagined and real cultural worlds discussed throughout the book. This will be set within a framework of cultural realism in which the social construction of culture is related to a false consciousness.

The rest of this chapter will introduce some basic concepts that structure this discussion and indicate issues which will be developed in the rest of the book.

Essentialism

I shall begin with essentialism because it is commonly felt to be a bad thing, and yet, as I shall argue, continues to sit at the centre of common perceptions of culture both in the academy and in everyday life. Essentialism presents people's individual behaviour as entirely defined and constrained by the cultures in which they live so that the stereotype becomes the essence of who they are.[1]

The most common aspects of essentialism are listed on the left of Table 1, and are to do with separate cultures as physical territories. Much of this essentialism will seem natural and normal because it is in many ways the default way of thinking about how we are different from each other. There is, however, only a short, easy distance from this apparently objective essentialist thinking to chauvinistic statements such as 'in Middle Eastern culture there is no concept of individualized critical thinking'. As I shall demonstrate later, this statement carries a moralistic judgement because of the positive status given to 'individualized critical thinking' in the mind of the speaker. This statement *Others* Middle Eastern people in the sense that they are lumped together as though all the same under a grossly simplistic, exaggerated and homogeneous, imagined, single culture. In Chapter 4 I shall explore in detail the indelible manner in which such Othering persists from an excuse for colonizing foreign societies into the present day. The discourse of Othering is so powerful that anyone who does not fit the essentialist definition is thought to be not a 'real' Chinese, Arab, Muslim or whatever; and in the case of non-Western cultures it is thought that they must be 'westernized' to have left their true nature behind. The serious implication here is that people are not allowed to step outside their designated cultural places.

Table 1   Essentialism and non-essentialism[7]

Essentialist view of culture	Non-essentialist view of culture
A physical place with evenly spread traits and membership	A social force which is evident where it is significant
Associated with a country and a language	Complex, with difficult to pin down characteristics
Has an onion-skin relationship with larger continental, religious, ethnic or racial cultures, and smaller sub-cultures	Can relate to any type or size of group for any period of time, and can be characterized by a discourse as much as by a language
Mutually exclusive with other national cultures. People in one culture are essentially different from people in another	Can flow, change, intermingle, cut across and through each other, regardless of national frontiers, and have blurred boundaries
What people say	
'I visited three cultures while on holiday. They were Spain, Morocco and Tunisia.'	'There was something culturally different about each of the countries I visited.'
'When crossing from Japanese culture to Chinese culture …', 'People from Egypt cannot … when they arrive in French culture'	'There is evidence of a more homogeneous culture of food in … than in ….' 'Private secondary schools in … tend to have a more evident culture of sport than state secondary schools in ….'
	'The culture of … in some businesses in … is changing.' 'The rapid influx of immigrants from … is having an impact on the work culture in the high street.'

Whereas essentialism, on the left of Table 1 , claims certainty about what sort of people can be found where, non-essentialism, on the right of the table, presents a more complex picture which is less easy to talk about. The statements are more cautious and shrink from pinning down the nature of individual cultures. There are serious disciplines implicit in these restrained statements, which I shall look at in detail in Chapter 2.

Neo-essentialism

While appreciating the artificiality of such dichotomies, and that there will be many positions in between and crossovers, I am going to base the discussions in this book around two basic paradigms – *neo-essentialism* and *critical cosmopolitanism*. I use the term neo-essentialism to refer to the dominant approach within the sub-discipline of intercultural communication studies which follows the essentialist and highly influential work of theorists such as Hofstede, while claiming a more liberal, non-essentialist vision. Critical cosmopolitanism is an established movement within sociology which I shall describe below. I will first briefly critique the work of Hofstede, and then demonstrate how neo-essentialism has developed from the type of thinking which he promotes.

The Hofstedian legacy

While the problems with essentialism are generally accepted, the temptation to be essentialist is quite deeply rooted in a long-standing desire to 'fix' the nature of culture and cultural difference. A particularly influential example is in the work of Hofstede. Based on data from IBM subsidiaries in 72 countries in 1968 and 1972 (Hofstede, 2001: x), Hofstede's model presents culture 'as a collective programming of the mind that distinguishes the members of one group or category of people from another' (ibid.: 9). Hofstede does acknowledge the dangers of ethnocentric stereotypes such as 'all Dutch people are honest' (ibid.: 14) and recognizes that a culture can be 'any human collectivity or category: a profession, an age group, an entire gender, or a family' (ibid.: 10). Nevertheless there is a tight comparison between national cultures as complete and self-sufficient social systems (ibid.). Each system governs the way in which the behaviour of individuals can be 'scored' within 'dimensions' such as power–distance, uncertainty–avoidance, individualism–collectivism, masculinity–femininity and long-term–short-term orientation (ibid.: 29).[2]

Despite sustained criticism of Hofstede's now ageing over-simplification of complex realities,[3] the systematic nature of his work has sustained theory building for more than 25 years, with his basic text going into further editions (2001, 2003). His 'macro-level laws' (Hofstede, 2001: 28) have been particularly attractive to intercultural communication theorists and trainers faced with what is considered to be an increase in international interaction during the past 20 years with the advent of globalization.[4] They provide the certainty of precise, tightly measurable behavioural formulae for how to act in the presence of people from specific cultural groups and the reassurance that one can calculate how to greet, for example, a Swedish business man on the basis of prescribed information about 'Swedish culture'.

Incomplete rejection of essentialism

Much current work in intercultural communication studies rejects essentialism and cultural overgeneralization and acknowledges cultural diversity. However, this work remains neo-essentialist because important essentialist elements are still maintained. While it does address a rich complexity that goes beyond national categories and deals with the smaller cultures or discourses of business or educational organizations, and so on, the same items of literature are invariably pulled back towards the traditional, essentialist use of national cultures as the basic unit, either employing Hofstedian categories of difference or others like them.[5] Behaviour which goes against national stereotypes is therefore nearly always framed as an exception to the essentialist rule rather than as a reality in its own right.

What I feel is implicit in the inconsistency of such neo-essentialist studies may be described as a *liberal–essentialist duality*. The liberal side of the duality represents Western society's genuine desire to oppose cultural chauvinism. The essentialist side represents its inability to recognize this cultural chauvinism within its own structure due to an inherent lack of criticality.[6] It may well be that this is a natural state of affairs, where essentialism is necessary for the tribalist survival of any group of people whether or not it has liberal intentions; and this may be the reason why for criticality to be sustained in any society it should not be too radical. This may go far to explain why it is possible to demonstrate political anger but not finally to change anything, for example the lack of action following massive anti-war demonstrations in London in 2002. The liberal–essentialist duality relates to a well-known critique of multiculturalism which will be described in Chapter 4. It may, however, run further and deeper than generally acknowledged, which is a difficult issue for intellectual elements of Western society who pride themselves on their critical support of the oppressed.

Figure 1 attempts a dangerously simplistic architecture of the ease with which a liberal intention sits alongside chauvinism. The inconsistency of essentialism, on the right of the figure, as already seen with Hofstede above, enables chauvinistic description [d] to be hidden by the apparent neutrality of description and the denial of ideology [c].[9] By *neutral* I mean a matter of technical fact or science which is therefore presumed devoid of chauvinism. By *ideology* I mean a system of ideas that promote the interests of a particular group of people.[10] (While ideology will be a focus of my discussion throughout, its specific role in culture formation will be discussed in Chapter 6.)

Liberalism		Essentialism	
a) Acceptance of diversity	b) The desire for truth and fairness	c) Belief in the neutrality of and the denial of ideology in cultural description	d) Chauvinistic description

Figure 1   The liberal–essentialist duality [8]

While the liberal ideal might morally dislike this degree of generalization, its desire for truth and fairness [b] feeds well, across a thick but porous line, on 'neutral' essentialist description because it needs something solidly different to be fair and truthful about. Diversity is thus accepted [a] as exception to an essentialist rule, distant though this rule might be. Neo-essentialist intercultural studies, as the scientific face of liberalism, also depend on the neutrality of description [c] to build theories about culture.

Shuter (2008: 38) argues that such theories thrive on tightly specialist concepts such as 'uncertainty reduction', 'initial interaction', 'intercultural communication competence', 'communication apprehension', 'intercultural adaptation' and 'relationship development'. Kumaravadivelu (2007a: 68) makes a similar point about the proliferation of technical terms such as 'accommodation, acculturation, adaptation, adoption, assimilation, enculturation, integration'. The need to get involved in such technical detail makes it hard for career academics to break away and address what Hall (1991a) and Hannerz (1991) refer to as the uncomfortable politics of global inequality. The liberal–essentialist duality thus represents a hybridity of critical awarenesses which is weakened by career research imperatives that depend on established scientific paradigms. Moon (2008: 15) notes the increased interest in tightly defined national cultures during the accountability regime of the Reagan and Thatcher era of the 1980s.

Individualism and collectivism

The common cultural labels of individualism and collectivism play a particularly powerful role in the neo-essentialist denial of ideology. These are most commonly associated with Triandis' (1995) classic text. They are presented as neutral labels for two 'prototypes' of national culture (Triandis, 2004: ix). While he acknowledges that both prototypes exist to varying degrees in all countries, it is well known in intercultural studies and training that they tend to be located in specific geographical locations. 'People from *individualist cultures*' are presented as 'North Americans of European backgrounds, North and West Europeans, Australians, New Zealanders', who perceive themselves as autonomous and prioritize personal over group goals. They prize linear progression, personal improvement, achievement, assertiveness, self-reliance, consistency, being open to new experiences, having fun and equal distribution of resources. Silence is associated with anger, bad mood or low competence. Face is personal. They like to have many choices of group membership, and they are good at making new relationships. According to one study, they prefer to ski alone. In contrast, 'people from *collectivist cultures*' are presented as 'Latin Americans, Southern Europeans, East and South Asians, Africans'. They perceive themselves primarily as group members with strong group loyalty and interdependence. They favour group members over outsiders. They prize stability, where norms and obligations do not change. They think in a circular manner. They think that silence is a virtue. Face is derived from the group. They are satisfied with very few choices, are members of few in-groups, with the family as the most important, of which they are members by right of birth or marriage. They find new relationships difficult. A recent study showed that they prefer to ski together (ibid.: x–xi).

However, despite the claim to neutrality, it seems clear that individualism represents imagined positive characteristics, and collectivism represents imagined negative characteristics. Individualism relates precisely to the geographical location associated with the Centre-West. Min-Sun Kim (2005: 108) insists that the collectivism label constructs non-Western people as 'barbarians'. Indeed, it is hard to imagine that associating individualism with being consistent, open to new experiences, having fun and self-reliance, and collectivism with circular thinking, being closed to new experiences and deferential to group tradition, can be anything but the projection of a positively imagined Self on a negatively imagined Other.[11] Evidence that the collectivism description relates more to a generalized notion of low achievement, rather than to specific national cultural groups, is evidenced by the fact that the same descriptions are used of low-achieving mainstream American schoolchildren (Kubota, 2001). Triandis (2006: 29) himself gives away his own association between collectivism and deficiency when he connects it with 'poverty', societies with '*only* one normative system' (emphasis added), which are 'not cosmopolitan', and with the 'lower social classes of any society' or among people who 'have not travelled', not 'been socially mobile' or who 'have not been exposed to the modern mass media'.

However, Min-Sun Kim (2005: 109) follows the neo-essentialist paradigm by quickly withdrawing from her attack with a reassessment of how the individualism–collectivism division can still be used as though a neutral set of categories. She may consider her reassessment to be a solution; but, in my view, realigning a concept that has chauvinism implicated within it simply shifts the issue elsewhere.

Far from being a neutral cultural quality, in the 1940s, 1950s and 1960s collectivism was associated with totalitarianism, 'closed societies' and the political curtailment of the human right of individualism. In *The Open Society and its Enemies*, Karl Popper states that collectivism is a doctrine that emphasizes the power of the collective over the individual (1966: 9, note 1) and inequality (ibid.: 99). It is perceived as an imposed order rather than as a cultural quality. While Popper does associate individualism with 'Western civilization' and Christianity, and collectivism with the political ideology of 'tribalism' (ibid.: 102) – not to be confused with tribe – he by no means sees this as an exclusive and fixed relationship, making it clear that Christianity imposed collectivism during the Inquisition and has the potential to do so again in the future (ibid.: 104). Similarly, individualism as a political strategy rather than a cultural quality is evident in Stråth's (2008: 22) observation that the individualist ideal of the liberal European nation state does not extend itself to immigrants from the non-West.

Popper also takes care to distinguish individualism from egoism and collectivism from unselfishness (1966: 100) and makes the point that Plato, in his construction of 'the Republic' as a perfect collectivist society, wrongly associates individualism with selfishness (ibid.: 101). We need to take the same sort of care in our use of these terminologies.

What the individualism-collectivism distinction does provide, however, is at least a hint of an imagined division in the minds of those who use it of something approaching a geographical division between the 'West' and the 'non-West'. These terms have a problematically unclear nature, hovering between geography and psychological concept, to the extent that it is impossible to use them in a logical, consistent manner, while at the same time using them is unavoidable because they are on everyone's lips. I feel I have no choice but to use them throughout the book, albeit in this unsatisfactory manner. There will, however, be an attempt to address them head-on in Chapter 5.

Cosmopolitanism

Imagining individualism and collectivism to be neutral cultural categories is thus a serious misrepresentation. To find an acknowledgement of the ideological forces that underpin such notions of culture it is necessary to go to the very different paradigm of critical cosmopolitanism. This derives largely from outside intercultural communication studies – from within a broader sociological and anthropological viewpoint. Writers within this movement say that the world is not neatly divided into national categories, but that boundaries are increasingly blurred and negotiable. There is a recognition of the complexity of cultural realities, and of the normality of behaviour which the neo-essentialists would consider exceptions to the rule.[12] There is an image of a vast complex of shifting, overlapping, swirling, combining and splitting discourses and literacies. In one sense this complexity and blurring of boundaries is connected with the advance of globalization and the movement of people. However, while globalization is often cited as a recent phenomenon, one only needs to read Herodotus (1972) to see a picture of 5th-century BC Greece in which cultural artefacts as basic as the gods are traced both in naming and character through a globalized relationship with North Africa and Asia.

There is a recognition that the preoccupation with national culture derives from a *methodological nationalism* that has dominated social science and created an oversimplistic impression of the way in which the world is organized. This stems from a 19th-century vision of European nation states and 'blinds' us to 'the multi-dimensional process of change' (Beck and Sznaider, 2006: 2).[13]

Global cosmopolitanism

However, not all cosmopolitanism manages to escape from neo-essentialism. Homi Bhabha warns us against a 'global cosmopolitanism' which imagines a globalized world from a 'nice' Centre-Western perspective:

> that configures the planet as a concentric world of national socie-
> ties extending to global villages. It is a cosmopolitanism of relative
> prosperity and privilege founded on ideas of progress. ... Global
> cosmopolitans of this ilk [that] frequently inhabit 'imagined com-
> munities' that consist of silicon valleys and software campuses ...
> call centres ... sweat shops ... readily celebrates a world of plural
> cultures and peoples located at the periphery, as long as they pro-
> duce a healthy profit margin. (Bhabha, 1994: xiv)

This Centre-constructed world defines 'proper' social life and is associated with the rhetoric of 'you are with us or against us' (ibid.: xvi) with which we are familiar in recent US foreign policy with regard to the militaristic spear of 'democracy'. Canagarajah (1999: 207–9) suggests that global cosmopolitanism presents an irresponsi-bly romantic and playful image which ignores inequality and seeks to obliterate the voice of the Periphery.[14]

The terms Centre and Periphery, like 'West' and 'non-West', need to be used with caution. For me Centre and Periphery only make sense as psychological concepts, though they are clearly related to West and non-West, which do have a geographical aspect as suggested above. Hannerz (1991) defines the relationship between Centre and Periphery as one of imposing and taking meaning within an unequal global order. This can apply strategically or emotionally to different groups of people, events or attitudes at different times. I will refer to the Centre-West as the economic and political powerhouse of the Centre within its current Western location. I shall explore the concept of the West in some detail in Chapter 5.

Critical cosmopolitanism

The critical cosmopolitanists therefore insist that Periphery cultural realities should be allowed room to express themselves in resist-ance to the dominant global cosmopolitan imagination. Homi Bhabha refers to this emergent Periphery voice as a 'vernacular cosmopolitanism which measures global progress from the minori-tarian perspective' and which 'begins at home' (1994: xv–xvi). Canagarajah (1999: 207–9) proposes that this Periphery cosmopoli-tanism 'has always been there in non-Western communities' with villagers dealing easily across small linguistic boundaries; but that it has largely been destroyed by colonial powers that have 'divided these communities arbitrarily into nation-states for their convenience'. Stuart Hall speaks of a revolution which is already taking place at the margins to reclaim conceptual space in a 'bottom-up' 'de-centred' process of change:

> The most profound cultural revolution has come about as a consequence of the ... margins coming into representation ... not just to be placed by the regime of some other, or imperializing eye but to reclaim some form of representation for themselves. ... Marginality has become a powerful space. It is a space of weak power but it is a space of power ... for the discourses of the dominant regimes, have been certainly threatened by this de-centred cultural empowerment of the marginal and the local. (1991a: 34)[15]

This critical cosmopolitan viewpoint thus places the issue of culture firmly within a global political arena. This view is encapsulated within King's edited volume, *Culture, Globalization and the World-System* (1991b), which includes Hall and Hannerz cited earlier in this chapter. The phenomenon of national culture is itself dependent on such forces in different ways in different places. For example, Hall (1991a: 20) suggests that the notion of British national culture is in decline because the old idea of 'English identity' can no longer be tied rigidly to a Protestant ethic due to the influence of 'global mass culture'. This does not, however, belittle the 'reality' of nation as a significant ideological force. Another key text, which I shall draw upon throughout the book, is Delanty et al.'s (2008b) *Identity, Belonging and Migration*, which deals with the dominant Western discourses of culture and race.

Imagined Certainty versus Acknowledged Complexity

Table 2 summarizes the two paradigms and lists concepts which will be picked up in later chapters. The more traditional and established neo-essentialism is marked by the definitions and certainties which make it so sustainable, while critical cosmopolitanism represents a complexity which is in a process of negotiation at every level within an unequal world which is marked by ideology.

There are some interesting but significant twists in the difference between critical cosmopolitanism and neo-essentialism. Critical cosmopolitanism is *postmodern* in the manner in which it sees ideology in everything and does not accept the stated neutrality of neo-essentialism, which appears *modernist* in its projection of

Table 2 Images of culture

	Neo-essentialism	Critical cosmopolitanism
Culture	National culture remains the basic unit Diversity is the exception to the rule	Non-essentialist Acknowledges a fluid complexity with blurred boundaries Diversity is the norm
Approach	Modernist – ideology only exists within the culture that is being described (Chapter 3) Liberal multiculturalism – different but equal national and ethnic cultures (Chapter 4) Cultural relativism – the protection of difference Positivist – a priori neutral cultural chorocteristics drive the analysis (Chapter 3)	Postmodern – both the subject and the methodology of investigation are ideologically constructed Recognition of deep Centre–Periphery inequality Emergent Periphery cultural realities struggling for recognition Contestation of principles Interpretivist – observation open to emergent, complex realities (Chapter 3)
The world	Global cosmopolitanism – globalization defined by the Centre image of a global political and economic order	Vernacular cosmopolitanism The Periphery claiming the world
Intercultural concerns	'Us' comparing 'our' culture with 'theirs'	All parties looking critically at cultural texts everywhere (Chapter 2)

a neatly organized world with accountable theories of difference. Critical cosmopolitanism thus takes inspiration from Kuhn's (1970) *The Structure of Scientific Revolutions* which blew apart the modernist illusion that science was neutral. He argues that the development of paradigms in science is influenced by the academic politics and the ideologies of schools of thought. Any statement that a description of culture is neutral and untouched by ideology thus appears naïve.

However, much postmodernism is accused of cultural relativism – the view that because there are no hard realities there is no basis on which to judge one culture to be better or more moral than another. Cultural relativism is ironically the stated position of neo-essentialism – that we should respect other cultures for what they are. An example of this is in the common preoccupation of language educators from the English-speaking West – 'we shouldn't expect *them* to be autonomous like *us*; we should respect *their* culture for not allowing it' (Holliday, 2004a, 2005: 82). However, from a critical cosmopolitanism point of view this is Othering and patronizing – to deny the foreign Other the possibility of autonomy, which in one way or another is a universal. Critical cosmopolitanism instead requires a 'self-problematization and the discursive examination of all claims', not keeping cultures separate, but 'promoting openness and public contestation', even of religion (Delanty, 2008: 92–3). I take this to mean that, while it is inappropriate to imagine the deficiencies of a whole culture, as is the case in the construction of collectivism, it is healthy to consider the instrumental efficiency or moral implications of a particular cultural practice. In Chapter 2 I will refer to business meetings between British and Chinese colleagues. If the traditional manner of conducting a meeting on *either* side is considered by relevant parties to be counterproductive or discriminatory against members, then this has to be addressed. Keeping from criticizing a practice because it is 'cultural' can only be patronizing, in assuming that individuals on *either* side are unable to move on from tradition. It needs to be remembered here that there can be complacency and ignorance of underlying prejudice even in practices that are constructed by their participants as 'progressive'. This seemingly harsh imperative of contestation will influence the disciplines in the methodology for intercultural understanding in Chapter 2.

Summary

The following points have been made:

- It is not possible to fix the nature of particular 'cultures' and then work out how best to help people to communicate between them. Although nations each provide structures which influence us differently, there are underlying cultural abilities that provide us all with the potential to expand and move across boundaries.
- There is a global politics that leads us to imagine that foreign cultures are such that their 'members' are less capable than 'we' are. The task in hand is to recognize individual potential against the deep and often invisible prejudice that such imaginations create.
- It is generally acknowledged that we must not indulge in essentialist Othering. We must not consider people's individual behaviour to be entirely defined and constrained by the cultures in which they live so that the stereotype becomes the essence of who they are.
- While dominant approaches in intercultural studies oppose essentialism, they remain neo-essentialist because they fall back on prescribed national cultural descriptions. These descriptions are seductive because they are convenient for theory building in the academy, and provide accountable solutions in intercultural communication

training. There is a prevailing liberal-essentialist duality in which liberal attempts at countering prejudice deny ideology. An example of this is the individualism-collectivism distinction which appears neutral but is in effect chauvinistic.

• A solution is a decentred, critical cosmopolitanism. The Centre-West must withdraw from imposing its own definitions and allow space for the Periphery to express its own cultural realities in its own terms.

Notes

1   Critiques of essentialism are well established (e.g. Dobbin, 1994; Grimshaw, 2007; Holliday, 1999, 2005: 17; Jensen, 2006; Keesing, 1994).

2   See also Hall's (e.g. 1976) influential concepts of 'high' and 'low' context cultures, later developed by Trompenaars (e.g. 2007).

3   Critiques of Hofstede are well established (e.g. Bond et al., 2000: 52–3; Fleming and Søborg, 2004; Gooderham and Nordhaug, 2004; McSweeny, 2002; Søndergaard, 2004).

4   See the following discussions of the increase in attention to intercultural issues: Kramsch (2005: 551), Moon (2008: 11), Pearce (2005: 36) and Reid et al. (2009: 4).

5   There are a number of examples of works beginning with anti-essentialist statements and then moving on to use potentially essentialist categories (e.g. Ellis and Moaz, 2006; Gudykunst et al., 2005; Jandt, 2001; M.-S. Kim, 2005; Y.Y. Kim, 2005, 2006; Pearce, 2005; Philipsen et al., 2005; Scollon and Scollon, 2001; Spencer-Oatey and Xing, 2000; Triandis, 2004).

6   See the following discussions of the lack of criticality in Western liberalism: Delanty et al. (2008a: 14), Jordan and Weedon (1995) and Y.Y. Kim (2005).

7   Source for Table 1: adapted from Holliday et al. (2010: 3).

8   Source for Figure 1: Holliday and Aboshiha (2009: 682).

9   See also the similar dichotomy between ideology and autonomy (Clark and Ivanič, 1997: 57; Street, 1984).

10   Other definitions of ideology include 'a set of ideas put to work in the justification and maintenance of vested interests' (Spears, 1999: 19), 'a system of ideas with powerful sex appeal' (Gellner, 2005: 2) – of course to the people who promote it – and communication which is 'systematically distorted' or 'bent out of shape' to legitimize a dominant political power (Wallace, 2003: 23, citing Eagleton and Habermas).

11   See other critiques of the collectivism label (e.g. Kumaravadivelu, 2007a: 15; Moon, 2008: 16).

12 There are several examples of claiming diversity to be the norm (e.g. Ahmed and Donnan, 1994; Delanty, 2006; Grande, 2006).

13 See discussions of methodological nationalism in critical sociology (Bhabha, 1994; Crane, 1994; Delanty, 2006; Grande, 2006; Schudson, 1994; Tomlinson, 1991) and in applied linguistics (Rajagopalan, 1999).

14 See also Centre-defined 'globalism' which claims that 'globalization is about the liberalization and global integration of markets ... is inevitable and irreversible ... benefits everyone ... furthers the democracy of the world ... requires a war on terror' and no power base (Fairclough, 2006: 40).

15 See also Stevenson (2003) on critical cosmopolitanism, and Guilherme (2007) on critical cosmopolitan citizenship. Also, Fairclough (2006: 121) describes 'globalization from below' or 'grounded globalizations' whereby local groups oppose Centre discourses and appropriate the networks created by globalization.

2

Critical Cultural Awareness

This chapter will propose a methodology for critical cultural awareness which will be applied throughout the ensuing chapters. The discussion in Chapter 1 proposes a critical cosmopolitan approach which suggests a cultural prejudice created by the Centre-West's ideological vision of the rest of the world, deeply coloured by a denial of this prejudice. However, many readers might consider that a lot of intercultural communication has nothing to do with prejudice or issues with the Centre-West, but with 'innocent' unfamiliar cultural events, practices, behaviour and values such as different management styles, family relations, dress codes, forms of address, attitudes to privacy, and modes of getting things done. This conflict of opinions needs to be cleared up before a methodology for cultural awareness can be determined. The chapter therefore begins with a sorting out of why a methodology for critical cultural awareness needs to address prejudice and ideology. It then moves on to a description of what this methodology should be in response to an ethnographically reconstructed example.

Models of Awareness

There is a considerable amount of attention in the intercultural communication literature regarding intercultural awareness; and there is clearly some movement toward a more critical non-essentialist position. Spencer-Oatey and Franklin (2009) provide an excellent overview of this literature. The eChina Programme papers (Spencer-Oatey and Stadler, 2009) suggest such experience-enhancing strategies as asking cultural informants, extending thinking beyond familiar fields of knowledge, understanding other people's goals (ibid.: 7), building wide networks, being aware of power systems, sensitivity to others' requirements for face (ibid.: 27), and appreciating the strangeness of one's own behaviour (ibid.: 31).[1] Byram's (2008: 162–3) work with state school language learners and European citizenship deals with developing critical evaluative abilities in looking at 'perspectives, practices and products', 'documents and events' with 'curiosity and openness, readiness to suspend disbelief about other cultures and belief about one's own'. A significant feature of Byram's approach is the concern that he and colleagues have with integrating language and cultural awareness development with broad educational aims and tertiary socialization – to take young people 'beyond the focus on their own society' (ibid.: 29).[2] A connection is made between communicative and political competence, in a 'fight against racism, prejudice and discrimination' in his broad citizenship approach (ibid.: 178). Guilherme's critical pedagogic approach to the 'critical intercultural speaker' recognizes the need for a postmodern, decentred 'critique of Western societies from the point of view of the Other' (2002: 92) in which 'no one should be regarded as culturally inferior or colonisable' (ibid.: 122).

I have two points of departure from these approaches. One is my opposition to their orientation towards a clear line between 'our culture' and 'their culture' which derives, especially in the case of Byram and Guilherme, from a strong association between learning a foreign language and a foreign culture and the methodological nationalism referred to in Chapter 1, and, especially in the case of the eChina Programme, from a notion of culturally exclusive values. The issues surrounding this intercultural line will be looked at specifically in Chapter 7.

My second point of departure is the attitude to what might be termed 'innocent' cases of intercultural misunderstanding. Examples of these can be found in the eChina Programme papers, in which British and Chinese teachers worked together to develop web-based teaching materials. They include:

- the British expecting planning meetings with specialist academics, whereas they met non-specialist administrators instead (Spencer-Oatey and Stadler, 2009: 14);
- the British practice of sending mass emails, offending higher-status Chinese colleagues (ibid.: 17);
- the Chinese finding it strange that the British raise issues immediately in meeting, and finding it hard to work out the urgency of instructions from the British side (ibid.: 19);
- the British surprised at the long turns and apparent lack of right to speak among the Chinese in meetings (ibid.: 25);
- the Chinese side wanting lots of speeches, festive room decoration and unmovable, heavy furniture in workshops, while the British side wanted more practical activity (ibid.: 26);
- the Chinese side wanting to spend more time on social networking than the British side (ibid.: 28);

- the discouragement of a British technical staff member from interrupting a Chinese ministry official to ask if he could ask a question in a crucial meeting and being told he could not (ibid.: 29).

My reaction to these cases is that very similar differences or conflicts can be found *within* national settings. I can think of a number of parallels within my own university in the relations between different academic departments, between academic and support departments, and between our and other universities – where practices may in many ways look very similar but represent individual cultural variations which lead to sustained miscommunication. A good example of this is in Chinese Wang's experience of working in a British university in Holliday et al. (2010: 52), where she found problematic structures similar to what she had experienced in a university in China. It may also be the case that things are simply done differently at an institutional and even government level in different places. I am thinking particularly of Byram's (2008: 70) example of a newcomer finding strange the 13th month's salary in Portugal. I prefer to think of these differences not so much as the result of harsh national cultural differences but rather as variations on what might be considered 'normal' within a particular person's experience. They may all find root in a wider set of *underlying universal cultural processes* which transcend national cultural boundaries, but the full variety of which may well be beyond the experience of individuals from particular societies or who have been brought up within particular social domains.[3] This principle will be discussed below and in detail in Chapter 6; and in Chapter 8 there will be a discussion of how newcomers from other places may bring an enriched and expanded cultural experience which will be relevant to foreign cultural practices to the degree that they may improve them. Indeed, Qing found that she was in a better position than her British colleagues to solve the sort of communication problems which are inherent in inter-departmental interaction, because she had experienced this sort of thing in a different system.

A positivist illusion

Thinking that such cases are 'innocent' stems from the naïve denial of ideology implicit in the liberal–essentialist duality described in Chapter 1. As suggested in Table 2 (rows 2 and 4), neo-essentialism, from which this duality springs, employs a positivist methodology following the approach of Hofstede described earlier. This produces a particular sequence of investigation such as that found in the eChina Programme papers, starting with an apparently neutral positivism which nevertheless leads to prejudice:

Positivist sequence

1 *A priori* national cultural descriptions are used to explain difference as though it is neutral.
2 National cultural stereotypes are acknowledged as problematic but remain as a starting point (Reid et al., 2009: 11–13).
3 'Us'–'them' overgeneralizations are made such as 'while the West focuses more on the learning process as a means in itself, the Chinese tradition is more oriented to learning outcomes' (ibid.: 18).
4 A sense of uncrossable boundaries: 'members of different cultures' have beliefs, values and practices which suit them but might 'compromise one's own values' (Spencer-Oatey and Stadler 2009: 9).
5 Not critiquing a British colleague's conclusion about what Chinese trainees said – 'the processes of articulating what you are thinking and why you're thinking it, is not generally practised in China' (ibid.).
6 A British colleague's statement that, in China, using English 'meant just absorbing and reproducing it, not thinking about how to present it' (ibid.).

There is no doubt that the people involved in the eChina Programme were struggling sincerely to make sense of the strangeness which they encountered in colleagues from a different country. However, the neo-essentialist rhetoric respects difference at a superficial level and is therefore too quick to draw naïve conclusions. The acceptance of stereotypical national cultural definitions (steps 1–3) is questioned but nevertheless maintained, and leads to an unquestioned sense of boundaries (4). This leads to an acceptance of statements about the other culture at face value (5) with no further reported analysis. The denial of ideology does not allow for the possibility that the definition (6) is a veiled, Othering, insinuation that Chinese people do not think. Even if the statement about not articulating thinking (5) came straight from a Chinese person, it should not be taken at face value. If such a statement were made about Britain, which I think would be very likely under certain circumstances, no one would think to generalize it to the whole society because the default belief is that British people do think about these things. The statement is accepted about Chinese society here because the default prejudice is that Chinese people do not. The statement that 'learning outcomes' are the main focus in China and not in 'the West' (3) is very unconvincing considering the huge emphasis on learning outcomes in British universities. There is too easy a cultural disbelief running through the sequence which will be discussed in Chapter 4 and further in Chapter 7.

A Reconstructed Narrative

As a contrast to the positivist sequence above, the following is an ethnographic reconstruction of interaction between two friends, John and Kayvan. There are several points to make about this narrative before reading it. It is not intended to be hard evidence. It is a fiction. Its purpose is not to prove that intercultural communication is such and such, but instead to demonstrate a critical cosmopolitan approach that will be supported by the statements of my informants and other discussions as the book proceeds.

The narrative is nevertheless based on empirical, ethnographic observation: (a) a long experience of spending time with a family like Kayvan's; (b) conversation with a member of the family about the hard decisions he needed to make as a businessman, and about self-determination and critical thinking in his life; (c) personal experience of being defined by other people; and (d) being told by a Hong Kong Chinese student that he refused to speak in my class because he felt everything he said and did was being scrutinized.

It is not intended that John and Kayvan represent national cultural types, for to do so would be to fall directly into the neo-essentialist trap. I believe there are people like them and that there is something of them in many of us; they both lead complex lives, a tiny bit of which is narrated here. They represent a trace of a conflicting attitude that runs through the Centre–Periphery predicament because John is Western and Kayvan is not. Although their names may situate them to a degree, just to add a necessary degree of uncertainty I am reluctant to name their respective countries. What can be said minimally is that John and Kayvan are individual actors who represent individual takes on a passing set of cultural realities.

> John was made very comfortable in Kayvan's country; but he began to feel uneasy when Kayvan invited him home and he found himself sitting for hour after hour during what seemed to him interminable weekend parties with his extended family. He was always surprised that Kayvan didn't seem to be able to just leave and do his own thing. One evening John had wanted to go with him to the cinema. Kayvan had refused to make a definite arrangement, saying that it would be impolite to discuss specific times with his family. As it happened, his uncle and aunt and two cousins had left at an opportune time; but just when John and Kayvan were about to leave, the door bell rang

and it was his brother and his family, and there seemed no choice but for Kayvan to stay and help his parents entertain them. Kayvan had once spent a month in John's country attending a course, and told John that one thing he'd experienced was a degree of privacy that he could never have at home.

One day John told Kayvan what he had learnt about individualism and collectivism when he was being briefed to come to his country. He said that he could explain Kayvan's family life on the basis of it being collectivist to always want to do things together and allowing loyalty to the group to get in the way of getting on with his own life. Kayvan at first went along with this idea and said it was certainly true that family loyalty was very important. John was pleased to begin to talk through these differences with Kayvan because he believed that it was important to learn as much as possible about the new cultures that one had the privilege of living in.

Kayvan was too polite to tell John that he was tiring of discussing cultural differences with him. Kayvan actually felt that the tone of the discussion was getting quite patronizing. John kept mentioning things like 'self-determination' and the ability to 'make personal decisions', as though they were restricted to 'Western culture'. Kayvan didn't feel that he could explain to John that his life was more complicated than he could imagine. John only really saw him when he was with his family, from whom he derived support and was able to relax, and did not have to make the sorts of decisions that John was talking about. What John didn't know about were the immense difficulties he faced in his business, which was currently failing because of the economy. He had to make very important and difficult decisions about laying off some of his workers, and perhaps even closing down the whole business and emigrating to North America.

Table 3 looks at the narrative in terms of emerging *categories of cultural action* which will be used throughout to make sense of other reconstructed narratives.[4] Once essentialist descriptions are left behind one no longer compares two cultural systems but instead begins to see social action which is partially universal in nature and against which cultural difference becomes a backdrop, with differences in cultural reference as a resource rather than an explaining structure or a set of confining features. The categories thus anticipate the social action theory introduced in Chapter 3. They represent the way in which perceptions of Self and Other are constructed around a strong undercurrent of politics and positioning which sits against a context of global inequality. Starting with statements *about* culture responds to the notion that people's representations of themselves are texts to be interrogated instead of taken at face value as in the positivist sequence above.

Table 3   An alternative explanation

Categories of cultural action	John	Kayvan
Statements about culture What people say about their culture	'My culture is individualist; Kayvan's is collectivist'	'I am not happy with being labelled collectivist, which implies lacking in self-determination'
Global position and politics How people position themselves with regard to foreign others, within a global order	Dominant language and economy, history of colonizing others. Conviction that he is able to improve things; the resources of technology, ideas, mobility, affluence and the media to do this; enacting the Centre	Isolated language and economy, history of having natural resources taken by others and his political institutions interfered with by others. Feeling that his positioning is not really recognized; problematic and limited resources; always being defined by others; feeling Periphery
Cultural resources What people draw on, in particular situations, from national or other cultural realities	Protestant ethic, the 1960s revolution, calm in the face of difficulty, cultural tourism, the image of individualism	Experience of political resistance, managing personal and business affairs without the support of state systems, a demonized religion
Underlying universal processes Cultural strategies shared by everyone	Rationalizing Self in contrast with Other, overgeneralizing in the face of uncertainty, perceiving Self as complex and the Other as simple, traditional and less civilized	Rationalizing Self in contrast with Other, not making opposition to ideas public when unsure of a dominant discourse

The individual categories will be looked at in detail in terms of how they fit within the context of culture formation in Figure 8 in Chapter 6, from which they are taken. Columns two and three in Table 3 enable a comparison of interpretations between the parties concerned. I place John's column before Kayvan's because he is the one who makes the first statement, which is itself indicative of the order of things.

The cultural references category in Table 3 indicates that cultural difference is certainly a major feature of what is going on between John and Kayvan, but that it is far from a finished matter of 'which culture' and what it contains. The misunderstanding between them has a lot to do with the very different cultural fabric of their societies on many levels. John finds Kayvan's family life very different from his own. Their institutions, politics, economy, geography, history, architecture, language, religion, social practices and so on are largely influenced by particular national configurations to the extent that Kayvan and John will necessarily have different world views. While there are the expected features in the case of John, for Kayvan, instead of the expected collectivism, there is a strong image of individualism which he brings to his business. Reference to Kayvan's religion is not to its cultural values, but to it being demonized. Individualism is presented as a resource in John's cell, not because it is a true descriptor of his society, but because it is an ideal which he draws on and believes in, as is evident in the statements section, which does not necessarily represent a true descriptor.

The individualism–collectivism differentiation thus appears not as a description of John's and Kayvan's respective cultures but as a concept claimed by John and resented by Kayvan. A key to the nature of this opposition comes from my Chinese colleague:

> I told Yuping the story about John and Kayvan. He seemed to recognize Kayvan's position. I asked him if the thought that Kayvan would be likely to note the chauvinism implicit in John's point of view. He said that this was not the point. Instead, he felt that, even with own his parents' generation, when there was massive government propaganda which told people that the collective was more important than the individual, the issue was not whether or not China was a collectivist society, but that the notion of collectivism was manufactured by foreigners who believed themselves to be individualists.

That Yuping is able to identify with what is going on between John and Kayvan might support Triandis's (2004) notion of collectivist cultures stretching across the non-West in Chapter 1. However, Yuping suggests that collectivism is a political rather than a cultural force, of the type referred to by Popper (1966), also in Chapter 1. What he recognizes in Kayvan is instead a shared experience of being defined by people like John. It is therefore the *act* of defining and being defined which is significant, and, following Hannerz's (1991) definition in Chapter 1, marks the Centre and Periphery condition. The 'dominance', 'conviction' and 'resources' associated with John's Western global position enable John to feel he has the knowledge to understand and then construct and indeed improve Kayvan. The confidence in John's behaviour can therefore be perceived as an 'enactment' of his Centre viewpoint. Kayvan's position is very different. It may well be that his personal wealth is far greater than John's, and it may be that he defines other people unfairly in other parts of his life, as we all do. However, within this scenario of global cultural relations he is marginalized by *always* being defined.

Another important element in their interaction, which I shall argue throughout and have already referred to above, is a universality of a pool of shared cultural processes. Both Kayvan and John are trying hard to rationalize Self in contrast with Other. They do this in different ways, but draw on the same pool of universal cultural skills. John rationalizes Kayvan's family as traditional and irrational; but Kayvan rationalizes his family's support. Kayvan's silence and decision not to tell John what he really thinks is a key move at the end of the narrative. Kumaravadivelu (2008: 17)[5] suggests that it is easier for John to Other Kayvan because 'Kayvan has actually failed to exercise his agency' and is in fact indulging in 'self-Othering'. My view is different. On the one hand, Kayvan had more important things to think about than to respond to John. Even though he was angry at the way in which John was thinking of him as lacking in self-direction, Kayvan had a lot of other problems to solve which were more important. Another explanation comes from comments from audience members in a number of seminar settings, who identified with Kayvan. They suggest this silence may be due to a strategic calculation that John's mastery of the dominant discourse concerning collectivism and individualism was too well articulated and established to be shaken. Indeed, if Kayvan had tried to explain to John the reasons why he would have to consult his father about his business, John would probably think that that was another example of 'collectivist' behaviour, so intent was he in finding collectivism in Kayvan's life. Were Kayvan's silence known to John, he would be likely to interpret it as the 'passivity' or deference to hosts which is also attributed to collectivist societies. I shall look at this discourse strategy against Centre dominance and the issue of self-Othering in more detail in Chapter 8.

Denial and resistance

Two larger themes that resonate through the narrative and the two halves of Table 3 are the denial of ideology on the part of John and resistance on the part of Kayvan. John enacts the liberal–essentialist duality described in Chapter 1 in that he believes his essentialist assessment of Kayvan is neutral and understanding – unaware of the possibility that Kayvan considers lack of 'self-determination' to be a simplistic, demeaning, one-dimensional, chauvinistic view of his society. John thus becomes Centre not just because he is defining Kayvan but also because his definition sustained within the public domain of their interaction; and Kayvan becomes Periphery because his meaning remains unheard. Because Kayvan does not tell John how he feels, John will depart thinking that Kayvan accepts collectivism as an adequate explanation of his behaviour, while, whatever Kayvan's motives for keeping silent, the irony is that, whereas individualism would have John as thinking critically, the expected roles are reversed and it is Kayvan who possesses this ability and understands more than John does. The specific realizations in John's and Kayvan's behaviour could be entirely different in circumstances different from those described in the narrative. However, I believe the overall tone is generally indicative of a Centre–Periphery relationship.

Searching for decentred solutions

The neo-essentialist solution to the miscommunication in the narrative might be to provide John with a better, non-chauvinistic description of Kayvan's culture. This would, however, be missing the point if it is the manner with which John describes, more than the actual description, which is the problem. To get out of this trap, within all domains of the Centre-West (e.g. interculturalist academics and professionals, the designers and purveyors of policies such as multiculturalism, discussed in Chapter 4, and intercultural travellers and collectors such as John, not to mention government and its foreign policy[6]) there needs to be a withdrawal from imposing definitions on the Periphery – to give space to decentred understandings.

The purpose of this book is not to understand the Periphery condition, which is well known in the Periphery. It is to explore what John has to do if he is going to appreciate Kayvan's deep sense of not being heard in the face of a profound inequality of who is defining whom, and if he is going to restrain himself from defining, categorizing, imagining Kayvan so that Kayvan can find space to claim the world in his own terms. The difficulty here for interculturalist researchers is that Kayvan's position is largely unsaid and invisible. It is only possible to complete the cells in Table 3 with a broader understanding of the two interactants from outside the setting. The aim must therefore be to:

- put aside established descriptions;
- seek a broader picture;
- look for the hidden and the unexpressed.

Critical Interpretivism

These three aims are addressed in the interpretivist methodology employed by critical cosmopolitanism, which is described in Table 2 as observation open to emergent, complex realities. Its basic aim is to allow meanings to emerge from the non-aligned piecing together of what is found, rather than imposing *a priori* narratives. This is an extremely difficult aim to achieve because of the inevitability of the influence of researcher subjectivity and ideology within the research setting, which is recognized within the postmodern underpinning of critical cosmopolitanism.[7] This difficulty is compounded by the division within the approach itself between more and less critical versions. Much interpretive attention is already given to cultural difference in the neo-essentialist paradigm; but it is not sufficient to undo the power of the essentialist roots in models like Hofstede's or to undo the denial of ideology. There is therefore a difference between what Collier (2005: 254) terms 'understanding culture as lived experience' and the more critical 'uncovering communicative forms of power at work in cultural systems in order to enable emancipation and change'.

Simply interpreting what we see will not be sufficient. A less critical interpretive approach may only make John less inclined to search for clear-cut descriptions of cultural difference. It would not be sufficient to allow him to see the full politics of Kayvan's opposition to his imagination of him, the full political nature of his relationship with Kayvan, or what underlies the constructions of inferiority and superiority. Even though an interpretive approach would shrink from defining Kayvan as a collectivist 'them', in its uncritical form it may still imagine him as someone who can be liberated to be just like 'us' – and certainly as a good market for globalized Western products as described in Chapter 1.

A more critical interpretivism therefore needs to employ particular researcher disciplines if it is to succeed in the thought-changing process of excavating the hidden aspects of what we choose to see – unlocking deeper political perspectives and enabling the undoing of the false political realities of neo-essentialism. The disciplines of *thick description*, *bracketing*, and *making the familiar strange* can be taken from critical, postmodern qualitative research.[8]

Thick description

Seeking the broader picture and looking for the hidden and unexpressed relates to the discipline of thick description. This can be defined as an analysis of all the facets of a social phenomenon that make up its full complexity, and involves piecing together interconnected data to build a picture of what it going on.[9] It encourages the exploratory juxtaposition of phenomena to create richer pictures of how things may be, rather than trying to fix how things are according to *a priori* hierarchies. In a thick description of, for example, a concert programme, the researcher will consider:

> the staffing, recent programme changes, the charisma of the choral director, the working relationship with a church organist, faculty interests in a critical vote of the school board, and the lack of student interest in taking up the clarinet. In these particularities lie the vitality, trauma, and uniqueness of the case. (Stake, 2005: 457)

This process is particularly relevant to sorting out truth and illusion in the discourses and ideologies of culture. This can be seen in the famous example of Geertz's (1993: 6) discussion of Gilbert Ryle's analysis of 'two boys rapidly contracting the eyelids of their right eyes'. A 'thin description' does no more than report the event in these limited terms. A thick description goes deeper to analyze the cultural meaning of the act, to explore whether it is an involuntary 'twitch' or a socially charged 'wink'. After investigating the boys' relationships with each other and with a larger group of boys standing at some distance, it is revealed that one of the boys is winking in parody of the other's twitch. Thus, the thick description delves into the depths of cultural realities in which there is 'a stratified hierarchy of meaningful structures of which twitches, winks, fakewinks, parodies, rehearsals of parodies are produced, perceived and interpreted, and without which they would not ... in fact exist' (ibid.: 7). Hence, thick description enables a recognition of the ways in which such dominant notions as individualism and collectivism are socially constructed, and a rejection of the 'taken for granted' and the naïve 'realism of conventional writing' which results in '"thin" description' (Atkinson and Coffey, 1995: 52). A thick description would similarly be necessary to sort out the reasons for Kayvan's silence in the narrative by looking widely into broad aspects of his life and experience. The implication is immense complexity which may well go beyond the surface knowledge of the actors involved. This piece of good advice from Goffman (1972: 135–6) would seem to be relevant here:

> When individuals come into one another's immediate presence, territories of the self bring to the scene a vast filigree of trip wires which individuals are uniquely equipped to trip over. This ensures that circumstances will constantly produce potentially offensive configurations that were not foreseen or were foreseen but undesired. ... In face-to-face interaction, the actor will have the task,

often the right, of providing clarifying information. ... [H]e will be in a position to try to cover improper intent and motive with false explanation. In brief, the individual will make an effort to provide correct information designed to prevent not only his being misunderstood, but also his being understood too well.

Covering 'improper intent and motive' applies not only to intercultural interactants but also to the researchers who study them.

Thick description is also an important part of the evidence base of this book, as described in the Preface. Figure 2 indicates how this works in relation to the discussion in Chapter 3. The grey core of the figure represents the part of the discussion focused on in the chapter. The immediate set of data is [a–c]. The narrative [c] is also constructed on the basis of [d–g]; and [h] indicates that there is a yet bigger set of interconnected data running through the whole book. The thick description here is wide-ranging and moves beyond a particular social location to suit the broad canvas of the book, and is therefore stretched further than the norm.[10] In [c] I refer to the 'composing' of the narrative because the act of composing itself becomes new data through the application of the other disciplines of bracketing, making the familiar strange, and generally being faithful to the data.

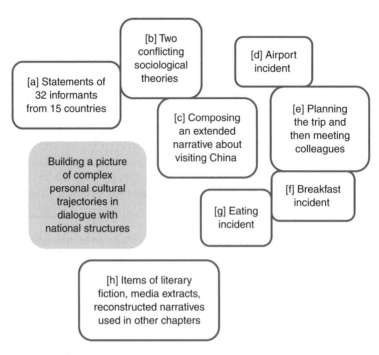

Figure 2   Applying thick description

Bracketing and making the familiar strange

Putting aside established descriptions relates to the discipline of bracketing. Often associated with phenomenology, this can be described as locating prejudices which will colour the viewpoint of the researcher and consciously putting them aside, to 'temporarily suspend all commonsense assumptions' in order to set aside judgements about the expected 'nature', 'essence' and 'reality' of things (Schutz, 1970: 316), and to 'make visible the practices through which taken-for-granted realities are accomplished' (Gubrium and Holstein, 1997: 40).[11] Bracketing is thus an essential device for seeing through the discourses and ideologies of culture. A good example is in Baumann's ethnography of the multicultural London borough of Southall. To avoid the essentialist trap of Othering the Sikhs who lived there, he made himself think of them first as 'Southallians', and made sure that any reference to their 'Sikhness' would be 'a matter of finding out, rather than knowing in advance' (Baumann, 1996: 2). This strategy was based on his knowledge of his own prejudices, which would lead him to non-critical 'easy answers'. In my own study of Hong Kong Chinese students (Holliday, 2005: 88ff.), I knew that the stereotype of Chinese culture was so deeply embedded in my thinking that I had to bracket it. If I was to avoid the 'easy answer' that Chinese students are 'collectivist' and 'passive', I had to work hard to think of them first as students, not as Chinese.

Bracketing is closely related to the discipline of *making the familiar strange*, which can be associated with Schutz's (1964) notion of the stranger approaching a new set of social practices and having to work out from first principles how the culture works in terms of its basic structures – indeed, becoming explicitly aware of all workings of culture formation as described in Chapter 6.

In my view, the collectivism–individualism distinction is an 'easy answer' and needs to be bracketed. If John had had no knowledge of the collectivism–individualism distinction he would have had a better chance of understanding Kayvan. If intercultural researchers put the distinction, or the possibility of such a distinction, aside, they may also see something else. Trying to see things differently is expressed well in this statement which implies actually travelling into a different world of perception:

> In the First World I had never paid any attention to the physical mechanisms which held my life together. It never occurred to me to figure out how the flush of a toilet worked, which secret route a gas pipe actually took, what a spark plug's purpose was. Their intrinsic nature had never concerned me ... To me the inner life of mechanical objects was as abstract as a cubist painting. (Marciano, 1998: 76)

Critical reading

The final ingredient of the critical interpretivist methodology is critical reading. The John–Kayvan narrative has provided a focus for analysis in this chapter. While it cannot be considered hard data, it demonstrates a set of complex interconnections between culture and ideology within a small space. It is a rich text that represents the nature of rich texts which mark cultural life. An important aspect of this is that John's statement about culture, Kayvan's silence, my Chinese colleague's comment about them, and indeed the British colleague's assumptions about Chinese culture in the positivist sequence earlier in this chapter, all need a to be viewed as rich texts – slices or instances of life which need to be interrogated critically, not taken at face value, and got to the bottom of.

For this reason the use of rich texts has been recognized as a powerful tool in intercultural awareness and will be a common focus of discussion throughout the rest of the book – more ethnographic reconstructions, critical incidents, extracts from the media and extracts from literary fiction. I am particularly influenced by Wallace's (2003) study of how students from diverse backgrounds work together to develop their critical reading of cultural texts. She states that every text reflects ideology and power relations (ibid.: 102). Here, critical discourse analysis plays an important role in asking basic questions about the ideological intentions of the writer and the content (ibid.: 25–6, citing Fairlcough, Kress and Halliday).

Transcending the intercultural line

Critical reading significantly transcends the preoccupation with the line between 'our culture' and 'their culture'. It is necessary not just to compare what people in different societies do, but to invite everyone to look at profound texts of interaction from every side. The texts should not be a depiction of 'the other, foreign culture', which would encourage a vision of how 'they' are different from or the same as 'us'. They should represent cultural interface. Critical cosmopolitanism is therefore not just one of the possible readings, but is also present in the choice of the text. Indeed, it is an advantage if there is a also strong cosmopolitan element among the intercultural trainee or student group, so that participants from different cultural backgrounds can look at texts with both familiar and unfamiliar content in each other's company. Wallace provides the example of a 'cross-cultural dialogue' within a classroom setting in a university in London 'where students, both from mainstream, dominant cultural groups and marginalized ones may make strange their own cultural practices', 'negotiate a range of different cultural understandings' and 'gain some distance from their readings of familiar texts'. Hence, 'in a multicultural classroom a diversity of readings provides a cultural and critical resource for the whole class' (2003: 75). I shall return to look more closely at the issue of the line between cultures in detail in Chapter 7.

A Decentred Reading

This description of Sara reading a newspaper article is an example of such a cross-cultural dialogue set around the critical reading of a text:

> Some time ago I showed a copy of the *Guardian* to Sara, 19, who lives in a 'developing' country. She has never travelled abroad nor seen a British newspaper before. Although illegal, she has seen CNN and BBC World television in friends' homes, and listens regularly to the BBC World Service on the radio. She has learnt English at school and is an enthusiastic member of an 'English group' – friends who meet regularly to practise their English. Her parents speak English, as do many of their educated compatriots.
>
> She read the newspaper eagerly from beginning to end, moving quickly over the extracts of the newly published tapes in which Clinton talked about his relationship with Monica Lewinsky. What she commented on in particular was a full-page article about famine relief in an African country. She wanted to know why the newspaper had chosen to publish this article at this time, when famine was ongoing, and why the journalist's name was highlighted at the beginning. She asked if the real purpose was to project the image of a 'caring' media who employed 'caring' journalists, while at the same time reducing the people in the African country to a starving 'foreign' other? When I asked her about the Monica Lewinsky affair she said that it was really no big deal in that everyone expects world leaders to behave in that way. [12]

Sara's reading problematizes the style and choice of content in the newspaper, which is a cultural product – an artefact of the way in which British society sees itself. She represents a Periphery voice in that she comes from a farther 'Eastern' place, where 'freedom' in whatever form still cannot be compared to that which we enjoy in the West, and is thus automatically critical. This compulsion by people from politically oppressed societies to 'read' more 'between the lines' is suggested in this statement which Wallace (1992: 59) places epigraphically at the head of her article on critical literary awareness:

> In 1977 banned Czech writer, Sdener Urbanak told me: 'You in the West have a problem. You are unsure of when you are being lied to, when you are being tricked. We do not suffer from this: and unlike you, we have acquired the skill of reading between the lines.' In Britain today we need to develop the skill urgently, for as freedom is being gained in the East, it is being lost here. John Pilger, the *Guardian*, March 1990

Sara thus, without instigation, asks some of the basic questions that are recommended in critical reading 'to help raise awareness of the ideology of texts' – about why the topic is being written about in the first place, how it is being written about, what other ways there are of writing about it, and why in this case it is being written about in this way (Wallace 1992: 71, citing Kress). There is nothing really new in the substance of her critical discourse analysis. One might say that Sara is overdoing her critique. It does not, however, matter whether she is right or not. It is the nature of the questioning which is important. Sara's critique is an important example of an outsider seeing through the taken-for-granted in the society represented by the article. Wallace has similar examples:

> My student Yuko ... was able to notice, more readily than the British student, the Orientalism which permeates popular culture texts produced for a Western readership. Students and scholars from non-Western countries and traditions will also offer not just richer, less writer-aligned interpretations of texts written in English but seek out different kinds of texts for critical analysis. ... Traditional ways of life, relations between men and women, ways of doing things, are necessarily open to challenge and can no longer be taken for granted in *any* society. (2003: 57–8, her emphasis)

Such readings from Sara and Yuko will help readers for whom such settings are familiar to achieve the discipline of making the familiar strange. To get to the bottom of our own prejudices we in the Centre-West need to see our familiar viewpoints through the strange-making eyes of the Periphery gaze. There is also employment of thick description in the manner in which Sara contextualizes the article about famine in Africa within the broader text of the newspaper as she browses through. Her passing over of the Lewinsky affair, to do with a sexual liaison between a US president and his aide, which was a major area of political critique for Western readers at that time, gave a sense that the more obvious intrigue was in danger of taking attention away from the deeper, more hidden issues of a journalism which represents a misplaced 'helping' society, as will be referred to in Chapter 4. The more acute, survival political sensibilities of a Periphery reader thus bring about a different sort of sociological imagination, from which Centre readers need to learn.

Suppose that Sara was comparing notes and discussing the newspaper extract with, say, British students, and their task was to locate neo-essentialist and critical cosmopolitan readings in something like the following manner:

- *Neo-essentialist reading* – African culture needs Western help if it is to be protected.
- *Critical cosmopolitan reading* – the imposition of a powerful Western discourse of help constructs 'African culture' in such a way that other cultural realities which may have nothing to do with this discourse will remain hidden.

This is of course not a straightforward matter by any means. The discussion might perhaps consider:

- that it cannot be denied that there *is* a starving population which *does* need to be helped;
- that this may have nothing to do with ideology;
- that there is also an undeniable colonial history of defining 'Africa' as culturally deficient;
- how far the image of 'Africa in need of help' colours the West's view of the whole of the continent;
- personal constructions, amongst the people carrying out the reading task, of people across the world who are associated with foreign communities needing help – and so on;
- how this relates to how we all construct people around us who we might consider different in terms of ethnicity, class, gender, sexuality, and so on.

The final query here is significant because it must not be assumed that the issues only connect with 'foreign' as 'far away'.

A very important implication here is that the distinction between the neo-essentialist and critical cosmopolitan categories is *not* to be held up as *the* definitive way of looking at things. It is instead a means – and there could be others – of beginning to sort out culture and ideology. However, one would hope that once the distinction has been made, whether or not one disagrees with it, it is not possible to see things in the same way again; and the process of interrogating established thought has begun.

On the one hand, it must be acknowledged that we all possess a natural methodology for making sense of the world around us – which will be discussed in detail in Chapter 6 within the context of underlying universal cultural processes. On the other hand, this clearly does not succeed in seeing through the narratives of Othering sufficiently to overcome the hidden racism of Western society. The universality of these underlying cultural processes provides everyone with the potential ability to read culture; but culture can be read in a variety of different ways dependent on the particular ideologies which come into play; and there are indeed no readings that can be devoid of ideology. It is therefore necessary to try and engineer the right readings – which is the aim of intercultural training or education. The task is therefore to introduce experience of a particular type that invites us to see hidden realities and disciplines to constrain the prejudice which gets in the way while encouraging the natural, underlying ability for reading culture. For a Centre-Western audience, untangling these neo-essentialist and critical cosmopolitan visions is a major task and underpins the need for a precise and disciplined methodology.

The principle that everyone has the potential to read culture everywhere is evidenced in the experience we all have of making sense of fictional narratives of foreign scenarios such as the exotic and science fiction. What is often overlooked in this respect is our ability to access our own histories which represent very different cultural realities from our present society. While many historical cultural references may be shared, the early 19th-century British society depicted by Jane Austen is no less alien than that of a so-called 'other culture'. The richness of thick description in Austen's literature as art enables greater understanding than the fragmentation of available information about such foreign locations. Understanding Austen's society is not inhibited by our long history of mistrust for the foreign Other. Studying Austen's society would be an excellent basis for studying the universals of the nature of culture.

Opening up Cultural Possibilities

Through the application of these disciplines, a critical interpretivist methodology applied to intercultural communication should open up possibilities not allowed within a positivist neo-essentialism. Such possibilities, discussed in ensuing chapters, include individuals' ability to expand their repertoire of cultural engagement and carry practices from one society to another, to share underlying universal cultural processes with people from other societies, and to dialogue with the environment provided by national social structures. The 'new thinking' advocated by the eChina Programme can be taken further by not taking things at face value. The presumptions in every step in the positivist sequence described earlier would be questioned along with *a priori* cultural descriptions and statements made by people about their own culture or implied as in the first of the categories of cultural action.

Implicit in this process, and very much connected with this notion of thick description, is a broad sociological perspective, or *sociological imagination* – the ability to locate oneself and one's actions critically within a world scenario – 'to grasp history and biography and the relations between the two within society' (Mills, 1970: 12). In trying to look at things freshly without baggage in the disciplines of *bracketing* and *making the familiar strange*, we also need to remember who we are in terms of where we come from and the ideological forces that have formed us. This tension is very evident in the title of Alibhai-Brown's (2000) book, *Who Do We Think We Are?*, which makes us reassess who we are with new thinking while reminding us of the history of what we have thought in our ignorance, to 'learn humility to look beyond our worlds, obsessions and interpretations' (ibid.: 17). It therefore takes a sociological imagination for someone who is brought up and wired by Centre-Western discourses and ideologies to be able to mobilize their underlying universal cultural skills in such a way to be able to see through these discourses and ideologies to appreciate the emergent realities of the Periphery.

The categories of cultural action referred to earlier automatically apply the discipline of thick description, by interconnecting a wide range of factors. They also apply bracketing, making the familiar strange and critical reading, by drawing attention to the ideology, positioning and politics of Self and thus glimpsing the perception of the person on the other side of the interaction, who is the Other which the Self constructs. This is how column three of Table 3 at least begins to reveal to the Centre gaze what has previously been hidden.

Summary

The following points have been made in this chapter:

- A positivist methodology which emerges from neo-essentialism places too much reliance on *a priori* descriptions of culture and insufficiently interrogates what goes on between people.
- The face value of what appears to be a difference between this or that culture needs to be interrogated by looking at categories of cultural action such as statements of culture as texts, the global positioning and politics of the actors, their 'cultures' as non-confining resources, and much of what they do and say as underlying universal cultural processes.

- Centre and Periphery conditions grow out of who defines and who is defined.
- An interpretivist methodology, which grows out of critical cosmopolitanism, is more suited to getting to the bottom of cultural interaction by putting aside dominant preoccupations (bracketing and making the familiar strange) and seeing broader interconnections (thick description and sociological imagination). It must, however, be sufficiently critical to uncover and address intercultural ideology and politics (critical reading).
- The John–Kayvan narrative reveals the value of rich texts in increasing critical intercultural awareness. Such texts must be looked at not from an 'us'–'them' perspective, but as texts which all parties need to interrogate critically.

Investigation

The following tasks are designed to apply principles connected with using an interpretive approach. Where possible, it would be useful to do these with people from other cultural backgrounds.

1 Consider Kayvan's predicament in the John–Kayvan narrative. Describe a time when your behaviour has been explained, or *defined*,[13] inaccurately by others and you have not been able to explain yourself to put things right.
   (a) The setting may or may not be to do with being a newcomer in another country; but it should be located within a workplace, family, community, friendship group, etc.
   (b) Employ a *thick description* by making interconnections between different elements in your life. Kayvan made connections with his business, employees and the economy.
   (c) Apply or adapt the *categories of cultural action* to your description and note unexpected findings.
2 Apply or adapt the *categories of cultural action* to the following scenarios, each time noting unexpected findings:
   (a) The interaction between the British and a Chinese colleague summarized in the positivist sequence near the beginning of the chapter.
      (i) This should generate a very different picture from that in the positivist sequence.
      (ii) The interactants could be the colleagues themselves, but may also include the authors of the report. You can get more details

from the actual report, if you can get access to it. This will involve a *critical reading* to uncover the ideologies implicit in the text.

(iii) You can reconstruct what you think might have happened in the form of a written account before you do the analysis. Take care to *bracket* your own ideological preoccupations as you do this.

(b) An instance of intercultural communication you have been involved in, applying all the interpretive disciplines.

3 As a result of using the *categories of cultural action*, what general advice could you give to people who find themselves in circumstances similar to those in 1(c) above?

4 Carry out a role-play in which you develop the idea of being explained by others. The actors should play the roles either of *defining* or *being defined*. Can you see what it feels like to be Othered and to feel on the Periphery (i.e. *always being defined*).

5 Write a narrative like the one about John and Kayvan. It should be about an incident you have witnessed or experienced as a participant, in which there was some sort of intercultural misunderstanding. It could be based on the above activities. It could also be reconstructed from different people and events. *Bracketing* and *making the familiar strange* can be aided by:

(a) describing only what you saw or heard, or what you know from what one of the characters has told you;

(b) not expressing your own opinions or judgements;

(c) not imposing any descriptions of national, ethnic or religious cultures. Allow issues to do with nation to emerge from what happens.

6 Consider the above activities.

(a) What role do *a priori* theories play in how people define the behaviour of others? These might include: national cultural stereotypes; definitions of being 'naïve', 'quiet', 'fake', etc.

(b) What positions of power do these theories represent? Relate this to the notion of Centre and Periphery. In what sense are they a denial of ideology?

(c) How does the difference between a less and a more critical interpretivism relate to the difference between a less and a more critical cosmopolitanism described in Chapter 1?

7 Plan an orientation session for people who might find themselves in John's position. Consider appropriate participants, presenters, texts and activities to ensure the following:

(a) the development of a non-aligned sociological imagination;

(b) a better understanding of Kayvan's background which is not dependent on images that define or confine it.

Notes

1   See also Antal and Friedman's (2008: 363) suggestion for 'developing "negotiating reality" as a key intercultural competence at an international business school in Europe'.

2   For a discussion of primary (childhood) and secondary socialization see Byram's discussion of Berger and Luckmann (Byram, 2008: 30, 133).

3   See Agar's (2007: 14) discussion of miscommunications which are common both within and across societies.

4   For other examples of the use of categories of cultural action see Holliday (in press) and Holliday and Aboshiha (2009). Lessons have also been learnt in the creation of the model from soft systems methodology (Checkland and Scholes, 1990; Holliday, 1990, 1994: 121).

5   Kumaravadivelu is commenting on an earlier appearance of this narrative (Holliday, 2007a).

6   Fairclough (2006: 5) lists five main sources of agency: 'academic analysis, governmental agencies, non-governmental agencies, the media, people in everyday life'.

7   See further discussion of the inevitability of subjectivity and the influence of the researcher's ideology (e.g. Gubrium and Holstein, 1997: vi, 38; Hammersley and Atkinson, 1995: 11; Holliday, 2007b: 19).

8   See Byram and colleague's use of ethnographic methods and autobiography in developing young people's intercultural awarenesses, which go into developed detail concerning the role and demeanour of the language learner as an integrative social researcher (2008: 115ff.).

9   See Denzin (1994: 505). Thick description can also be considered as a break from the more positivist device of triangulation which checks things out through comparison (Holliday, 2007b: 76; Stenhouse, 1985a, 1985b).

10 See my discussion with Alan Waters regarding the validity of data used in this manner (Holliday, 2007c; Waters, 2007a, 2007c).

11 See my discussion of bracketing with respect to combating cultural chauvinism, in Holliday (2007b: 173ff), and with specific reference to the Othering of the 'non-native speaker' of English in Holliday (2005: 88ff.).

12 This extract is used and discussed further in Holliday (2000).

13 *Defining* involves explaining in such a way that a rule is established for future occasions. Defining someone else's behaviour in effect sets up an expectation for how they should behave in the future. It also fixes what someone is thought to be able and not able to do.

3

Cultural Complexity

The purpose of this chapter is to develop the critical cosmopolitan view of culture presented in Chapter 1 and implicit in the methodology for critical cultural awareness in Chapter 2. I shall relate some of the thoughts arising from interviews with expert informants to demonstrate how the complexity of personal cultural realities which transcend boundaries is sometimes in creative conflict with the external cultural structures of nation. I shall then move on to develop the difference between neo-essentialist and critical cosmopolitan views of culture, growing out of the interviews, by looking at the opposing sociological theories of structural-functionalism and social action.

Informants

The first part of this chapter is based on a body of data emerging from interviews with 32 people who were selected according to their conscious engagement with issues of culture. It was my presupposition that this would be through crossing or otherwise encountering cultural boundaries of one type or another. They also represent a diversity of nationalities. The characteristics of the group were thus as follows. Two were Australian, 11 English, two Chinese, two German, one Greek, two Italian, one Mexican, two Indian, one Northern Irish, one South Korean, one Tunisian, three Turkish, one American, one Welsh, and one Zimbabwean. Of these, five were first- or second-generation immigrants to Britain or Australia from Iran, Jamaica or Pakistan, 16 were or had recently been expatriates from Australia, England, India, Italy, China, Ireland, Greece or Wales, living in England, France, Holland, Japan, Malaysia, Saudi Arabia or the United Arab Emirates, seven had spouses or partners of another nationality, 20 were female, two were gay or lesbian, 18 were academics, of whom 14 were applied linguists. The medium of email in the case of 28 of the interviews allowed the informants to reply at their leisure, with the opportunity to explore diverse interpretations. As appropriate for an exploratory, qualitative study, two questions designed to invite rich responses were asked of the email informants: (1) What are the major features of your cultural identity? (2) What role does nation play in this?

They responded with 23,000 words of raw data. A further four interviews were carried out face to face, sometimes with meetings on several occasions. Here the informants were asked more specifically about modernity and Westernization. All the informants spoke freely and creatively; and it became clear that many of them found this a daunting, difficult and perhaps self-revealing task. Their comments provide a major input to this chapter and will also appear intermittently to support the discussion in ensuing chapters.[1] (There is a section in the index which shows where references to each informant can be located.)

An Emergent Methodology

The approach to the data provided by these informants follows the critical interpretivism described in Chapter 2, within a broadly postmodern qualitative research paradigm.[2] The struggle to balance my own agendas with submitting to emergent meaning is represented in the following dialogic steps:

Research sequence

1 Ask exploratory questions.
2 Submit to the data to allow themes to emerge.
3 Select extracts to support each theme.
4 Engage with each extract in a discussion of the theme.
5 Reassess the themes and the placing of extracts as the discussion develops.

In several ways what emerged from my informants led me seriously to reassess both my beliefs about culture and my methodology of presentation. I was forced unexpectedly to appreciate the importance of nation, but not in ways I had predicted. I was forced to reconsider the placing of my own voice in talking about the data (Holliday, 2007b: 107), and to take the eventual decision to present longer strings of two or three data extracts, introduced minimally, in an attempt to reduce the clutter of discussion as much as possible. Especially in step 2, I had seriously to reassess my image of the informants – to withdraw from grouping them as cultural types. I was not able to employ the Western–non-Western categories which suited my own interest in cultural politics because none of the informants indicated them as relevant. Neither was there any evidence to allow me to say that, for example, Asians had different types of views from Europeans, or that there were different cultural types such as collectivist and individualist. Indeed, there was little to distinguish between what different types of people told me in terms of the overall tenor of the responses. I thus experienced the important principle of shedding researcher ideology in favour of a deeper, more cautious and disciplined personal knowledge of life (Holliday, 2007b: 90, 127, 69) and making the familiar strange was forced.

Emergent themes were therefore less about difference than about process. Each theme was expressed by between 70 and 25 per cent of the informants, regardless of their personal details. The roughness of these figures indicates complex interconnections and shades of meaning. The diversity of the informants, which was important to the purpose of the study, could only therefore be represented by the atomistic listing of nationalities above. Even here the apparently objective categories of passport nationality proved inadequate because one informant rejected 'British' in favour of 'Welsh' as a nationalist cause. As I will indicate in my findings below, I had to find a new set of terms to express the aspects of culture which emerged, and to rediscover forgotten theories. Throughout I provide minimal detail of their nationality or other aspects of their identity unless they emerge in the informants' own words. Although I had chosen informants partly because of their range of nationalities, ethically I felt I could not declare their nationality unless they gave me permission.

The following themes and sub-themes emerged from the data, most of which will be dealt with in this chapter and the rest later in the book:

- national culture as an external reality – this chapter;
- complexity (movable groups, trajectories of multiple, shifting realities, defying definition, layered and compartmentalized, language and reference) – this chapter;
- struggling with Otherness – Chapter 4;
- cultural references (resources, relativity to group) – Chapter 6;
- global circumstances and politics – Chapter 6.

The face-to-face interviews on the subject of modernity and the West are also used in Chapter 5. I have listed complexity as a separate theme; but in many ways it also characterizes all the others and contributes to the overall image of a strong cosmopolitan dimension. The names I use are either actual, where permission was given, or pseudonyms chosen by the informants, or anonymous codes.

Statements of Cultural Identity

Evidence that my informants engaged fully with the complexity of cultural identity is in how daunting, difficult and perhaps self-revealing they found the task of writing their responses to be:

So you start with the easy questions then. Like who are you? What I have thought about the answer to number one has been different each time I thought about it. For example now I am inclined to think that it is best not even to approach this question because anything said will be at best partial and therefore misleading and more likely just wrong. So here is my wrong answer for today. (David)

The 'cultural interface' to which you refer has led to new ways of thinking about all of the above [measures of cultural identity], putting features into relief by comparison with other views. ... It's like a layer painted over the other features but allowing them to show through. Or, if we stay with the painting imagery, it's like defining objects in a still-life through painting the shadows they cast. (Beth)

Nation as an external reality

My informants generally made it clear that nation *is* an important category, but an external one which may be in conflict with more personal cultural realities. Here, Chin describes nation as an undeniably powerful source of identity, security and belonging:

Nation plays a very important role. 'Home'land or 'mother'land appears to have a real and somewhat more powerful meaning because it always draws me back to things related to my country of origin, and my cultural root. It is like a base deep inside me – a base that is very important to me because it gives me a sense of cultural identity which will never change. (Chin)

Other informants, however, place nation in conflict with other cultural realities. Alba speaks about nation first as an external and established frame within which Mexican people can place themselves, but then moves on to conflicts with the details of daily life, gender issues, and her personal identity as a married woman:

Every Mexican fits under the blanket of their country's name. It's curious how romantic that sounds too. I like to be called Mexican. I like to belong to this country, what that actually means, it's hard to describe. I guess I have a hate and love relationship with my country and its people, and so it's hard to see what parts of me come from having grown up accepting them or rejecting them.

There's an important note on this question and it is that it immediately brought up one of my high school memories when I learnt a definition of nation and its components: territory, government, language and culture. So I guess my problem is that for some reason I feel it excludes diversity, and the possibility to dissent.

Of course it's hard to talk about this jumping from a macro level into daily lives but I would like to give an example of this. Take for instance the construction of a Mexican woman; what do you expect her to be like?

I am 28 years old, I'm 'married'. What is the idea of a Mexican woman, married at 28? I'm not like most of them, the ones I know anyway. I do not have children yet, my husband is in charge of the shopping and the meals, I care very much about my career and want to keep on studying. So when I talk to other Mexican women of 28–30 years old that are married I do not quite feel in the right group. (Alba)

All informants express similar tensions with personal diversity. In the following extracts Park also talks about nation in conflict with her identity as a woman; and Farzad, as a first-generation Australian, talks about resistance to imposed norms in his country of birth and the way in which nation imposes unrepresentative cultural unity:

What the Korean society asks me as a woman, a mother, and a wife to be, is unreasonable and even outraging. … I come to realize that I just want to settle in the conventional images of a competent female and enjoy what I have achieved as the result of compromising with the society. (Park)

As I grew up in my country of birth, I increasingly became conscious of the cultural norms of my society and I felt that I couldn't blindly agree with some of those norms. It came to a point where I had to leave my country as I couldn't stand the cultural environment of where I was living. I was in a sense rebellious towards the culture of my society.

I think the concept of 'nation' is problematic in that it can refer to several entities at the same time, such as a country or a group of people who share a particular language and culture. For example, in Australia, the term 'nation' can refer to all the people who live in this country, who as we know are of different cultural and linguistic backgrounds. I am personally a bit cautious of terms such as 'nation', 'race', and 'nationality'. I think politicians would like to keep these terms in currency so that they can, so to speak, keep the people of their country 'under one roof'. (Farzad)

Personal cultural realities work in a variety of ways in resistance or dialogue with nation. David and Ursula refer to nation almost as a place where they find themselves through the accident of birth; and the way in which they see it and it treats them is largely to do with what they personally bring to it. David talks about nation as the place which he has grown to associate with certain aspects of his life, but which does not prevent him from affinities elsewhere and which is very much in the background of who he is; his ambivalence about the politics is shared quite aggressively by Ursula, who is highly critical of the way her particular nation projects itself on the rest of the world and internally on the people it does not want to fit. Her reference to the greater reality of family history, colour and sexuality is shared by several informants and will be picked up in the next theme.

Nation plays more role than I choose to admit or wish. I would like to think of myself as merely accidentally British and marginal and wary of my native culture but obviously I actually identify myself through language, shared expectations, knowledge and belief, a certain attitude, a certain affectionate familiarity even with less pleasant aspects of Britishness and of course football and other unknown ways. All of this is the expected consequence of remaining throughout my formative years and most of my life in this country. On the other hand I also feel lesser but significant loyalties to other categories of humanity e.g. Turks, Muslims, victims of injustice, writers/artists, parents ...

No. I am pleased to be British in my head but not British as understood by nearly everyone else in this country or the world and never English. By this I mean Britain as a geographical location with natural historical and social associations not a political entity. And actually I do not like being defined whatsoever. (David)

I am the granddaughter of a poor economic migrant, and I don't know how I would be telling this if I were black. Being a white UK citizen I take my acceptance in this culture for granted, although I wonder at our island mentality sometimes, and how it seems to be expressed in a veiled hostility to foreigners. ... My cultural identity is formed by my family history, and my colour and my sexual identity which is freely chosen and accepted in liberal circles where I feel safe. I have learned where not to disclose my sexuality. I feel ashamed of the assumed historic and cultural superiority of this island repeating its xenophobia by encouraging foreign workers to come here to do low paid work, treating them with contempt and urging repatriation. (Ursula)

The last word in this section on nation goes to Stephan, with the important idea that nation is also something that can be left behind:

I was born in Germany and hold German citizenship. I have been living abroad for more than 10 years now and cannot identify with many features of German culture. When travelling in Germany, I feel mainly as a stranger. Before I came to England I lived in the Netherlands and married there. I would have taken a Dutch passport, if I hadn't come to England; Dutch culture held and holds great appeal to me up to the point that if pressed about national identity I was inclined to think about myself rather as Dutch than as German. (Stephan)

These accounts of personal cultural diversity in conflict with the external definitions of nation lead me to look at other aspects of cultural diversity.

Movable groups and realities

While the informants come from startlingly different backgrounds, they each draw on a range of interrelated cultural factors. Some do talk about the confusing aspect of being at cultural interfaces: 'Please don't forget that, as an itinerant, my cultural identity is messed up (but maybe that's not a bad thing!)' (Mario); 'Having lived abroad for most of my adult life I often feel I do not really belong to one culture' (Victoria). However, the majority speak of a complexity that enriches cultural identity.

A number of people talk about smaller groups and realities that are more negotiable and movable than nation. Mario is labelled as belonging to different regions depending on the setting; and Katharina also describes the contextual variability of the realities which are meaningful to her:

> Region is a very powerful identity marker in Italy, often more powerful than nation. I'm not sure what role 'nation' plays in defining my cultural identity, but I guess I'd probably replace the concept of 'nation' here with that of 'territory', which can be expanded or restricted in different situations. When I was in Thailand, I was a 'farang' (Caucasian), in England I'm an Italian, in Italy I'm an Abruzzese, in Abruzzo I'm someone from the north of the region, and this could go on until individual areas of the village where I used to live before I left Italy. (Mario)

> Though German, I do not feel particularly German, and care very little about the idea of Germany as a nation. This does not mean that I am not very attached to Germany and certain ways of doing things ... in a country in which I no longer live. I am fortunate enough to live in an area of the world where my nationality only plays a marginal role, where the only times when I re-think of myself as German is when I go through passport control at the airport or opening a bank account, things where one is limited to one's passport identity. In everyday life my nationality does not come to the fore when I ask myself who I am, rather these little things, the little cultures under the roof of the German nation state which I take as characteristic of me: I like German bread, tea, cosmetic products, I am very attached to my family and friends in Germany, there are certain areas which I am attached to and to which the way that I see myself is connected because they were the stage for certain moments in my personal development. ... I also acknowledge the

influence of the UK, and again small 'cultures' within it, as formative. People I have met, being a student and part of an international community within the student population, also the food, the books, the movies, are all things which have impacted on the way I see myself and have formed part of my cultural identity. (Katharina)

Katharina's 'little cultures' are also meaningful to Sarah, Faye, Ulysses and Laura, often also in contrast to nation, and relate to the 'small culture' described in Chapter 6. They include religion, ethnicity and class, but also the communities, workplaces, skills and artefacts such as clothing and housing which cluster around people as they move through life, and the more physical aspects of appearance, age and sexuality:

> The major features of my cultural identity (in no specific order) are: religion, ethnicity, linguistic repertoire, education, profession, and also skills and abilities. These features interact to give rise to individual values and beliefs that give me a cultural identity. (Sarah)

> I have lived and been part of many different 'cultures'. I was born in N Ireland, but moved to Papua New Guinea when I was 22, where I lived for two years. I then lived for three and a half years in Indonesia, six years in Mozambique, four years in Kenya and 17 years in the Netherlands. Within each one of these 'cultures' I moved between different 'small cultures'. My cultural identity feels complex, enriched by the various cultures in which I have lived. Being N Irish feels like a relatively small part of my identity. (Faye)

> The major features of my cultural identity are, I think, very strongly interwoven with my physical identity, the one I would have had even if mankind had not evolved in the direction it has in the last few thousands of years. So, being 36 years old, healthy, male and heterosexual are a significant part of the context of … cultural identity. (Ulysses)

> Where I live, the area, the house the people I live with. My past, upbringing, attitudes got from upbringing. Language, speaking and communicating. Where I work, work colleagues, how we interact. Activities outside work, friends. Extended family. What I wear. Mostly nation doesn't play a part at all. I don't think about it, but I share similar upbringing and attitudes with other southern English lower middle class Methodist types, and I am more similar culturally to other Brits than probably to other nationalities. So it is easier to predict their attitudes and relate to them. But the political entity of nation doesn't come into it, it's purely cultural. (Laura)

On one level Laura's experience may seem more local than that of other informants; but on another level she refers to a collection of realities as complex as those of Faye who has travelled across three continents.

A picture therefore begins to emerge that while nation is certainly there, it is mediated by other realities that will vary depending on who people are and the contexts within which they find themselves.

Trajectories of multiple, shifting realities

The next theme relates complexity not only to location but also to movement – to trajectories, which also cut through the external realities of nation, and region.[3] Personal realities which emerge strongly are religion, already referred to by Ursula, Sarah and Laura, and ancestry. Sadia relates to a family which has emigrated huge distances over generations. This journey breaks apart the relationship between ethnicity and nationality, neither of which she is prepared to label, which leaves her with religion as the one constant, but within a range of other factors and ambivalences:

> I think the most important feature of my cultural identity is religion because it steers my life. I am Muslim which means whether or not I am Arab by ethnicity, I have adopted certain aspects of Arab culture that are directly related to my religion. Ethnicity is another feature of my cultural identity which co-exists with nationality (another feature) even though my ethnicity is not the same as my nationality. Then there is race which is again different from my ethnicity in being related more or less to biological ancestry. My ancestors came from Persia to India so that is how I would describe my race. Another feature of my cultural identity is my gender. Philosophically speaking, nation should play an important role in defining cultural identity by referring to ancestry and race. However, I don't really know if one particular nation plays a role in defining my cultural identity as can be seen from my response above. I presume colonialism and globalization has changed that forever. (Sadia)

Religion and ancestry here clearly cannot be untangled. Even though Arab culture seems external to her, the power of religion makes it very significant in Sadia's life. This is a description of a personal trajectory from which a variety of 'features' have been culled.

Beth and Park also talk about ancestry and trajectories. Beth refers to her upbringing in Australia and speaks liberally about religion in a more historical sense which is connected with a trail of identity which her family brought as immigrants, making the connection with the broader, transnational notion of ancestry; Park speaks of a journey from Japan to Korea which also connects with class, education and political identities:

Ancestry … relates to 'nation' but I think it transcends any definition of 'national' characteristics. What was impressed on me from an early age was the way my ancestors worked to make a life for their families when they came out to harsh conditions in this country. More important than their countries of origin (to me, at least) was their resilience and adaptability. Indeed, succeeding waves of successful immigrants have exhibited the same characteristics, regardless of origins. Religion is a strong part of my cultural identity that I cannot escape, regardless of how my beliefs have changed. Being brought up in a strong religious tradition means that one has to think very deeply about ingrained beliefs before rejecting them – now the term 'cultural catholic' probably covers where that has brought me. (Beth)

Both my parents spent a substantial period of their life in Japan during the colonial period. My paternal grandfather was working in a mine or sometimes a construction site and my maternal father was an oriental doctor there. When my family moved into Korea … (which led to … a great loss in terms of socio-economic benefits), the general atmosphere of our house was somewhat different from the rest of Korean traditional families due to my father's educational background in Japan. And because of my father's working-class background which had been built up in Japan, nearly all my siblings were exposed to modern education earlier than other poor ordinary Koreans and naturally showed strong opinions about social and political affairs. (Park)

Other informants speak of moving, changing identities which defy definition. Riti's 'fluid' and 'organic' cultural trajectory is hard to place within a linear pattern:

My cultural identity is extremely fluid. It has to be because for me the individual is always either moving beyond who s/he was a minute before or moving backwards/behind who s/he is in the moment. For me, identity is understood in terms of the movement of waves, rather than being something linear. Identity rises and falls, and flows and continues, or recedes.

I believe that my identity is very strongly anchored in being Bengali and in being Indian, although I don't accept that these are static or truly knowable ways of being human. I dislike the idea that being either Bengali or Indian can be understood in terms of physiognomy or any other so called racial characteristics. Because I am also an actor, I have played an American, an Italian, an English girl – and characters about whom it wasn't necessary for the audience to know anything in terms of their national, or racial, classification.

Put simply, my identity is organic and cannot be contained within the noose created by that form of the human thirst for knowledge which seeks to 'understand' by limiting people to closed definitions. ... In scholarly/creative terms I think of it as the School of Categorists – populated by people who are uncomfortable with lateral ways of seeing and living. (Riti)

She expresses a confidence to imposing herself on the roles she wishes to play across different national cultures. Katharina also defies categories by rejecting even 'features' as being too solid:

I find it difficult to think of my cultural identity as comprised of 'features', as you put it in your question. For me, 'features' implies some definable entities of which the sum makes the recipe of my identity. I acknowledge that there are many different factors which impact on the way I think of my identity but the boundaries between them are blurry and they, and their importance change over time. So rather than thinking about my cultural identity as clearly defined by my nationality, my language, my skin colour, my class or religion, I see it as something which always accompanies me but is ever changeable from context to context and from time to time. (Katharina)

For Katharina the blurring of cultural boundaries thus seems to be a moral necessity. She projects an image of someone who collects different cultural realities around her, shedding some and gaining others, depending on her circumstances.

Layered and compartmentalized

A further theme is that of different dimensions existing side by side as simultaneous layers or compartments. Arpita feels able to place herself within two cultures as layered, parallel, simultaneous universes separated by her passport. Peyvand, living in one place with another in his history, expresses a different type of physically layered existence within one household which has deep temporal and political fault-lines. Both their cultural personas seem to have grown to accommodate several dimensions of who they are.

I am carrying two different cultural identities – Indian and British. Each identity has its own features. As an Indian, the major features ... are Indian ethnic clothes, education, my accent, my upbringing and my passport. And my British identity, the culture that has rubbed in me a bit, the features are my accent, clothes, education, experiences, friends and my body language. (Arpita)

Downstairs (I am at my father's study, as I write) a satellite TV station is broadcasting a performance of the famous Iranian singer Elahe, who died this week. This afternoon my mother attended a memorial service in honour of the singer at the Churchill hotel in London. ... My grandmother who is visiting from Iran is watching TV too. She cannot read or write, is ill and will soon leave for Iran. Not having spent my childhood with her, there is little to connect me to my grandmother other than a history linked inextricably to other Iranian personal histories (and to those of other colonized third world peoples). My father just arrived. He has been in Cologne for two days to do a stand-up comedy show in support of political prisoners in Iran (he's a well-known satirist). Nation is downstairs. (Peyvand)

Identities are located physically in these two accounts. Arpita can pass between two very different places easily; and for at least a moment, Peyvand finds the different parts of his cultural identity in different parts of his house. This detailed account from Peter demonstrates similarly that in one place is the history of his extended family which seems a sort of sustained enclave within a second place where he was brought up and finds his future. These layered places are marked by an immense richness of food, music, family disciplines and locations:

My cultural identity is a mixture of two cultures, that of my West Indian roots, which stem from my Jamaican parents, and my British identity. The features of my Jamaican identity centre around family, relatives and friends, through social gatherings, eating West Indian food (rice and peas, ackee and salt fish, fried dumplings, etc.), listening and dancing to music (Reggae and Calypso), supporting sport teams from the Caribbean (in particular cricket and athletics), attending church, youth and social clubs where patois is spoken. Additionally, my cultural identity was also influenced by my parents' upbringing and the close contact with relatives in my London community where discipline was strict.

... My British identity comes from the fact that I was born in London and ever since have continuously interacted with non-black British friends in school, college, social clubs, and in various working environments both in Britain and abroad. ... We speak English and understand British culture. We may also share similar interests on some things such as sports, music, certain hobbies and perhaps even some television soap programmes. (Peter)

Perhaps the most important aspect of living within, rather between these two worlds is the comfortable manner in which Peter manages them:

Despite these different responses, I am comfortable with my mixed cultural identity which is a state of mind that combines and moves within British, West Indian and other cultures. Such mixture allows me to participate and interact with people depending on the environment I am in, similar to children speaking two languages who are able to change from one to the other with very little difficulty adjusting. … This fluid flexible cultural identity, I believe, forms the essence of making any society culturally 'richer' and stronger through cultural interchanges which help to promote tolerance and acceptance of others from various backgrounds regardless of race and cultural differences in a culturally mixing world. (Peter)

Language and reference

Salim describes the power of Arabic as a 'major player' in his cultural identity. As a medium for cultural reference, the way he talks about language resonates with what other informants have presented as markers of cultural reality such as food and music (Peter), clothing (Laura, Arpita), art and even cosmetic products (Katharina). Such things communicate universes of experience, and, in the case of Arabic, for Salim, a sense of transnational nation:

Language, for me, is a major player. Arabic is still shaping who I am. … As I moved out of Tunis and lived in other parts of the Arab world I came into contact with Gulf dialects in daily interactions and in the media and music again. Arabic is now, that I live in the UK, much more than it used to be. It has always been there but now I seek it and make conscious efforts to read, use it and even teach it. I am making an effort in my daily life to use Arabic, feel it and live it.

The issue of nation in its modern socio-political sense used to be a major definer of who I am when I was in my twenties. It ceased to be. My sense of belonging has gone beyond the boundaries of Tunisia. I think it is the effect of age, contacts with others who share Arabic with me and the realization of how much in common I have with many Arabs in the Arab world. I think it is language that plays a major role in redefining the meaning of nation in my mind. I am now very interested in the Arab world as cultural, linguistic and political entity. Tunisia is where my cultural roots are but my intellectual and even emotional interests lie in a bigger world. (Salim)

I began this analysis by speaking about nation as an external frame. Salim gives a very different impression of nation as an inspiration. It needs, however, to be noted that what he says about Arabic may not apply, for example, to English as the two languages represent very different types of histories, global impact and cultural diversity. It is not a simple matter of a national language representing a national culture. Different languages can therefore carry different types of cultural universe. Different informants express different types of relationship with language as a cultural marker. For Peyvand, relationships with different languages mark a further facet of the physical locatedness of the different cultural aspects of his life common to several of the informants already cited:

> Primarily, I am a native English-language speaker. To refine it, I am a speaker of British English. I am also a fluent but not native speaker of Persian. Add why I speak these languages (my history as the child of Iranian immigrants and the shared histories of Iran and the UK) to the fact that I am a non-white and you have the crackle on the radio that is cultural identity. (Peyvand)

The crackle on the radio resonates with Peyvand's previous reference to Iranian culture located physically 'downstairs' where his grandmother is watching Iranian satellite television. English-speakerhood thus contributes to the cultural pastiche.

For Beth, language marks the capacity to be at ease with cultural realities across boundaries:

> Being a non-native speaker of a language doesn't prevent someone from claiming that language as part of their cultural heritage/identity. I can appreciate the poetry of Baudelaire or Verlaine just as the Japanese colleague I once knew was an expert on the English Metaphysical Poets. (Beth)

This notion of 'claiming' implies committed ownership and the capacity to expand culturally into different domains. As implied by Katharina above, cultural capacity is carried by the individual to absorb whatever environmental reality is encountered.

The dimensions of cultural complexity

From these statements there has emerged a picture not so much of the nature of culture, but of how a particular group of people work with the cultural realities in their lives:

- Nation is often an external cultural reality which provides a framing for identities which may be in conflict with personal cultural realities. It can also represent an idea which stimulates personal cultural realities.

- Cultural identities can be made up of a variety of things such as religion, ancestry, skin colour, language, discourse, class, education, profession, skills, community, family, activities, region, friends, food, dress, political attitudes, many of which can cross national boundaries.
- Cultural reality can form around and be carried with individuals as they move from one cultural arena to another. Being part of one cultural reality does not close off membership and indeed ownership of another. Individuals can have the capacity to feel a belonging to several cultural realities simultaneously.
- Language can be many things – a cultural reality, a cultural marker, artefact, a cultural arena, the location of a cultural universe. It may or may not be strongly associated with nationality or nation.

Although few of my informants may be easily categorized as coming from Periphery communities which are struggling to claim a cosmopolitan cultural status, their accounts project a clear message that who they feel they are is not about to be subsumed beneath established cultural descriptions such as individualism and collectivism. They therefore support a critical cosmopolitan view of the world in which cultures are emergent and expressive.

During the discussion I have found myself having to withdraw from the traditional terms with which we speak about culture. 'Culture' or 'a culture' seems too definite and defining. I find myself instead using the following terminology which seems more appropriate to capture the less tangible, floating, organic, uncertain, yet highly impactful quality of what my informants are talking about:

- Cultural reality = something which is going on around the individual which carries broad cultural meaning. 'Reality' implies that it is real to the person concerned, but may not be to other people. A psychological entity.
- Cultural arena = a setting, environment or context within which cultural realities are situated. A psychological place. It could be a country, region, religion, ideology, language (perhaps large), or a community, institution, group, discourse, etc. (perhaps small culture).
- Cultural universe = a broad, rich complex of cultural realities which generates a large number of cultural references. A big psychological entity or place.
- Cultural marker = something which signifies a cultural reality. An artefact.
- Cultural trajectory = a personal journey through a series of cultural realities.

Competing Social Theories

A significant overarching feature of what my informants have to say about the way in which they construct cultural reality is that of social action. I shall now explore this notion with regard to two opposing sociological theories, which locate social action in very different ways and go some way towards explaining the current dominance of neo-essentialism and the rationales behind critical cosmopolitanism.

Structural-functionalism

Figure 3 represents a structural-functional model which can be traced back to the sociology of Emile Durkheim (e.g. 1964), which presented society as an organic system that achieves equilibrium through the functioning of its parts. Derived from biological science, this gave the impression of a society as a solid object, and enabled the development of social theory based on detailed descriptions of how the parts of society, such as the institutions of education, the military, the family and politics, contributed to the whole. Talcott Parsons's *The Social System* (1951), which provides a detailed description of all the interconnected parts of society, is a development of this idea, and did provide an undeniable understanding of the way in which society worked. As the primary unit, the Figure indicates that each national

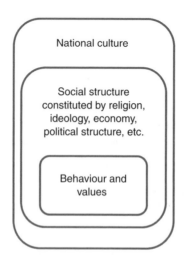

Figure 3   Structural-functional model

culture contains all aspects of that particular society and that behaviour and values are in turn defined by the social structure of the culture. Because of the solid nature of society within the structural-functional model, it is believed that individual national cultures can be described; and these descriptions can therefore be used to explain and indeed predict cultural behaviour.

What is observed about social behaviour can thus be explained in terms of the functions of the social system (or national culture). If a culture is deemed collectivist, any behaviour within it can be explained as contributing to (or as an exception to) its collectivism. Each countable culture is considered as a differentiated unit between which precise comparisons can be made. This approach underpins the essentialist work of Hofstede, described in Chapter 1, who draws on Talcott Parsons to gain support for the notion of cultures as '"complete" human groups that exist; a society is a social system "characterized by the highest level of self-sufficiency in relation to its environments"' (Hofstede, 2001: 10).

However, there are several problems with the structural-functional model, all of which relate to its holistic manner of incorporating everything within its vision of a solid, describable system. There is a normative dimension which enables the evaluation of behaviour and values depending on whether they are functional or dysfunctional (or deviant) to the equilibrium of the whole. There is a sense that all behaviour is contained within the system, which impacts on the degree to which individual behaviour is determined rather than autonomous. Ideology is contained as a product of the culture.

The methodology for describing and predicting culture is therefore positivist in the manner adopted by neo-essentialism as described in Chapter 1, in that it takes as a starting point the notion that national cultures do exist as solid entities with a known type of structure within a world that is organized in a known manner. Social science then takes on the business of confirming, measuring and pinning down the details in such a way that their social truth is enhanced. The approach encourages looking at the world as though it is a place that can be described in objective terms, and denies that ideology may influence science as well as being a subject of study.

A final point is that which is being, because ideology is perceived to be locked within the system described, it is not acknowledged as part of the act of describing. Descriptions of culture appear neutral. While social action is very much the concern of some theorists in this area (e.g. Parsons, 1937), it is locked within a positivist system – as an atomistic, rationalist, scientifically determinable response to a systemic social context (Martindale, 1960: 422–3).

Social action theory

Social action theory presents a very different model from that of structural-functionalism by asserting the independence of social action, and can be argued to throw light on at least some the thinking in critical cosmopolitanism. Here culture is much more of a negotiated *process* which is far more difficult to pin down than the structural-functional system. Social action theory can be traced back to the work of Max Weber (e.g. 1968b) who, while carrying out extensive investigations of the nature of society and culture, made it a major point that the precise nature of human behaviour could never be determined. Part of his strategy against pinning things down was remembering that coherent ideas about societies should be regarded as 'ideal types' that might be used to imagine what society *might* be like – imagined models against which to look at reality, heuristic devices (i.e. for the purpose of investigation) – but which should never be taken as descriptions of how things actually are (Weber, 1968a: 23).[4] There was therefore no way that national culture, social structure and behaviour and values could be neatly packaged into a solid organic system. Weber did in fact produce detailed explorations of Confucianism and Protestantism, but only to suggest how they might influence the social structures against which the social action of individuals needed to be expressed (Bendix, 1966: 261; Dobbin, 1994: 118). The interpretivism associated with critical cosmopolitanism is also derived from social action theory (Weber, 1968b).

It is important, however, to remember that sometimes political and other circumstances may severely reduce the degree to which such choices can be acted out;[5] and it is in such cases that mistaken images of a deficient Other begin to emerge. In circumstances of political oppression, or, more commonly, in educational settings which do not encourage certain types of expression, people may not display critical thought in public; but this does not in any way mean that they do not think critically. For all sorts of reasons they may continue not to display critical thinking when they find themselves in changed circumstances which allow it; but this still does not mean that they do not think critically. Indeed the Western classroom, for example, which requires a public display of critical thought, might well appear to be yet another thought-controlling regime – an immediate turn-off to real critical discussion (Holliday, 2005: 89ff.).

Rather than a confining structural-functional organism, Figure 4 therefore presents a trajectory of action which is certainly influenced by a combination of such major forces as politics, religion and the economy, related as they are to the social structure of the society in question, and to an integral sense of culture connected to *but not*

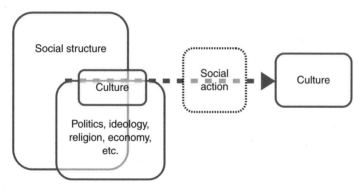

Figure 4 Social action model

contained by these forces. This more independent social action is able to generate something that has at least the potential of something different. Indicative of this, Weber is interested in the power of individuals to change existing orders, for example by means of charisma (Bendix, 1966: 265). One of my interviewees expresses well the way in which the individual is able to make their own decisions about what is going on culturally around them:

> Ultimately, I suppose it's each individual's response to those societal/cultural factors, or indeed to what extent each factor is viewed as having directly affected the lifestyle of an individual *by* that individual, that will shape a person's own ideas about what 'their' culture is. I hope that makes some sort of sense?! (Helen)

Unlike the neat layering of structural-functionalism in Figure 3, Figure 4 indicates a messy complexity with an indefinite movement from a more established culture (on the left of the figure), which may be seen as a dominant discourse, to a more expressive one (on the right of the figure) which is the product of a personal trajectory similar to those expressed by some of my informants above. The double appearance of culture indicates its presence both at the production (creating) and the product (created) ends of the action trajectory. In his study of the London suburb of Southall, Baumann notes:

> Culture-making is not an *ex tempore* improvization, but a project of social continuity placed within, and contending with, moments of social change. Southallians engage the dominant discourse as well as the demotic one. They reify *cultures* while at the same time making culture. Even when they explicitly engage the demotic discourse, the faultlines of the dominant one are effective and, moreover, empirically visible. (Baumann, 1996: 31)

Hence, the structural-functionalist approach may produce more straightforward descriptions beginning with 'the culture' such as:

> Culture X is hierarchical due to its political and religious systems. Members of culture X therefore value loyalty to the group more than to the individual and are more likely to seek peer support in making decisions. Culture X is collectivist.[6]

In contrast, the social action approach will seek to begin with action and attempt to suggest more complex interconnections such as:

> The show of individualistic values which is common in society X is associated with cultures of resistance against a particular type of hierarchy within institutional structures of government and education. Whereas these structures can be derived from aspects of religion X there are other elements in religion X which encourage this type of resistance.

This more shifting, uncertain picture is dependent on the perspectives of the people concerned and resonates with the notion of personal cultural trajectory expressed by my informants above. Hannerz describes it thus:

> Many people have biographies entailing various cross-cutting allegiances – they share different parts of their personal cultural repertoires with different collections of people. And if there is an 'integrated whole', it may be quite an individual thing. Under such circumstances, people may well value some parts of these personal repertoires more highly than others, identify themselves particularly in terms of them, and identify in collective terms more strongly with those other people with whom they share them. It could also be, on the other hand, that they may resist attempts to categorize them unidimensionally in terms of any single cultural characteristic. (Hannerz, 1999: 402)

An understanding of what might be going on is thus built up by looking at the various aspects of culture and society (remembering the impossibility of defining precisely what these might be) and clearly necessitates the thick description suggested in Chapter 2.

One must, however, avoid projecting too neat a case for social action theory – as with all arguments regarding people and society. Some people argue that Weber is still preoccupied with nation to the degree of being a methodological nationalist (Schudson, 1994: 21), actually 'failing to treat it as problematic social and historical construction'.

Complexity and Politics

What can be learnt by juxtaposing the comments of my informants with social action theory can be rationalized in three ideas as follows. (1) Social action theory supports the critical cosmopolitanism view that social structures do not by their generic nature contain and limit cultural behaviour. (2) My informants suggest that cultural realities are individually constructed around individual circumstances, and can transcend national culture description and boundaries. Putting these two together, it can be said that (3) how people wish to be seen is a complex business that cannot be predefined. Cultural description is thus defied. The boundaries which they set on their cultural identities are very much of their own individual making. Individuals have the potential to claim the world as their own cultural universe.

However, these claims are not always recognized for all sorts of reasons (domestic, interpersonal, political). The statements of my informants in the first part of the chapter can be read simply as different people with different realities that are moulded by their individual life trajectories and left there. These people do not themselves state the politics in the interview extracts cited in this chapter. Even though there are statements of conflict between the individual and nation, the political stakes seem low. But what if the stakes change, and the norms imagined by nation, or by bigger regimes of imagined and explicitly or tacitly manufactured truth – the dominant discourses that shape how the powerful view the less powerful – prevent these voices of complexity from being recognized?

In the next two chapters I will therefore explore the struggle which some people have to establish their cultural potential. I shall do this by looking at particular cases which are situated within a global political climate that perceives people to be very different from their potentials. But first I shall see how the three principles above are worked out in another reconstructed ethnographic narrative.

Thinking about China

This narrative is based upon my own direct experience of a number of trips to China as a visiting academic. The three incidents which follow the main narrative are separate events but contribute to the same change of impression seen in the narrative:

Mark had been to China several times in the previous ten years, had had a number of Chinese students, and had become aware of the inaccuracy of the stereotypes of Chinese culture. However, this awareness was not sufficient to prevent some anxiety while planning a trip to China to speak at a conference at provincial University A, and also at University B in Beijing on his way back.

The arrangements were complex. University A would pay for the return flight to Beijing and take care of all the expenses and arrangements while visiting them; and University B would pay for the internal flight from Beijing and take care of all the arrangements while visiting them in Beijing. After Mark made sure that the two parties were in touch with each other by copying them into each other's emails, he thought he would be able to leave them to finalize everything. However, he began to get conflicting message from the different parties, who did not always seem to copying their messages to each other, and felt he had to do a lot of coordination work himself.

Mark was also anxious about having some free time while he was there, to get on with writing his book. On a previous visit to China he felt that the hospitality had been so intense that he had no private time. There were several messages from University A about taking him to 'the lake', which he imagined was far away and would require a long excursion; and the University B people wanted to take him to the Great Wall, which he had already visited, and to the Olympic Village.

Before he left for China, Mark had coffee with a Chinese colleague, Ming, and they talked through his anxieties. It became clear, as their conversation progressed, that Mark's anxiety about travelling to a strange place had led him to build up images of cultural difference. These were based on two theories. The first was that non-Western people did not know how to organize things. The second, connected to this, was the theory that this was a collectivist culture in which it was impolite to question things like hospitality. Putting these two together, he had become angry that collectivist hospitality was ignoring, not listening to, the needs of the individual traveller. Ming told him that he was wrong on all counts and that actually there was simply the normal amount of inefficiency that one would find everywhere. Moreover, Ming believed that Mark might find, when he got there, that the people who had been tasked to look after him would be delighted not to have to take him to the Great Wall and the lake once they could meet face to face and talk about it. Surely, Ming felt, he must realize that email was not the easiest medium for working out such issues.

When Mark arrived he discovered that Ming was right. One of the University B organizers complained to him that it was so annoying that her colleague was not copying other people into her emails and causing breaks in the planning. Moreover, she was delighted not to have to take him to the Great Wall. Also, at University A, 'the lake' turned out to be just next to the city centre with cafés by the water, and no distance at all.

Incident 1

Mark was going for his first breakfast in the Chinese university hotel. As he entered the self-service restaurant he was faced with an array of plates and bowls which he did not know how to use and with items of food he had not seen before. Fortunately an English-speaking student just behind him saw his plight and explained how to proceed. The following morning Mark was sitting comfortably eating his breakfast when he saw a young Chinese man and older Chinese woman, perhaps son and mother, looking as confused as he had been about how to use the different bowls and plates. They also found a friendly informant to show them what to do. Mark then realized that his problem was not that of a non-Chinese being unfamiliar with 'Chinese culture', but simply of a foreigner to that particular situation. He learned quickly that he possessed the underlying experience of a rich variety of different types of self-service restaurants and 'food courts' both at home and abroad, with all their differing practices. The 'mother and son' would do the same. They had the language which Mark did not, and therefore did not depend on an English-speaking advisor.

Incident 2

Mark was with his Chinese colleague, Tong, getting lunch in a fairly high-class self-service Thai restaurant at Hong Kong International Airport. The Chinese cashier accidentally knocked over Mark's glass of fresh fruit cocktail juice and drowned the tray that it was standing on in liquid. Mark complained in an explicit manner. (He had acquired the courage to complain about restaurant service from his daughter who used to work in a restaurant, and from his Italian friend who was brought up with less embarrassment about sticking up for customer standards than he had been.) Tong said that *he* was embarrassed because Chinese people did not normally behave in such a confrontational manner in restaurants.

Incident 3

Tong taught Mark how to hold a rice bowl properly and how only to take food from the nearest parts of the plates of food in the centre of the table. Mark's mother had told him not to put his elbows on the table when eating, and never to take the last item of food from the plates of food in the centre of the table. When some students later invited Mark to a formal lunch in their university they were very careful to show him how to use chopsticks. When he told them that he had observed students in the refectory eating with plastic forks, they said they were making a special effort because it was a formal occasion. On another occasion when they were having dinner together in a restaurant, Mark noted how his Chinese colleagues didn't seem to follow the rules that Tong had taught him. When he mentioned this, quite a discussion ensued about the correct way to hold chopsticks, and Mark was surprised to note how several of his hosts admitted they had not been taught properly.

I shall use the categories of cultural action to help analyze Mark's experience. Instead of comparing two actors, I shall compare his two different types of impression, which are also contributed to by Ming and other Chinese interactants. It is important to note here that the framework is not something with definite categories, but something to be used creatively to help make sense of things. Following the two readings of the *Guardian* in Chapter 2, I have used essentialism and critical cosmopolitanism as the base conceptual markers for two and three columns in Table 4, but only as starting points. I have added a further phrase in the 'statements' cell to indicate that these statements in effect represent theories about culture. I have also added 'personal trajectories' to the resources cell to reflect what has been learnt from my informants in this chapter.

This is not an easy analysis, marked as it is by complexity. There emerges a considerable amount of essentialist thinking on all sides, both in terms of the statements and theories about culture, and the resources that people draw upon. Mark's theories about Chinese culture can be traced to the way he positions himself regarding a non-Western Other, which is marked by the strong element of cultural deficiency. Intervention by Ming leads him to reflect and move to the critical cosmopolitan side. It is this movement that begins to place Ming's statement and Chinese rules of eating in a different light. The realization that they are resources which can be drawn upon rather than confining essences is actually part of this movement to a critical cosmopolitan viewpoint. It is worth noting here the role of Mark's personal cultural trajectory influenced by his Italian friend. The underlying universal cultural processes cell indicates that actually all of the above is part of the process of making sense that Mark begins to share in the discussions with Chinese colleagues about eating habits. No doubt his memory of the enforcement of rules in his childhood, which started as evidence for the essentialist position, also a significant part of his own cultural trajectory, will be thrown into the conversation as part of this sense-making process.

On the one hand, Mark's experience might be seen as a fairly innocent journey of sense-making. However, what I wish to draw attention to is the ease with which he falls into the trap of constructing chauvinistic theories about China. Ming's intervention

Table 4 Developing impressions

Categories of cultural action	Essentialist appearance	Critical cosmopolitan reflection
Statements and theories about culture	Mark: Chinese culture does not encourage effective organization and planning. Collectivism inhibits the questioning of hospitality and the needs of the individual The rules for eating in Chinese culture are impenetrable to foreigners Ming: Chinese people normally avoid confrontation in restaurants and have precise rules for eating Mark: Italians are not embarrassed about confrontation in restaurants	Mark and Ming: anxieties about travelling have led Mark to build up theories about cultural difference which were not true
Global position and politics	Mark: the non-West is inferior in organizing, planning, and considering the needs of the individual. The West has to take charge	
Cultural resources and personal trajectories	Mark: strict rules about table manners in his childhood Ming: rules about how to use a rice bowl and take food Chinese colleagues: there is a tradition of hospitality Chinese students: rules about how to use chopsticks	Mark: experience of a rich variety of different types of self-service restaurants and 'food courts' both at home and abroad, with all their differing practices His Italian friend who didn't mind complaining. His daughter who used to work in a restaurant
Underlying universal processes	Building theories about culture is part of coping with pressures and uncertainty; *but* they are counter-productive Both Mark and his Chinese hosts are trying to work out how to behave with each other before they meet; and the Chinese have issues with communication and efficiency just like anyone else Both the Chinese mother and son and Mark have to work out how to behave in the university hotel breakfast room by asking other people Shared negotiation between Mark and Chinese colleagues and students regarding rules for eating	

pulls him out and takes him elsewhere; but I am sufficiently familiar with Mark to know that he will slip into these 'easy' responses to his anxieties about the foreign again and again. The reason for this is the powerful narratives with which he has been brought up, which populate and colour his cultural resources – which I will now turn to in Chapter 4.

Summary

The points raised in this chapter are as follows:

- When describing people's cultural realities one must refrain from imposing prior agendas, categories or means of organization that will inhibit their expression.
- When considering what people say about themselves it may be more realistic to speak not of individual cultures but of cultural identities that are built differently for different people around diverse cultural realities, arenas, universes and markers, and dependent on personal cultural trajectories. Language may be a constituent part of this complex, and dependent on different histories and politics.
- Nation is often an external frame which may be in conflict with personal cultural identities.
- The *structural-functional* model constructs culture as a total structure which contains and determines all aspects of social life and defines what sort of behaviour is good for the whole society. This lends itself to an essentialist view of culture and a denial of the ideologies that underpin cultural stereotypes because the science of looking at culture is considered neutral and ideology is considered a product of the culture.
- The *social action* model allows greater cultural agency – in dialogue with, rather than contained by, social structure. This supports the notion of individually emergent and expressive cultural identities that defy established descriptions and allow for individual cultural trajectories.
- Individual perceptions about other cultural realities, and the manner in which they present their own cultural realities to others, are also highly complex and influenced by their individual cultural trajectories.

Investigation

The following activities are based on the principle of individual cultural identity in dialogue with national structures raised in this chapter. Again, it is preferable to do these with someone from a different cultural background.

1 In what ways are the disciplines of *thick description, bracketing, making the familiar strange* and *critical reading* employed in the research project described in this chapter?

2 Describe your own life in terms of a cultural trajectory. The statements of the informants, especially Katharina's, may help you here. Describe the cultural realities for each stage and explain what has influenced them. *Bracket* the 'easy' national narratives and excavate deeply.

3 Consider Beth's statement about claiming new languages as part of her own cultural heritage. Find similar examples in your own life. What 'foreign' realities have you incorporated into your cultural universe and taken ownership of? What are the circumstances for this?

4 Consider Peyvand and his grandmother. Describe ways in which different aspects of your cultural universe are embodied in different places in your everyday life.

5 Describe someone who has moved from one country to another and become successful within the structures of the new location. Is it the case that they have:
   (a) left their old culture behind and learnt something completely new, or
   (b) been able to develop a creative mixture of existing cultural abilities and new opportunities?

6 What is the equivalent in your society to Protestantism (if you are British) or Confucianism (if you are Chinese)?
   (a) Consider the degree to which you are confined by or in dialogue with this influence. How far is this a matter of personal choice?
   (b) Is it possible for a person to have more than one such influence? Where do they come from and how do you interact with them?
   (c) Construct a narrative about someone who revises her or his cultural theories about a foreign location.
   (d) Because 'easy answers' will prevail it will be necessary to do some hard searching and bracketing for an alternative critical cosmopolitan impression, which will require noticing aspects of an experience which might have previously gone unnoticed.
   (e) Reconstruct the precise nature of the intervention which led to these alternative, previously unnoticed features. Employ thick description to demonstrate the roots of the impact of the intervention.
   (f) Use or adapt the categories of cultural action to make sense of the narrative.

7 Plan an orientation session for people who might find themselves in Mark's position. Consider appropriate participants, presenters, texts and activities to ensure the following:
   (a) an understanding of the shared complexity surrounding professional behaviour in different societal settings;
   (b) an analysis of the prejudices that can be invoked when someone is anxious about travelling.

Notes

1   An earlier version of the discussion of my informants' contribution in this chapter can be found in Holliday (2010b), and a further discussion of the research process can be found in Holliday (2010a).

2   A postmodern approach, in response to a critique of the postpositivist paradigm which pretends an objective detachment of the research, can be found in a number of places (Clifford, 1986: 2; Clifford and Marcus, 1986; Faubion, 2001; Guba and Lincoln, 2005; Gubrium and Holstein, 1997: 9, 19–33; Hammersley and Atkinson, 1995: 1, 16; Holliday, 2007b: 16; Lincoln and Guba, 2000; MacDonald, 2001; Spencer, 2001).

3   This notion of a personal cultural trajectory through diverse cultural settings is not to be confused with – and is indeed far more dynamic and less essentialist than – the idea of carrying one's culture, unchanged, into different settings as suggested by Geoffroy (2007).

4   See Stråth's (2008: 33–4) reference to Weber as a starting point for new understandings which oppose the fixity of national boundaries.

5   See, for example, Giddens's (1991: 53ff.) discussion of the complex social factors in individuals' narratives of Self, and Mathews's (2000: 93) reference to the constraints brought by power relations and poverty.

6   Elsewhere I describe a conference presentation in which the presenters explain the behaviour of students in the classroom by connecting it with the political structure of their society and their driving behaviour (Holliday, 2005: 25).

4

The Indelible Politics of Self and Other

Neo-essentialism remains a dominant force in both the academy and popular perceptions. A major reason is that its apparently straightforward, neutral categories of cultural description remain successful in hiding the complexity of the foreign Other and the prejudices of the Western Self. In this chapter I will focus on the deep but common forces that sustain the process of Othering and will try to reveal why they so easily remain hidden.

I will do this by interconnecting a series of social pictures. First there is the long-standing Western historical and cultural narrative of Orientalism which results in the pervading ideology of cultural disbelief in everyday experience. Second, on another level, there is, on the one hand, the sensitive criticality with which we see through and rise above the societal and psychological forces which breed prejudicial ignorance, and, on the other, the way in which we commonly, naïvely and often unconsciously submit to these forces. In other words, we live and perpetuate the prejudices which we abhor. I will attempt to show how this can happen at a discoursal level in professional and media locations. This will reveal complexities which are so vulnerable that they can be made invisible, resulting in gross and aggressive misunderstandings of what people are and what they can be. Third, I will discuss this paradox as it is realized within a liberal multiculturalism which mixes the desire to help with a chauvinistic commodification of the Other. These contexts will be set alongside the perceptions of my informants.

Othering

The process of Othering is complex and in many ways basic in the formation and maintenance of group behaviour. It can be defined as constructing, or imagining, a demonized image of 'them', or the Other, which supports an idealized image of 'us', or the Self. Othering is also essentialist in that the demonized image is applied to all members of the group or society which is being Othered. Othering operates at all levels of society, as a basic means whereby social groups sustain a positive sense of identity, as indicated in this sequence:

Othering sequence

1 Identify 'our' group by contrasting it with 'their' group.
2 Strengthen the contrasted images of Self and Other by emphasizing and reifying respective proficient and deficient values, artefacts and behaviours.
3 Do this by manipulating selected cultural resources such as Protestantism or Confucianism.
4 Position Self and Other by constructing moral reasons to attack, colonize or help.
5 The Other culture becomes a definable commodity.
6 The imagined Other works with or resists imposed definitions.

The sequence represents a neutral politics in the sense that we may have no idea that we are on the road to Othering as we set up who we are in contrast to others (step 1). A good everyday example of this could be a family moving into a new neighbourhood where they do not know anyone. They are naturally interested in appearing of good status (2), but have to build an outward sense of this by looking around them to see which resources they have brought with them will make the best impact – clothes, curtains, car, garden, football team, and so on (3). It is by small degrees that this self-imaging arrives at Othering on a world level. There is an imagination of neutrality while in effect the constructions that are generated are not neutral. Construction is by its nature a non-neutral and therefore ideological projection on the world. The Self can thus be 'we the strong' or 'we the pure'. Within the conceptualization of individualism and collectivism, the Self is 'we the efficient'. In order to maintain these images it is necessary to construct the Other as 'they the weak', 'they the impure' or 'they the deficient'.[1]

The construction of 'values'

The categories of cultural action (statements about culture, global position and politics, and cultural resources) are key parts of the sequence as it develops (steps 3–4). Of course the idealization of Self must have some relationship with actual behaviour; but it will enhance and exaggerate positive attributes and play down less positive attributes. An example of this is the common statement that people from individualist cultures are always punctual and get straight to the point in business meetings. This statement is sustained even though a lot of the time people are not punctual and people do not stick to the point. In Britain there is certainly an emphasis on this sort of thing, which can be traced to the Protestant work ethic. Whether or not most people in 'our' culture are punctual and stick to the point, because these are the 'ideals' that have been set up by the group, the Other is imagined to be certainly *not* punctual and *not* getting to the point. Values which explain this behaviour then have to be dreamt up; and collectivism fits the bill very well, rationalizing that there are other, group loyalties that override the need to be on time and make the point. Because these values appear to 'prevent' what the Self considers to be the rational behaviour of being on time and punctual, they must be preventive, backward looking, the opposite to being modern, therefore traditional. This is where the difference between a structural-functionalist and a social action theory, presented in Chapter 3, comes into play. Structural-functionalism would tend to view the Protestant work ethic as part of a containing social system in which everyone would conform to the ethic unless they were exceptional. Social action theory would consider Protestantism to be a structural backdrop against which people would act independently. I take the social action position. The Protestant ethic is there and can be a strong cultural influence; but this does not mean that everyone is punctual and gets to the point. A packaged image of the Other thus begins to be formed, and lends itself to the process of commodification (step 5), which will be dealt with below. The manner in which the Self constructs a morality with which to deal with the Other (step 4) is at the centre of the manner in which the West hides its aggression, where helping becomes a justification for attack and colonization. This will be discussed later in this chapter. The process of reification – making the imagined real through a process of routinization (stage 2), is a basic building-block in this process, and will be looked at in detail in Chapters 6 and 7. The final step (6) concerns the response of the people who are being Othered and their strategies for resistance or compliance, which will be looked at in Chapter 8.

Orientalism

Orientalism refers to the long-standing manner in which the Centre-West has Othered the cultures of the 'exotic' East and the South.[2] The essentialist element of Orientalism is in the manner in which entire societies are packaged into simplistic images. The Self versus Other psychology is brought out in different

Figure 5   Image of the foreign Other [3]

ways. The example represented in the detail of a 19th-century painting in Figure 5 (Gérôme's *Le Marché d Esclaves*, 1857) in many ways projects the Orientalist stereotype. (I use the word 'stereotype' because Orientalism is also an ideology and can itself overgeneralize – an important point which I shall come back to below.) The painting depicts a slave market in an Arab country. The men are examining a naked slave as though she is an animal, while other seated women are completely covered in what seems to be a male-dominated public space. Kabbani (1986: 76) argues that this is an imagined image of Middle Eastern society which is characterized by lascivious sexuality and the objectification of indolent women in slave markets and harems. She argues that this imagined depiction of Other is actually a projection of a European Self preoccupied with a sexuality it cannot express at home.

The more political projection of Orientalism is imagining the non-West to be culturally morally deficient or in need of liberation as a justification for Western imperialism. While this is often described with respect to European colonization in the 19th century and before, Edward Said argues that it also underpins the imagery surrounding more recent Western foreign policy in the Middle East. Here he characterizes well the psychology of the Self:

> But there is a difference between knowledge of other peoples and other times that is the result of understanding, compassion, careful study and analysis for their own sakes, and knowledge that is part of an overall campaign of self-affirmation. There is, after all, a profound difference between the will to understand for purposes of coexistence and enlargement of horizons, and the will to dominate for the purposes of control. (Said, 2003)

This extract from Hanan Al-Sheykh's novel, *Only in London*, characterizes the persistence of Orientalism in the everyday lives of a diverse group of Arabs living in the capital. Here, Lamis, a young Iraqi woman, finds herself at a social event encountering a particularly common Western reading of who she is and where she comes from:

> 'Listen, Lisam. Sorry. Ah, Lamis. I like your name. I've been thinking about Arabia all this week, and then I meet you! … Did you know the harem is a sadomasochistic institution? … Nobody realized that before me, not even the Orientalists. The women in the harem used to help each other bathing, beautifying, massaging, getting dressed and made up, preparing themselves for one man. Then they sat there waiting for him to choose one of them. Just like that. Can you imagine the torture? I want to take some photos portraying the harem. I don't know how to do it but I've got an idea about how the Sultan should look.' … Lamis and Nicholas finally caught one another's eye and the tension evaporated as they burst out laughing. (Al-Sheykh, 2002: 158)

While this fairly uniformly distorted image is rampant, supported by film and paintings in much of the West, it bears little relationship to depictions of strong, combative women in Middle Eastern literature and paintings (Mernissi, 2001: 14–15), or indeed to the image of modern domestic life with its career building and national politics (Honarbin-Holliday, 2009: 14–49). The images nevertheless persist even with the most sensitive of us. The interactant in the extract could so easily be any of us; and although what he says looks so crass in hindsight, he may well just have been trying to be friendly by making a cultural connection or even teasing. (I shall look further at this sort of mistake in Chapter 7.) It is easy for Nicholas to laugh in hindsight. A journalist known for his sensitivity towards the politics of Orientalism was heard to say, while commenting on widespread nose surgery in a Middle Eastern country, 'in this land of the veil appearance is surprisingly important – even reaching Western standards'.

Cultural disbelief

It is not the purpose of this book to look further at the images which Orientalism creates, which are well known, but to get to the bottom of the psychology which underpins it within the Centre-Western picture of the world. My purpose is to get to the bottom of why it is that when, for example, 'Arab' or 'Iranian' is mentioned, the West imagines problems. The cultural 'problem' corresponds in varying degrees with the boundaries which Triandis (2004) sets for collectivist cultures (Chapter 1). At the current moment in history people of Middle Eastern origin suffer worse because of the association between Islam and terrorism (Delanty, 2008: 81). Across British educational institutions, 'Chinese' or 'East Asian' also represent 'problems' (Reid et al., 2009: 4). Regardless of massive education and access to more information than has ever before been made available, the possibility of a shared normality with the non-Western Other somehow escapes the dominant Western perception.

This lack of belief that the non-Western Other can be complex and sophisticated just like 'us' may certainly be due to a lack of insider knowledge of other people's societies. I remember seeing some footage on a television documentary with two women sitting in front of their dwelling in an African village. Because their conversation was subtitled in English I noticed less the details of their 'traditional' ornamentation, and was instead overcome by the surprise at how they were analysing everyday life in the same personal and uncertain manner as any pair of people from the West. We naturally project simple categories and hypotheses about other people in order to help understanding. While it is often argued that this creation of stereotypes is a natural and helpful method for initial understanding, it is doubtful that it is able to develop into a deeper understanding which is able to overcome prejudice.[4] I shall look in Chapter 7 at how the construction of discourses naturally works against deeper understandings. However, many of us who travel and gain insider knowledge of other places still maintain a deep cultural disbelief because of the way we are wired through our own long-standing social narratives.

Greeks, Persians and Martians

It is not difficult to find examples of cultural disbelief in daily life and the media. I can begin with my own life experience. I recall images of the foreign Other in the stories and books of my childhood which had a strong neo-colonialist flavour. Foreign lands and people were the rich canvas for exploration and imagination. The recurring 'Chinaman' in Rupert Bear stories (e.g. Betsall, 1979) was an example of this. Rider Haggard made clear the breeding and civility of the almost godlike tall blond Englishman, Sir Henry Curtis, and Allan Quartermain, the doughty English hunter whose very existence seemed there to make sense of the foreign in *King Solomon's Mines* (Haggard, 1985). Being of a generation where history was still taught chronologically at school, the conflict between the 'democratic' Greeks and the 'despotic' Persians was introduced early, and therefore simplistically. The reasons for Greek success appealed easily to the schoolchild mentality. Every Greek soldier became an individual fighting for his personal freedom, while the Persian army was depicted as pressed into service from the far corners of a soulless empire for which they had no personal loyalty. The narrative was quickly extended to a blond and blue-eyed Alexander invading a Persia that was depicted as already burned out before the birth of Christ.

At that point in my school career Asian history was abandoned except for a brief mention of the Crusades. Brief images of exotic and chivalrous 'Saracens' appeared on television depictions of *Ivanhoe*, with a 'Saladin' who was able to cut through a flimsy silk handkerchief with his fine scimitar, and associated with images of Sinbad the Sailor and harem heroines with bejewelled bikini tops and see-through billowy trousers. These images of West versus East also connected with biblical icons – uncannily Westernized David against a spiritless oriental Goliath, and Delilah corrupted by the same 'painted', 'gaudy' Philistines.

The narrative of small bands of freedom fighters succeeding against despotic armies is then shifted to the Spanish Armada, where Catholics became the 'corrupt', 'collectivist' foreigners. In my schooldays of the 1950s and 1960s Islam was not a concern, subsumed under images of 'Sheikhs', 'harems' and oil. The East was simply the corrupt despot, which eventually merged into Soviet Russia. There was, however, a romance around Sinbad and the Sheikhs – my parents' fascination with the *Desert Song*, the romantic King Hussein of Jordan and the fabulously wealthy Shah of Persia. The exotic, dark-skinned harem woman was not far in my imagination from the almost naked Martian princess, Dejah Thoris, depicted by Edgar Rice Burroughs (2007). I took for granted the popular myth of an organized, autonomous and competent Robinson Crusoe civilizing the tribal Man Friday.[5]

The fascination with the dark native was complex. Haggard's *Nada The Lily* (2001), also part of my teenage reading, is a Zulu love story without a single Englishman present, and yet the Western authorial imagination is total. Haggard the author may not be to blame for this, as he may have been describing faithfully what he saw and indeed loved. There may have been no alternative written account from 19th-century Zulu society. This presents a dilemma of the Western imagination being all there was to write the foreign to itself. Orhan Pamuk, in his autobiographical account of growing up in Istanbul, expresses this dilemma well when he explains that:

> Whatever we call it – false consciousness, fantasy, or old-style ideology – there is, in each of our heads, a half legible, half secret text that makes sense of what we've done in life, and for each of us in Istanbul, a large section of this text is given over to what Western observers have said about us. … So whenever I sense the absence of Western eyes, I become my own Westerner. (2005: 260)

Is it therefore the nature of the West itself to describe the Other as it so consistently describes itself – but because the Other is so much more obscure to the Western eye it suffers from overgeneralization? The most renowned early description comes from Herodotus (1972). His text appears to me critically analytical about his sources; and he is equally as critical of the Greeks as he is of the Persians. He accuses the Spartans of being duplicitous,[6] and he makes a comment, which he says would also surprise his current Greek readers, about the Persians replacing the tyrannies of the Ionian Greek states with democracies (1972: 337–8). However, what he says of Persia is inevitably much more distant and less complex than his detailed discussion of the Greeks. The Greeks thus have a more rounded character with which to absorb criticism, while the Persians remain a stereotypical caricature.

The same can be said of Oliver Stone's 2004 film, *Alexander*, in which he traces the Macedonian conquest of Persia and India. I cite this not as an indication of what happened in history, but of how the narrative of the West versus the East has been sustained in current popular fiction and imagery. The characters of the Macedonians are explored in depth, so that Alexander's brutal, autocratic killing of the people within his party is tempered by complexity. The individualism versus collectivism narrative is evident in several places. The renowned Greek philosopher Aristotle tells the boy Alexander and his companions that the Persians are 'an inferior race', that the 'oriental races are known for their barbarity and their slavish devotion to their senses and excess in all things', and that 'we Greeks are superior, we practise control of our senses, moderation'. At the beginning of the battle of Gaugamela, Alexander tells his army that the Persian soldiers 'do not fight for their homes but because this king', Darius, 'tells them they must', and that they, the Macedonians, in contrast, are 'free men'. When Alexander and his companions arrive at the harem in the newly taken Babylon, he says that the women may 'fool us with their beauty and degrade our souls'. Alexander tells his companion Hephaestion while standing on the parapet of Babylon that he is there to 'free the people of the world' – which takes us right to the current rhetoric regarding the military liberation of the 'Iraqi people'. (See my discussion of this term below.) Most of the audience would recognize all of this as the normal rhetoric of war; but in the absence of complex images of the Persian Other it sticks to the less consciously thinking aspects of the mind as the dominant image.

There is an irony in the manner in which the idea of Greece is still used as an icon of Western individualism while at the same time being firmly planted within the collectivist domain as described by Triandis (2004) in Chapter 1. When I visited Washington, DC, I saw in gigantic scale the Greek columns of US government buildings. A direct descent can be traced in the architecture and language of government and power from Greece, through Rome, through European and then US world domination.

Professional English teaching

My work as an English teacher in Iran in the early 1970s brought me into contact with professional scenarios where the interface between the West and a foreign Other is particularly poignant. Much has been written recently about how the apparently professional distinction between 'native speakers' and 'non-native speakers' hides a racist distinction between White and non-White.[7] Under the cover of this apparent neutrality, the Centre-Western discourse seeks to 'correct' the cultures of 'non-native-speaker' teachers and students based on the conviction that these cultures are lacking in individualist abilities to think critically, to be autonomous, to speak out, and to plan and manage. I have continued to observe this phenomenon into the present, as marked by the following very recent observation:

> We were discussing what sort of research could be carried out to inform practice in a university language centre in the UK. A genuinely caring British colleague who has worked with students from all over the world said that it would be interesting to look at 'Arab students' because they have an 'oral tradition' that means they find reading and writing problematic. I immediately thought of the folded newspapers under the arms of Egyptian men going about their business in crowded Cairo streets.

This reflects the myth of non-Western students which also pervades the training of language teachers, where 'problems' are often associated with national culture (Holliday, 2005: 71, citing Baxter). Cultural disbelief was not only levelled at students:

> On one occasion my Syrian colleague told me that much of what
> I saw around me in his society was to do with temporary problems
> with the administration of the country rather than being a feature
> of their deeper culture. I felt he was just playing with words; and
> neither did I believe him when he told me, on returning from doing
> his master's degree at a British university, that he had encountered
> racial abuse from his tutor in the classroom.

This distinction between political and cultural dimensions is difficult
to untangle, and will be discussed further in Chapter 6.

Innocent soldiers

Coming to the current time, with the invasion of Iraq in 2003, there
was and has been a constant flood of rhetoric both for and against
the need to combat terrorism. Widespread anti-war awareness has,
however, not touched deeper prejudices. The complexity of this double thinking is hinted at in these extracts from television documen-
taries about British and US soldiers in Iraq.

> A young woman British soldier is standing guard in a bunker and
> looking out over a city roundabout in Basra, on the edge of which taxi
> drivers are washing their cars. She says: 'The traffic here is chaos.
> That roundabout is just mad. There's a bus stop, taxi rank. It's where
> they all stop and wash their cars. They've got no rules over here. A
> suicide bomber could come from anywhere. ... There's nothing I
> like about Iraq. ..... The palm trees are pretty; but everything else is
> terrible. The people are quite nice.' (Beaton et al., 2005)

> A male British soldier on patrol on a road into the city comments
> that 'they're just getting on with their lives. ... But when you look at
> the state of it, it's not as if it's Manchester or London, is it?' (ibid.)

> In Fallujah a US soldier asks, 'Why can't they understand that they
> need to commit themselves, to do something, if they want to have
> freedom and democracy. They don't seem to want liberating.'
> (Langan, 2004)

The reader may ask why examples should be taken from soldiers,
who are after all party to the war effort. The significance is that
the roundabout with the taxi drivers washing their cars and the
road into the city are very 'normal' throughout the Middle East and
Asia. The soldiers' statements therefore represent the complexity
within which views are held. They are employed to fight terrorism;
they are also ordinary young people engaged with making sense of

the everydayness of what they see around them. At one level they express an innocence, but through which they are unable to accept the normality of the life they observe; and there is the overriding view that the 'quite nice' people they see around them need to change culturally in order to be 'liberated'.

How can it therefore be that the internationally experienced language educator continues to miss the point that Arab students can read as well as anyone else, that the intellectually sensitive 'Left' British academic can still be racist, that the sincere soldiers cannot see any normality but their own – despite being exposed to more information about the world than anyone else in history, often through a critical press and media, going so far as Channel 4 News broadcasting from the doorsteps of clerics in Iran?

The Morality of 'Helping'

Underlying this deep and almost inevitable chauvinism within the Western gaze and making it even harder to see the real problem is the embedded belief that the foreign Other is being helped. There are several domains both in the present and in the past where this can be seen.

Reference has already been made at the beginning of the chapter to the Orientalist argument that it was in the Western interest to imagine a culturally deficient non-Western Other, to provide an excuse for colonization. Embedded here is a belief that the Other is being 'civilized', educated and improved through its contact with the West. This narrative of a cultural improvement implicit in education recurs in a number of places. Zimmermann cites letters from US Peace Corps volunteers in 1901, in which education is a weapon against a foreign threat:

> 'Our nation has found herself confronted by a great problem dealing with a people who neither know nor understand the underlying principles of our civilization, yet who, for our mutual happiness and liberty, must be brought into accord with us.' (2006: 1)

> '… a bridging of the chasm, through the common schools'. (ibid.)

> 'The fact that so much has been done for the civilization and uplift of the Hawaiians gave us courage to believe that a similar mission would be crowned with success.' (ibid.: 2)

There is a sense in this 'mission' that 'they' must learn about 'us' and not the other way round. This might be connected with Rostami-Povey's discussion of the lives of Afghan women within the context of Western aid to Afghanistan after the invasion of 1991. She explains how the objective of educating the Other is realized if *it fails actually to reach the Other;* and there is a Western disbelief that the Other has the cultural ability to participate in a meaningful manner:

> Everywhere women feel disappointed and angry. Bibisafia said: 'In reality the money which comes in to Afghanistan from one door goes out from another door, because Afghans are not being absorbed into the NGOs and UN organizations.' Tajbanoo similarly argued that: 'Their aim was not liberating Afghanistan; their aim was to steal our resources. Afghanistan has become a workplace for foreign specialists either through western governments or international organizations. ... Why don't they employ Afghan specialists? We have doctors and engineers and all kinds of specialists, even if there are shortages of Afghan specialists, why don't they employ and train us?' (Rostami-Povey, 2007: 52)

A display of engagement which actually fails to engage resonates with accounts of 'democracy training' in Iraq after the 2003 invasion being restricted to five-star hotels, where courses are well advertised but do not venture outside.

While it cannot be denied that Western aid has had significant impact in many locations, its greater contribution to the well-being of an idealized Self can certainly be greater than an actual understanding of what may or may not need to be improved in the foreign Other. The Western Self *needs* the foreign Other to be inferior to fulfil this purpose, and therefore constructs an imagination that it is so. The common Western comment about Islamic society – that women are treated badly – may be intended as support for the women, whereas in effect it can be an act of demonizing the society which forms a direct line of argument to 'we must liberate the women by destroying their society'. Naghibi (2007: xxiii) claims that 'British patriarchs focused on certain practices in other cultures that they identified as oppressive ... and used the rhetoric of feminism to justify their colonial presence in the offending country', even though they were not themselves feminists. This practice continues into the present as the US administration used a discourse of women's rights in Iran to justify the 'war on terror' (Osanloo, 2009: 201). Rostami-Povey, again reporting the narratives of Afghan women, has the following to say:

> These women challenge the western concept of freeing the female body from the hijab. For them the female body desires freedom from war, rape and unwanted pregnancy and not the hijab. In the West, the hijab of Muslim women is simplistically interpreted as an imposition by patriarchal Muslim men ... and the hijab seems to epitomize

Islamic cultural inferiority. This Orientalist view portrays the Muslim woman as having no voice. In post-9/11 and 7/7, the hijab is used as a tool to portray Muslim women, in particular Afghan practising Muslim women, as the barbarian Other, who should be kept in check.... Alma from Los Angeles, whose mother wears the hijab, said: 'They look at us as terrorists and they blame us for 9/11. My mother wears a scarf and when she comes to school many are abusive of her. They are really racist and ignorant.' (2007: 113)

She thus relocates the possibility of ignorance and repression from the women's home societies to the West (which is also a source of some of the war referred to), and then moves on to critique Western feminism – one of the pinnacles of Western criticality:

Today, in a similar way to the colonial era ... western feminists do not challenge the imperial agenda and do not perceive its relationship to their own feminism. They do not attempt to understand women in Muslim societies ... [and there is a] deployment of feminism against Islamic cultures ... as a tool serving US-led military domination in Afghanistan and the region. (ibid.: 139)

At the same time there is a denial of a powerful feminism coming from Muslim societies in women's long-standing struggle for rights which are not in conflict with their religion (Afshar, 2007).

In defence of Rostami-Povey's image of Western feminism, one can concede that each of us has only so much capacity for criticality. All of one's energy might be spent in particular locations; and, indeed, great things can be achieved. This does not, however, mean that one cannot be at the same time ignorant of the deeper realities of other locations, and that ignorant, uninformed criticality can result in chauvinism. This is, however, not an excuse, even though the barriers to understanding the Other may be deep in our histories.

Liberal multiculturalism

The ethos of helping the Other[8] is an ingredient in the liberal multiculturalist response to the 'foreign' within Western societies. What appears to be an inclusive, celebratory recognition of cultural diversity through a presentation and sharing of artefacts, festivals, ceremonies, dress, food and customs has now been widely criticized as hiding a deeper racism. Its superficiality has resulted in a commodified packaging which has been far from faithful to the complexity of lived cultural experience.

I classify this approach to cultural description within the neo-essentialist paradigm because, while there is a celebration of diversity, it is based on the same overgeneralization and packaging found in Orientalism. While it may be argued that Orientalism is out of date because the 'foreign' described by Edward Said is no longer simply located in the East,[9] it may be the case that the psychology of Orientalism is simply being applied to the 'foreign' everywhere. In multicultural Britain, Othering feeds 'the ideology underlying the construction of minority group cultures based on the principle of differences' (Sarangi, 1995: 11). Baumann, in the introduction to his ethnography of the uses of the concept of 'culture' in Southall, observes that:

> In Britain this Ethnic reductionism seemed to reign supreme, and the greater number even of academic community studies I read seemed to echo it. Whatever any 'Asian' informant was reported to have said or done was interpreted with stunning regularity as a consequence of their 'Asianness', their 'ethnic identity', or the 'culture' of their 'community'. (Baumann, 1995: 1)

Within the multiculturalist approach 'other cultures' are presented to schoolchildren around the themes of food, ceremonies, religious festivals, clothing and so on. The critics of the approach have accused this attempted celebration of difference as 'bland', 'indulgent', 'spectacle', 'the exotica of difference' and 'ethnic cheerleading' to express how they are demeaned and alienated by such policy-driven intrusions into their personal identities.[10] The annoyance at the superficiality of representation is expressed well in these statements:

> Ritualized celebration of difference has become an end in itself ... aestheticized and packaged as an exciting consumable collage: brown hands holding yellow hands holding white hands holding male hands holding female hands holding black hands ... 'boutique multiculturalism'. (Kumaravadivelu, 2007a: 109, citing Radhakrishnan, and Stanley and Fish)

> Nobody would talk of racism but they were perfectly prepared to have 'International Evenings', when we would all come and cook our native dishes, sing our native songs, and appear in our own native costume. ... I have been deracinated for four hundred years. The last thing I am going to do is to dress up in some native Jamaican costume and appear in the spectacle of multiculturalism. (Hall, 1991b: 55–6)

The reference to not talking of racism resonates with the notion of neo-racism where race is rationalized, hidden and denied under the 'nice' heading of culture (Delanty et al., 2008a: 1; Spears, 1999). At a macro level, the self-perception of a democratic West as 'de facto anti-racist' leads to a 'depoliticization' which 'masks the embeddedness of the idea of "race"' (Lentin, 2008: 102–3). At a micro level there are everyday 'disclaimer' statements of denial – "'I have nothing against [...], but", "my best friends are [...], but", "we are tolerant, but", "we would like to help, but"' (Wodak, 2008: 65). This agenda of Othering is thus subtle and is often hidden beneath the apparent humanity of modernism. Latour explains the political irony of how the desire to be efficient and clear in tying down who everyone is revealed instead to be a veiled form of aggression:

> The modernists never really waged war.... Quite the contrary! All they did was to spread, by force of arms, profound peace, indisputable civilization, uninterrupted progress. They had no adversaries, nor enemies in the proper sense of the word – just bad pupils. Yes, their wars, their conquests, even their massacres were educational, of course! (Latour, 2006)

Rather than building bridges, a naïve multiculturalism has thus failed to escape from a deeper Centre-Western psychosis, which we see in the expanding world of tourism, where ethnic imagery is reconstructed, generalized, mythologized and fixed for the best effect in satisfying the high-status activity of what amounts to 'shopping for difference' and 'authenticity'.[11] While writing this in a restaurant in a central Mexican city, I overhear an Argentinian-American telling his friends that he and his wife are 'culture buffs' when they travel, how, while in Vietnam they therefore went to see 'the local Buddhist culture' in the market, while the hotel where they stayed was 'Westernized' and 'clean'. Jordan and Weedon state strongly that:

> Blackness, for example, is often celebrated in the dominant – that is to say, racist – culture, especially by those in the dominant group who regard themselves as liberal, avant-garde and/or cosmopolitan. The celebration of racial and cultural difference is a marked feature of the radical twentieth-century avant-garde (both modernist and postmodernist) in the West. (Jordan and Weedon, 1995: 150)

This point of view may seem extreme, but the question is important:

> Our questions simply are these – Isn't the Cosmopolitan often inadvertently a Racist? – How innocent is shopping for difference? ... Doesn't this particular recreation often reproduce again, inadvertently – racist imagery and fantasy? (ibid.)

Commodification

Underlying this 'shopping for difference' and the overall 'celebration' of the foreign Other is the process of commodification – treating something as a commodity which can be bought, sold, collected, stockpiled, displayed, budgeted for and so on. The term is often used to refer to things that have previously been considered of intrinsic value, such as education, knowledge, health, political correctness, travel, leisure and culture. Including culture in this list relates to cultural difference as a commodity within the multiculturalist ethos. A question which may be asked here, especially as many people would not admit to commodification, is why anyone should *want* to commodify the Other. What is the psychological urge and why is it so powerful? The following may be surmised:

1 Commodification is a natural step in the politics of an idealized Self constructing a demonized Other, where an imagined, simplified, reduced Other is so packaged that it becomes an object which *can* be collected, bought and sold. This is implicit in the stylized images of the naked slave, lascivious men and covered women in the Orientalist painting in Figure 5. Once commodified, the group of people concerned can become an object of perusal and manipulation.

2 Constructing the Other as a commodity facilitates ownership – of a manufactured image.

3 Commodification enables accountability within the quest to help and improve. This mirrors the postmodern critique of learner-centredness in dominant Western discourses of education, where a stylized notion of 'learner' is useful because it can be constructed as a set of skills which can be defined, counted and then ticked off as they are addressed by the teacher.[12] This process can be seen in the common media presentation of 'the Iraqi people'. Delanty et al. (2008a: 8) argue that the Western liberal state emphasizes diversity and autonomy within its notion of sovereign 'peoplehood', but does not extend the notion of 'the people' to foreigners, especially when they are non-Christian. Hence, to make the invasion of Iraq look humanitarian, governments and the media spin the commodified image of 'the Iraqi people', thus signing them up to the Western club and making them appear to be 'like us', whereas in fact the complexity of the population of Iraq is something quite different.

4 There is a special allure related to the exotic image of the commodified Other – the sense of an older, less rational, therefore 'mysterious' traditionalism, which carries with it the images of lascivious sex, the secrecy of the harem, and the person as an object of art or beauty with a sense of the animal which can

be collected, owned and displayed. This detracts from the idea that the Other can be a person 'like us', and therefore not to be Othered. This is not of course an issue with Othering generally; and it would be inaccurate to suggest that it should always apply to the non-Western Other.

5 A commodified Other becomes a convenient subject matter for Western study. This relates to the notion suggested in Chapter 1 that the intercultural studies academy needs a foreign Other which is theorized and constructed in a particular manner to be able to build its theories and careers. This is evident in the case of Orientalism:

> Orientalism inscribes its European scholars as learners and teachers adding to the store of western enlightenment. A powerful interpretive paradigm of carrying knowledge of the orient to the west for European improvement and advantage takes shape, in which Orientalism, obsessed with antiquity, chronology, the common origins of language, mythology, science and race becomes a foundational history of the West. (Sangari, 1994: 41)

The reference here to 'the common origins of language, mythology, science and race' provides a useful basis for methodological nationalism and also to the neatness of a global cosmopolitan dream. Interest in 'antiquity' and 'chronology' diverts the gaze from the diverse complexities of modern everyday life which might break the essentialist illusion of Other.

Jumping to conclusions

It is, however, necessary to indicate caution. We need to be careful not too easily to interpret all Western depictions of a non-Western Other as being chauvinistic and not to indulge in the overextending of accusations which give political correctness a bad name. The Orientalist imagination of a deficient Eastern culture was introduced above with specific reference to 19th-century paintings in which women are depicted either as (often naked) in marketplaces (Figure 5), or as indolent 'odalisques', or servants. We need, however, to be cautious not to generalize this Othering of women to all 19th-century European paintings of Middle Eastern scenes. The painting in Figure 6 (Lewis, *The Seraff – A Doubtful Coin*, 1869) is of two women in dispute with a moneylender, or *seraff*, in a Cairo marketplace over a coin which either he or they are unwilling to accept.[13] A critical interpretation of the painting as an Orientalist artefact is that the painter is depicting the people in the painting falsely.

Figure 6   *The Seraff – A Doubtful Coin* [14]

Yeğenoğlu posted the following comment next to the painting when it was exhibited at Tate Britain, London, in 2008:

> The Orient is nothing but endless dissemblance and dissimulation. Not only its women, but also the whole Orient itself are deceptive and theatrical. With 'them' everything is enigma. The veil is not a simple dress that covers their bodies and faces, but is everything that is Oriental, covering their true nature. This European Orientalist fantasy turns the Orient into an enigma which implies that the real nature of these people is concealed – that they are therefore not what they appear to be. According to the logic of the Orientalist, one should always go beyond false appearances, be on guard against the possibility of deception; their duplicitous character is heightened when women are involved in transaction. Doubt and mistrust mark every encounter.

My interpretation is different from that of Yeğenoğlu. The men in the painting do not look to me to be to be duplicitous. The expressions on their faces are not remarkable and no different from those of ordinary people anywhere in the world. The veils of the women are depicted simply as their everyday clothing, with nothing sinister about them. The artist himself may simply have been engaged in depicting what was to him an intriguing scene; and, indeed, the detail in the fabrics and carpets indicates a high degree of engagement with the attractiveness of a market scene which is in many ways unremarkably common throughout the Middle East. The allure of the foreign is certainly present and may indeed have engendered a style not always found in European subjects at the time; and ideology is bound to be present as it is in all pieces of art and indeed all texts; but nevertheless the overall tenor is descriptive.

However, the issue may not be what is depicted in the painting, but what people read into it when they look at the painting now. As with the British soldiers watching the taxi drivers above, the problem is what people imagine about scenes of normality because of the histories and prejudices they are brought up with. We do not know what was in the head of this particular painter; but what might be in the heads of modern viewers who read duplicity into the faces of the characters standing there? Othering can take many forms and can be dealt with in a multiplicity of ways in the everyday circumstances of social life.

Struggling with Identity Recognition

To bring the issues with Othering to a more personal level, I turn again to my email informants. Half of them refer to some sort of struggle with how other people see them. It would be inappropriate for me to connect this explicitly with Othering in every case, where they themselves do not use the term. They instead raise a series of issues relating more generally to how it feels to be perceived as having problematic ~~the oute~~ cultural identities in either some or a whole range of circumstances. ~~limits or~~ While few of my informants would see themselves as Periphery, their ~~eage of an~~ accounts of the everyday struggles with being understood add an ~~area or~~ important extra dimension with which to understand something of ~~object.~~ what it may be like to be defined by others all the time. They remind us that on one level we have all experienced being misunderstood in a variety of circumstances – by our families, colleagues, friends – and this can have varying degrees and types of impact. Teenagers being misunderstood by their parents or children by their peers can be part of growing up or can result in serious trauma or bullying.

I need to make the point again that it is not my intention to try and speak for any of my informants, and therefore not to go deeply into their experiences and their struggles. My purpose throughout the book is to focus instead on the Western predicament which leads to the sorts of surveillance and treatment which my informants report.

Dealing with appearance

Peter and Arpita both have physical appearances which draw attention and which for many people signal foreignness which cannot be placed because of their presence 'here' rather than 'there':

> The way in which others define my cultural identity varies depending on the environment I am in, and how the people I interact with perceive me. For example, as a young lad growing up in London, some white people saw me as a black person first and then British. Whenever they asked me where I came from and I replied London, I could see they felt uncomfortable with my answer. Sometimes they probed further and ask me, where my parents came from to which I would reply 'Jamaica'. On hearing this, they responded with more interest and would ask me further questions about it. It was as if they were more interested in hearing more about Jamaica than of me telling them that I came from London. It seemed they would have preferred I had said Jamaica when they first asked me where it was I came from.
>
> Similarly, when working in Africa, some people would, on first meeting me, assume I was from one of the tribes in the country and therefore, would initially greet me in the local language. When they later realized I was not from their country, and were informed that I came from Britain, some people found it difficult to believe, especially when I was in the company of my white British friends or working colleagues. Not entirely convinced about my place of birth, they too would also probe and ask me further questions about my parents, grandparents and that of my ancestors. When I said they came from Jamaica, they could not relate to its geographical location and understood it to mean America instead, which required further explanation.
>
> On the other hand, whenever I am in Denmark, the Danes initially assume I am American and not African, perhaps based on my dress code. Not until some verbal exchange and discourse had occurred, would they then realize that I was not American but British. In Jamaica the perception some people have of me ... is different again in that there I am seen as a black Englishman and not a Jamaican. These different responses have as much to do with skin colour and race as [with] my cultural identity. (Peter)

None of the instances Peter describes seem particularly threatening, perhaps because he seems to deal with them well, and to brush them off. This does not, however, mean that there are not issues. Arpita does not experience the same directness referred to by Peter, but a degree of discomfort in the constant questioning and sometimes embarrassed surveillance:

My South-east Asian looks ... have created awkward situations for me. I have been asked if I am Pakistani, Sri Lankan or African. I wish people could simply ask me where do I come from, talk to me and then make their opinion about me. I walk in a conference hall and people turn their face around or ignore having any eye contact, not probably because I am Indian but most probably because of the things they have heard or experienced about Indians. (Arpita)

White, British, older Ursula does not have the attributes of nationality or skin colour that one would normally associate with Othering. Neither do the issues surrounding her gender seem to be sexist. Nevertheless, the questioning of her identity definitely appears far more aggressive than in the cases of Peter or Arpita:

Who defines me? Times when I have felt uncomfortable: In a group where a woman asks (and it is always a woman) 'do you have children?' I say no, which then makes it difficult to categorize me. I must be prepared for a line of questioning that seeks to define my status as a woman. This could raise questions about my sexuality, which in turn can make me feel vulnerable.

When in Pakistan with my friend Shaukat and his two young children, I was acutely aware of the hostility of the women expressed in their direct unblinking stares, but without language it was impossible for me to do other than guess that they assumed we were married, and that they didn't agree with such things.

I had the experience of being defined in a negative way and it was very uncomfortable. Recently at the Mela in London walking alongside many Indians toward the station I had the experience of a threatening attack by a thug with a savage dog. The lout allowed his dog to force us into the road with its aggression and was very frightening. My cultural identity at that moment was seen by another, namely the lout, as other. (Ursula)

There is an interesting movement across these three accounts of what may be considered innocent curiosity, in the case of Peter, to embarrassment, perhaps connected with the uncomfortable dangers of 'political correctness' discussed in Chapter 7; in the case of Arpita, aggression which seems to come from a far more basic inability simply to cope with lack of compliance with traditional role expectations, in the case of Ursula, that cuts across nations and cultural realities. This relates to the underlying universal cultural processes referred to in Chapter 1.

Dealing with definitions

Whereas Peter, Arpita and Ursula experience a questioning of their identities because they do not fit, Sabina and Gwyn have identities thrust upon them because they seem to fit stereotypes too well. Sabina suffers from being too easily placed, ironically, as coming from a country of which everyone has a romantic, positive image. At the same time she can appreciate how easy the stereotype is because of her own picture of England:

> When I first moved to England, people seemed to think of me almost as some kind of exotic creature, coming from a beautiful country, where it never rains and everybody is happy and ridiculously stylish, etc., etc. I can deal with these stereotypes (with less and less graciousness and patience as the years go by), but at first I think I really thrived on the positive qualities immediately associated with me because of my culture of origin.
>
> Of course, I also came here to escape some of those associations, such as the over-reliance on the support of one's family in Italy. I myself was guilty of stereotyping England into a country of fiercely independent people, at best mildly eccentric, at worst a little too insular. (Sabina)

However, she can still feel 'flattened' into a national and accented stereotype even though it may be classified as affectionate teasing:

> I am fairly comfortable with how people define my cultural identity, although 'cultural identity' in this case is certainly synonymous with 'national origin'. I only ever notice that people are pigeon-holing me when they see me as 'the Italian lady' or, more often these days, if they have only just met me and I'm having a 'good-English-accent day', as 'the foreign person'. In fact, the only other instance of (gratuitous) assumptions on my cultural identity is to do with my job as an academic: some people immediately assume that I am some kind of bookworm or pretentiously artsy or scarily clever and aloof. One thing that really annoys me, however, is when people who do know me socially insist on making spurious references to my being Italian (and it is even worse when they do so with a mock-Italian accent!). There is one person in particular who manages to do so

every time she sees me, and I find that unbelievably annoying. I resent that for two (related) reasons: it flattens my entire personality onto my nationality and it overlooks the fact that I have spent the best part of my adult life in this country – as far as recent popular culture is concerned, I am much less of a foreigner here than 'at home'. One of these days I'll probably just have to punch that woman, but I wouldn't want this to be on record in your research. (Sabina)

Gwyn is different again – also being categorized into a common, though perhaps less positive stereotype, but which seems instrumental in not recognizing a national identity which he finds central:

It is irritating when others cannot comprehend what I represent or my background, and particularly so when I as a welshman am presumed to be stupid, comic, amusing, exotic, or to be a 'frequent complainer' as is often the case with certain English people in particular. Representations of my compatriots in the media do not help this, with recent examples being a 'Pot Noodle' advert, a trailer for Channel 4's 'the Charlotte Church Show' (who is welsh), and Tony Blair complaining about the 'fucking welsh' when one of his policy decisions was met with hostility in wales.

What makes this all the more aggressive is the fact that the voiced stereotype is *so* common that it may well go unnoticed by the instigators. This apparent lack of attention is compounded by the following observation, which explains Gwyn's ironic use of 'welsh' without capitalization:

I've just noticed during the writing of this reply that Microsoft Word … treats the adjectives/nouns welsh, wales, Scottish, Scotland, English and England differently. The programme auto-corrects the words Scottish, Scotland, English and England to have a capital letter, whilst welsh and wales are not corrected, remaining with a lower-case 'w' or even as misspellings. (Gwyn)

Large and small narratives

This lack of attention to the damaging effects of a national stereotype, which is also present in the casual references to accent in the case of Sabina, may have something to do with Gwyn and Sabina both being 'white' and European, and therefore not registering on the West–non-West danger scale that might be making people nervous of being seen looking at Arpita. There might here be a differentiation between individual responses and broader narratives of history and civilization such as those described above. Whereas Peter, Arpita and Sabina speak mainly of responses to their identity from individuals, Gwyn refers to less personal narratives within the media, politics and Microsoft. Here, Salim makes this distinction, between misdefinitions he can personally counter on a daily basis, and the larger Orientalist narratives he just does not have the time to address:

> I am aware of the complexity of being defined in a number of ways by others. This of course depends on who the other is. The UK other, for example is generally similar in many ways to the European others. This in itself depends on how aware of other cultural features this other is. In my last six years in the UK I intervened whenever possible to clarify and even correct some definitions of my cultural identity. The issue is with the bigger other, i.e. the media which is often seen to be the official discourse in any country. Because of lack of time I have not started writing and replying to many gross generalizations about Arabs in this country. (Salim)

Personal standing

A final observation comes from Duan and Ulysses, both speaking in different ways about personal standing in their relationship with others. Ironically, in China, Duan feels he is constructed as a 'nobody' on account of being a brief returnee to his home country without the normal official credentials, while Ulysses feels he does well because, as a foreigner, he stands outside and is immune from local markers of status:

> I went to a local Bank of China in Xi An City to change some US dollars into Chinese currency Renminbi. The bank staff, a lady, asked me to show my ID card. I said that I had not got an ID card since I have been away from China for more than seven years (in China, an ID card has to be constantly updated), but I had got a Chinese passport. She said 'you do not have an ID card so I cannot do the exchanging of currency for you.' I said 'I have got a Chinese passport.' She said that that did not count. She further said, 'if you are a Chinese, you should have an ID card. If you are a foreigner, you should have a foreign passport.' ... Therefore, I was reconstructed in China as a 'nobody'. I was lost in the discursive reconstruction of my identity. ... This reminds me of Kumar's [claim] ... that he could live comfortably and happily in two cultures – an American culture,

when he works outside and an Indian culture, when he comes back home from work. Such comfort and happiness might be attributed more to his social status as a well known academic and professor in an American university rather than America being more friendly or open to its immigrants. (Duan)

I am from 'outside' of this. I didn't go to public school, did not grow up in Knightsbridge, and so on. So, I think most English people find it easy and possibly comforting to talk to me, being on the other side (but an understandable and not offending, hence safe, side) of the Queen's English. This is not simple and it doesn't happen automatically. Those who understand it are usually either also foreigners in the UK, people who have found themselves in a similar position or those who have studied the subject. Interaction with these people usually works very well. I can't say things would be like that if I was a foreigner in another country. (Ulysses)

Personal standing, status, prestige and social skills, as well as how they are positioned globally by the people who look at them, will all play a major role for all the informants in this analysis. It is not possible to determine these factors in such a brief analysis and would also be inappropriate because these are complex and only represented by passing instances in these accounts.

The purpose of listening to my informants in this way has been, as with their appearance in Chapter 3, to indicate an enhanced picture of cultural complexity. The following thoughts emerge:

- Factors in how people are perceived, positioned and treated are diverse, including physical appearance, skin colour, conformity to traditional expectations, association with well-known stereotypes.
- Degrees of annoyance with these perceptions are to do with how far they can be negotiated and put right, and how far the struggle to be recognized accurately is successful.

Understanding the Discourse Politics of Othering

A major lesson from this chapter is that there seems to be a wiring, deep in the discourses of Western civilization, which in turn derives from deeper interpersonal universals, which makes the Othering of the non-West inescapable. In many ways, the liberal intention to help does not help at all, in that helping in itself mistakenly implies a deficient Other which is in need of help and improvement. The massive resources of the West are indeed often lacking in the locations of the Other; but this fact should not be extended to a belief that they are also lacking in cultural ability. Solutions will require a deep understanding of the mechanisms of these Centre discourses.

Summary

The following points have been made:

- Othering is built on the idealization of the Self and the demonization of an imagined foreign Other. It is common in many aspects of everyday life, from sexism and racism to Orientalism.
- The cultural disbelief in the non-Western Other is rooted in an ancient narrative which is sustained into modern times through histories, stories and the media, often with an imagined individualist and clever few defeating an imagined large, despotic collectivism.
- This disbelief can be so deep that it becomes an innocent response to the unknown. The imagined features of the Other become routine and considered real. There is a general denial in everyday thinking of the ideology that underlies Othering so that few people acknowledge that they are implicated.
- An established 'morality of helping' the imagined deficient Other, embedded in liberal multiculturalism, takes people further away from acknowledging Othering, and results in commodifying aspects of the non-Western Other rather than appreciating deeper cultural complexities.
- At a more personal level there is a diversity of social and physical factors in how people are perceived and positioned everywhere in relation to traditional expectations and stereotypes; and they have diverse ways of dealing with these issues.
- There are, however, also dangers of reading Othering into places where it does not apply.

Investigation

The following tasks are connected with the principle that Othering is a deep and integral part of everyday life. Preferably carry these out with a person from a different cultural background.

1 Consider Arpita's statement. Go to a public place and look around you. When you see someone who seems to be foreign:
   (a) Take time to unearth the stories, histories, references, images and so on which are behind what comes into your mind as you try to work out who they are and what they are about.

(b) How do these things influence how you see the person, in terms of superiority and inferiority?

(c) If you are with someone from another cultural background, compare your description with theirs and describe how the differences and commonalities in perception throw light on the roots of your prejudices.

2 Consider Peter's, Sabina's and Gwyn's accounts of being misplaced, 'flattened' or misrepresented.

(a) Describe instances when you have inadvertently fallen into traps in which you might have had this effect on people.

(b) What is expected or unexpected about their accounts?

3 Find a text which has some connection with an image of the foreign (from a travel brochure, the press, advertising, fashion, music, art, literature, popular culture, etc.). Apply critical reading and search for the underlying ideologies in the text. What evidence is there of (a) commodification, (b) the Centre-West helping, or (c) the narratives described in this chapter?

4 Apply or adapt the *categories of cultural action* to Lamis's encounter and to the statements of the soldiers in Iraq.

5 Take your experience of the above tasks and work out what you need to *bracket* to do this effectively. Write a *thick description* based on the analysis.

6 What is substantially different between being Othered within one's own society and being Othered as a foreigner from the non-West?

(a) Design a research project to address this question.

(b) How would you employ the disciplines of *thick description, bracketing, making the familiar strange* and critical reading within the project?

7 Plan an orientation session for people who are going to spend long periods in other societies. Consider appropriate participants, presenters, texts and activities to ensure the following:

(a) an understanding of how a universal sense of standards and quality of life are expressed in societies with different structures and economic and political circumstances;

(b) a withdrawal from the notion that doing a specific job implies helping an entire society or group of people to improve itself.

Notes

1 See Agar's (2007: 20) reference to 'number-one identity' nations applying a 'deficit-theory approach' to the foreign Other.

2 The Orientalism thesis is well established in the literature (e.g. Asad, 1973; Comaroff and Comaroff, 1992; Florean, 2007; Jack, 2009;

Mernissi, 2001; Morawska and Spohn, 1994; Nzimiro, 1979; Pennycook, 1998; Said, 1978, 1993, 2003; Sangari, 1994; Sarangi, 1995).

3   Source for Figure 5: http://commons.wikimedia.org/wiki/File:G%C3%A9r%C3%B4me_Jean-L%C3%A9on_The_Slave_Market.jpg, image retrieved 22 December 2009.

4   There are several discussions of the value or otherwise of stereotyping (e.g. Holliday, 2009; Kumaravadivelu, 2007a: 48; Waters, 2007c).

5   Pennycook (1998: 10–16) provides a full discussion of the social construction of the Robinson Crusoe myth.

6   A discussion of the common theme of Spartan duplicity in classical Greek literature can be found in Bradford (1994).

7   The Othering of 'non-native speakers' in English language education has now been acknowledged by a number of researchers (Holliday, 2005; Kubota and Lin, 2006; Kumaravadivelu, 2003; Nayar, 2002; Pennycook, 1998). The historical perspective of the setting up of the 'native speaker' teacher as the world norm is described in Phillipson (1992).

8   A discussion of the related notion of 'tolerance', but mainly only of Christian communities, can be found in Delanty et al. (2008a: 9).

9   This is argued by Ahmed and Donnan (1994: 5).

10 See other critiques of multiculturalism (e.g. Delanty et al., 2008b; Hall, 1991b: 55; Kubota, 2004: 35; Kumaravadivelu, 2007a: 104–6; Wallace, 2003: 55).

11 See discussions of boutique tourism (Jordan and Weedon, 1995: 150; McCannell, 1992: 158–70; Urry, 2002: 2, 5, 10).

12 Discussions of constructing 'the learner' as countable skills rather than as whole people can be found in various places (Clark and Ivanič, 1997; Holliday, 2005; Usher and Edwards, 1994). In Holliday (ibid.) there is also a parallel discussion of constructing 'stakeholders' in English language curriculum projects.

13 For a further discussion of this painting see Tromans (2008: 82).

14 Source for Figure 6: http://www.bmagic.org.uk/objects/1891P28/images/136155, image retrieved 22 December 2009.

5

Unnoticed Periphery Identities

In this chapter I will continue with the theme of Othering and look at how people in Periphery situations, who, like Kayvan in Chapter 2, have been used to having their 'cultures' defined for them, struggle to make visible unexpected, complex, creative cultural realities. My aim is not to explore the identities of the Periphery *per se*, for this is not the purpose of this book, but to try and understand the processes through which the Centre-West defines the rest of the world.

Claiming the World

Critical cosmopolitanism tries to understand that the Periphery, in being constantly defined by the Centre-West, needs to work hard to assert the cultural realities that it finds meaningful, and in effect to claim the world. Claiming cultural space does not always result in this claim being recognized by others.

The struggle for visibility

Honarbin-Holliday's (2009) study of young women, *Becoming Visible in Iran*, is significant in this respect. It resists the common images within Western media and political institutions which associate Middle Eastern societies with forms of mindlessness, religious fundamentalism, terrorism and the oppression of women.[1] A parallel would be to associate Western society with child abuse to the extent that this becomes its defining characteristic. Honarbin-Holliday takes us deeply into the lived experiences of a number of young women from a variety of class and religious backgrounds. A major thread throughout her book is how the personal is political and how young women resist cultural and political restrictions through presence and living their daily lives. As independently minded and working women, they tell us about the ways in which they change

Figure 7 Whose heritage? [2]

the mindset of their male relatives with regard to women's creative autonomy and place within the family and such unexpected activity as demonstrating against government restrictions on women attending football matches and proposals for changes in legal systems and family law.

Among the women are fine art students who represent a particular interface with global cultural practices. The photograph in Figure 7 is of one such student sitting next to two of her own paintings.[3] She claims that the European tradition implicit in the paintings is as much a part of her own heritage as the expected traditional Persian schools. Other students carry out what is normally considered to be the European practice of life drawing in the privacy of their homes because nudism is illegal. Honarbin-Holliday explores the manner in which they claim ownership of this practice in this description of a conversation with one of the students, Nokteh, who tells her how European art is a normal part of her education:

'When we studied the Renaissance, our tutor covered almost every single painter and every single brushstroke placed on a church wall in Italy during that period. We would do project work and often I would be given the job of researching topics in art history to investigate and report to the class. You see I love art history, and it is ridiculous to separate West and East too much. If I am to be an artist, all of art history is my heritage. After all, we wouldn't tell a quantum physicist or a philosopher to skip the parts not related to their own geographical location, would we? Besides, I am a citizen of the globe, a member of the global village, I don't want to see myself as an artist who does not know what world art is all about. ... I like to paint prostitutes, women working hard in boring offices behind desks and young couples in coffee shops, I paint them as saints.' (Honarbin-Holliday, 2009: 77)

Honarbin-Holliday then speaks about the significance of this:

I am intrigued and inspired by this young woman. With just a few words she draws a picture of her world; this is a big world where her ideas, mind, and imagination can rise beyond geographical and cultural boundaries. She has determined her artistic identity to be complex and multi-dimensional. (ibid.)

Nokteh's easy reference to project-based and creative educational practices also implies they are a normal part of her cultural universe, whereas they may be expected, by the authors of the individualism–collectivism distinction, not to be a feature of her supposedly 'collectivist' culture. Honarbin-Holliday includes in her book a photograph of a university lecturer and his students sitting around a seminar table in a manner normally expected only in Western universities (ibid.: 154). Nokteh continues to talk about a European Renaissance painting of an interior as part of her cultural universe:

'These are familiar to us, we have interiors like these; I look at the organization of the space and the whole content, the story, and I look at the colour palette. The subject in painting during these periods was usually about some aspect of Christ's life, that is true, but many ideas in these paintings are not dissimilar to some Persian paintings we have discussed in the history of painting in Islamic civilization. If you study art history you can see the connections between early *Bizance* art, and the late Gothic period and some Persian illuminated manuscripts. There have been influences from East to West.' (ibid.: 82)

The ownership which these students claim for European art resonates with my informant Australian Beth's affinity with French literature in Chapter 3. However, in the case of the Iranian students there is a heightened moral dimension to the issue of cultural ownership. An essentialist view contributes to the Othering of people from Middle Eastern societies by reducing the art students to something far less than what they are able to be, by denying the cultural richness implicit in being able to expand their cultural universes to include these apparently foreign genres.

Cafés and cultural resistance

There is therefore a sense of resistance both against the dominant essentialist view and also against the strictures of national structures. This latter is evidenced in young Iranians' use of cafés, or 'coffee shops', as a means of cultural and political resistance. In many ways these coffee shops are related to the global trend of latte cafés, which I shall talk about in detail later, in that they sell European style coffees and pastries, and are therefore as alien to the common stereotype of Iranian culture as the abstract paintings in Figure 7. Nevertheless, Honarbin-Holliday is careful to trace the phenomenon to a combination of current and past cultural practices in Iran as well as to more global economic trends:

> This is understood as a new concept different to the traditional tea houses for men which have been part of the culture for centuries, and to the cake shops serving hot drinks. The idea of coffee drinking as a daily refreshment remains an alien concept for the great majority of Iranians, this is except for Iranian Armenians who drink the short thick coffee much like the Turks, Greeks and Arabs. Amongst urban Muslim Iranians drinking bitter coffee is a symbolic act when visiting those mourning the loss of a loved one. The coffee shop in its contemporary sense has developed in parallel with the opening of the internet cafes in the 1990s. As an entrepreneurial idea and mild capitalist enterprise, a venue for consuming commodities and a source of income by the young, the coffee shop has found its place in most shopping centres. As a marker of socio-political change and a site for holding a dialogue with the opposite sex. The coffee shop is thus claimed as a young idea viewed with enthusiasm and excitement by the secular youth; it is nevertheless a subject of disdain and verbal attack by the clergy and sporadic harassment by the Heraasat [morality police]. (Honarbin-Holliday, 2009: 109)

This sense of ownership of the coffee shop phenomenon by young middle-class Iranians is demonstrated in the following ethnographic description:

> The coffee shop is just a large room with 12 tables for two with square wooden tops and two chairs in wood and woven raffia. There is a smart wooden counter at one end with facilities for preparing refreshments. Two young attendants with sculpted hair styles await orders. Young men and women are sitting at most of the tables drinking milky looking drinks in tall glasses and in dialogue with one another. Some smoke. Soft light is let through the

windows, half covered with finely woven netting material. The simplicity and minimalism here contrasts with the commercial allure of the boutiques on the street, the colour and atmosphere is provided by the young women's bright and shiny headscarves, fitted short coats, cropped trousers over different designs of boots, and makeup. (ibid.: 111)

The significance here is not so much whether or not Tehran coffee shops are rooted in mainstream cultural practice. It is instead that *even* this 'Muslim Middle Eastern' society, which is often considered relatively 'closed', is sufficiently cosmopolitan to be complexly diverse. So why shouldn't they have coffee shops in Tehran? Attention is thus drawn to the 'public presence' of the women, a juxtaposition of 'traditional' and 'contemporary', 'dialogue' and the 'secular', and Muslim headscarves which can also be 'bright and shiny'. The detailed richness of Honarbin-Holliday's *thick description* is an important factor in this 'making visible'.

The Iranian coffee shop is one of the many sites in the cityscape, such as university campuses, numerous cultural centres, public transport, workplaces and parks, where young women demonstrate their modern visibility and what Honarbin-Holliday (2009: 165) refers to as 'a quiet march of self-realization'. This 'quiet march' became all too evident on a global scale through YouTube, Facebook and Twitter during the events following the 2009 Iranian election. This is actually not the same thing at all as the image implied by John Simpson that the estimated 2 million Iranians coming onto the street marks a resistance which has not been seen since the 1979 revolution, since which time they have 'accepted authority'.[4] His statement is a veiled essentialist reference to the view that in a collectivist society people are mostly 'passive' towards authority and lack self-determination.

Honarbin-Holliday describes a cosmopolitan reality which is implicit in the very fibre of a youthful, rather than just traditional or theocratic Iran in which 60 per cent of the population are under 30:

To begin to understand the dimensions of such cosmopolitanism, one needs to imagine three million students on the move, coming together for the first time, passing one another in the public sphere, curious about each other's ideas and expressions, and consequently forming new dynamics of socialization and interaction not experienced or imagined by their elders. The public sphere in Tehran, comprising various corners of the city, university campuses and public transport, underground and overland trains and buses, assumes different and new spatial meanings. The exchange of ideas and behaviours, and the rapid development of particular youth cultures become inevitable. (ibid.: 9)

There is a strong implication that the discussion of cultural ownership should not actually need to take place at all. This is expressed by another art student, Saara:

> 'I never think about what belongs to who in art, maybe I know a lot more about Western art than many in the West. I am doing what I like, I don't really care, there is no need to make a speech about it.' (Honarbin-Holliday, 2009: 82)

This tone resonates with another Middle Eastern location, where Kamal's students at Kuwait University told her what to say about them when she was going to speak at a conference in the US – like the Iranian students, they resist just by being themselves, also with reference to cafés:

> 'I think teachers need to understand that it's OK if they don't get everything about our culture and behaviour. As long as we're not hurting anybody, why does it matter if I am different from someone else?' (Kamal, 2003)[5]

> 'We're just students you know; why have you got to understand us?' (ibid.)

> Sitting in Starbucks and sipping their lattes … whether these students are dressed in traditional Arab clothing or they are in jeans and Eminem tee-shirts, the Arabs do not want to be pigeonholed. They resent the stereotypes including bearded fundamentalist images that represent a lot of what is wrong in the world today; but then they equally resent being seen as products of external influences. (ibid., also cited in Holliday, 2005: 36)

Multiple realities

The theme of cafés as sites of cultural complexity is picked up in the following ethnographic reconstruction which is based on a series of events and locations: visits to Starbucks and other latte cafés in Beijing and Jinhua in China, Istanbul, Seoul, Singapore, Athens and Canterbury; conversations with colleagues from Hong Kong, China, Turkey and South Korea, while sitting in such cafés; and a personal ambivalence towards the Starbucks invasion in Britain:

The latte café phenomenon

Zhang, Ming[6] and Caroline were in Beijing international airport after attending a conference. They were in a café that sold the whole range from latte to cappuccino and a range of cakes and Danish pastries. Zhang suggested that Caroline must feel at home because it was an example of Westernization just like Starbucks.

While Caroline could see how such a café could not be part of Chinese culture, she tried to explain that the 'latte café' had also invaded her culture. She recounted how in the 1990s a lot of British people were also angry when American Starbucks began to invade every high street, with corporate packaging of French and Italian coffee in mugs. She mentioned a TV documentary she had just seen, with the pop artist, Derek Boshier, in 1962, complaining about cornflakes packets being American culture.[7]

Neither Zhang nor Ming were prepared to accept her position on this, but for two very different reasons. Zhang said that her sense of invasion by Starbucks could in no way be compared to his. He said that because she was already Western, an American café chain could be no more than just an irritating business venture coming from a 'different but equal' culture to hers – whereas for him the latte café was an invasion by a superior power which was inflicting a major loss of traditional culture.

Ming's take was very different. He said that both Caroline and Zhang were underestimating the complexity, richness and resilience of culture. In his view the latte café was simply a very attractive commodity that people everywhere wanted to buy, with their own cultural stamp. He explained that this café was part of a Chinese chain which had another branch in Beijing with a very local ambiance. Britain had its own latte café chains, so why shouldn't China? Why should it be presumed that anywhere outside the West that took on new, modern cultural forms was being Westernized? Zhang replied that Ming was just Westernized but didn't realize it.

Caroline had no idea that there were British latte cafés. She thought they were all foreign like Starbucks. She got more confused when later on she went to the internet and found that Costa, Caffè Nero and Coffee Republic were indeed British. However, one was *originally* founded by a British *Italian* and another by British *Iranians*, and in the Costa café in Canterbury there was a large poster of a very Italian looking man and the caption 'Beans selected by Gino – Costa Coffee Maestro since 1976'. So even the local was selling a foreign image.

Next time Caroline met Ming she suggested it all had something to do with globalization. Ming said this was far too neat and recent an answer for something that had been going on in a complicated manner for a long time. On the one hand, cafés were like cultural concepts which had always been carried from place to place all around the world by different people on the basis of trade and the exchange of ideas. He believed the first coffee shops were Arab or Turkish and one was opened in Istanbul in 1457. On the other hand, this cultural trading could present immense threat for some people, Zhang being an example, and that this would depend on how they positioned themselves or were positioned in global politics. Terms like 'globalization' or 'Westernization' were used by different people at different times to make sense of these things.

The different views portrayed through Zhang, Ming and Caroline are laid out in Table 5, again in terms of categories of cultural action. This time I have headed each column with what emerge as the three major themes expressed by the three participants.

A general point to note, which is put into the views of Ming, is that there can be more than one cultural reality operating at the same time, even if they are in conflict with each other. The café, though appearing on the surface to be a single type of location which may seem very similar in different cultural locations, is itself a complex reality with its own history of cultural trajectory, carried from society to society, as Ming points out, by different people at different times and for different reasons. This single type of location will mean different things for different people, as is evident in the three characters themselves. While I locate the characters within three views of culture in the figure, they each take on a life of their own. Zhang's essentialism is political, while Caroline's preserves the claim for neutrality which might be expected of her multicultural-ist background in Britain. Ming's cosmopolitanism is critical; but Zhang accuses it of being naïve. The stereotypes of collectivism and individualism are by no means maintained. As with John in Chapter 2, Caroline comes out the least critical of all, once again defying the cultural stereotype of a critical culture of individualism. Ming and Zhang are not collectively the same.

At the same time, Caroline does not want to be the politicized Westerner imagined by Zhang. Her dilemma is key though. Whether she likes it or not, as with John in Chapter 2, she has no choice but to be placed in a political inequality with Zhang, simply because, unlike Zhang or Ming, and whether Ming likes it or not, she can *only* be Western. For Zhang, and perhaps implicitly for Ming too, being Westernized does not mean taking on new cultural traits, but selling out to a superior force and stopping being who they are – traitors of collaborators. This political divide is irremovable. For Zhang, Caroline pretending to be something culturally in common with him is pretending to be something she cannot be – not so far from the Western traveller dressing up in oriental clothes, which can never be the same as the non-Westerner wearing European clothes – playing with the 'ethnic' versus claiming the right.

Table 5   Multiple realities of the latte café phenomenon

Cultural action	Zhang – cultural invasion and inequality	Ming – cultural appropriation	Caroline – cultural equality
Theories about culture	Cultures are essentially separate Cultural descriptions are not neutral Ming's cosmopolitanism is naïve and Westernized	A particular cultural universe has the richness and resilience to absorb new cultural realities in its own terms It is not Westernized to enjoy latte cafés	Cultures are essentially separate Cultural descriptions are neutral
Global position and politics	He feels he has a culture which is being invaded by another, more powerful one within a process of Westernization, resulting in cultural loss Caroline is associated with the invading Western culture	He thinks that both Zhang's and Caroline's notions of invasion are too simplistic, but acknowledges the cultural and political reality of Zhang's essentialism	She does not like being thought of as part of the same 'Western' culture as the latte café This might be because of a rejection of the notion of cultural inequality She does not accept that she is part of an invading force
Cultural resources	An image of Chinese culture which does not include latte cafés Starbucks is associated with Westernization A belief that people from the West cannot feel invaded	An entrepreneurial China which can absorb and appropriate foreign influence Histories of global cultural exchange	Popular resistance to Americanization in cornflakes and mugs An image of Chinese culture which does not include latte cafés
Underlying universal cultural processes	Rationalizing Self and other relationships with respect to the latte café phenomenon Speaks out, unlike Kayvan in Chapter 2 Represents the expected stereotype of upholding Chinese culture, but does not seem particularly collectivist Takes on essentialism as a form of resistance	Rationalizing Self and other relationships with respect to the latte café phenomenon Employs a critical cosmopolitan viewpoint to make sense of diversity	Rationalizing Self and other relationships with respect to the latte café phenomenon. Looks into the histories of her own cultural universe – unlike John in Chapter 2 Remains naïvely neo-essentialist

'Westernization' and Modernity

The issue of Westernization is thus an important theme in the view-points of Zhang and Ming in Table 5, which runs as follows:

- *The essentialist view* – someone who appears to have stepped out of the behaviour expected within the national culture stereotype, and appears to be adopting behaviour normally associated with the individualist West, must have learnt this from the West, and must be 'Westernized'.
- *The non-essentialist view* – there is no reason why someone with a non-Western cultural background should not adopt behaviour which might appear to be Western, because there are underlying universal cultural processes which underpin such behaviour.

Modernity and individualism

A further dimension to the issue of Westernization is that of moder-nity, which I believe is implicit in the imagined, idealized notion of individualism. Like so many other concepts discussed in this book, modernity is not easy to define. Like 'culture', 'modern' is in our everyday language as well as being a subject of academic contro-versy. As I am concerned with everyday perceptions, I will allow one of my informants, British Helen, in her twenties, who describes herself as a 'modern young lady', to define it:

> There is a freedom to believe in what you want, wear what you want, be what you want. This is being modern. This seemed to be also the case in Japan, though there was still a strong family tradition with some arranged marriages. Strong family tradition can also be found in Britain though. There are people with Catholic back-grounds. In one case a woman who had a child out of wedlock had to sit in a pew further back in the church. The term 'out of wedlock' is still used. Morality is important; but it is something you can work out for yourself, with examples from family and friends. This is being modern, and has to do with the relationship between politics, reli-gion and the family. The norm in this society is that everyone has these freedoms. One gets the impression from the news and the media that such freedoms do not always exist in other societies. (Helen, notes from interview)

There is a strong sense here that modernity is connected with some form of self-determination.[8] I would like to locate this with Honarbin-Holliday's (2009: 7) characterization of the young women in her study as suggesting 'patterns in thought and courageous behaviour which push boundaries and resist forms of subordination'. Helen places this in opposition to family and religious traditions. However, while Helen acknowledges that such tradition exists in Britain, it is more expected in 'other' countries, and self-determination is the expected norm in Britain. I do not wish to hold Helen responsible for idealizing individualism here. She is cautious and reflective in what she says, and I feel she represents the discourses around her while learning from travel. She continues to talk about her brief stay in Japan, and indeed to problematize the notion of 'modernity':

> I was always struck by how 'American' lots of young 'cool' Japanese students and friends seemed to dress! Bandanas and lots of denim – very 'Bon Jovi' if that means anything to you?! And just the way that they would 'hang out' together in the city – groups of skateboarders, or people roaming around with guitars slung over their shoulders, like you might imagine the cover of a Bob Dylan album or something! But then I would often think to myself, *is* this 'American'? Or would I be as likely to see these sorts of styles/fashions back in London? Did it appear so much more 'American' *because* I was in Japan, and I hadn't expected to see that sort of thing in Japan? But then, what *is* 'modernity'? Is it about dressing to fashions, or having the latest gadgets and gizmos? Or is it about a way of thinking? Someone who dresses in 'traditional' styles may not necessarily have 'traditional' or 'old fashioned' views on family, religion, politics, education. ... Perhaps modernity *is* a cultural thing – or simply an individual thing even – differing perceptions of what is 'modern'? (Helen)

Like Caroline's impression of latte cafés above, she does not immediately associate the 'Western' traits she observes among Japanese youth with herself, but with 'America'; but she adjusts her views as she writes, and again returns to 'modernity' in opposition to 'tradition'. However, while she acknowledges its underlying universality, the tendency is still there for 'modern' to be more associated with 'Western'.

The major question, which is central to the entire thesis of this book, is therefore: *is it possible to be modern without being Western?* The possible answers revolve around the break between essentialism and cosmopolitanism as expressed in Table 6, which summarizes the key observations of this chapter so far. In the left-hand column is a summary of instances seen so far in the chapter. In the other two columns are what I view as essentialist and critical cosmopolitan views, largely as expressed by Zhang and Ming in the latte café narrative. The critical cosmopolitan view is also supported by Beck and Sznaider's (2006: 9) concept of 'divergent modernities' rather than a single Western model, in which the potential for individualism and self-determination is therefore also present in these non-Western cultural realities.

Modernity and religion

It is worth pausing for a moment to consider the relationship between modernity and religion. Putting aside West or non-West, in her interview Helen stays with the idea of religion (the Catholic friend) in opposition to modernity. This is indeed a common theme in everyday thinking about the issue. Delanty (2008: 94) opposes this idea by arguing that 'Islamic fundamentalism in Europe, like all

Table 6 The issue of modernity and Westernization

Modern behaviour which *looks* European	Discoursal explanations	
	Essentialist: 'It is not possible to be modern without being Western'	Critical cosmopolitan: 'It is possible to be modern in non-Western terms'
Iranian students claiming ownership of European art, carrying out individualized projects, sitting in seminars, drawing from life at home, painting prostitutes, frequenting cafés	Their behaviour does not conform to the collectivist Iranian, Middle Eastern, Muslim, Chinese, Japanese cultural stereotype	The behaviour may or may not be widely prevalent in their society; but their society, and their personal cultural universes are sufficiently complex and rich to accommodate a wide range of cultural practice
Chinese entrepreneurs setting up latte cafés Young Japanese with 'Bon Jovi' styles of clothing	They must therefore be Westernized – having adopted Western cultural practices and values – and have therefore left behind aspects of their own culture	Structural aspects of their societies (e.g. theocratic government) do not necessarily prevent, and indeed may sharpen, individualistic resistance in personal expression and (with the Iranian students) educational practice

fundamentalist movements, is opposed to the traditional teachings of the past and is modernist in the pursuit of personal liberation', which follows his general point that modernity is to do with the rationalization of religion in opposition to magic, which has also been a cause of secularism.[9]

It is significant that several of the Iranian university professors who support their students by tutoring their drawing and painting of the nude in private (Honarbin-Holliday, 2005: 100) had built their careers on the Islamic revolution and were staunch supporters of the theocracy (ibid.: 6). While some of them may have supported the anti-government reformist presence on the streets of Iranian cities in the summer of 2009, their opposition to the theocracy does not make them secular. 'God is great' is the slogan of their demonstrations; and the wearing of green symbolizes Islam. The potential conflict between modernity and religion does not seem to be an issue with the 19-year old British Muslim medical student who demonstrates Helen's freedom regarding dress alongside her perception of religious dress code, among the everyday artefacts of the British high street:

> Standing in front of the mirror each morning my thoughts travel along familiar lines. Are the sleeves long enough? How can I cover up that plunging neckline? ... If I face my wardrobe in the morning with a sense of adventure, it quickly vanishes in favour of the same one or two outfits – mainly those jeans with a white shirt dress – bleary-eyed and weary as I am after long nights spent with my nose buried in a book. ... Wearing hijab is about more than throwing on a headscarf. It means committing to a broader dress code – for me clothing needs to cover everything but the hands and face, and be loose enough to hide my body shape. Since I like to shop on the high street, that's a bit of a tall order. ... 'Cardigans to cover your bum, trench coats, and lots of bangles,' advises Hasna Abby, 22, who works at H&M in London's Oxford Street. 'When you're wearing hijab all the attraction goes to the face.' So, she says, 'create an alternative focus. Shoes, bangles [...] And then all my money goes on bags, bags, bags.' ... Last season almost every Yves Saint Laurent model was sent down the catwalk in a polo neck. Good news for me, as the extra neck coverage allowed me to be more creative with the way I tied my headscarf. (Kossaibati, 2009)

Indeed, the modern women in Honarbin-Holliday's study are neither particularly secular nor the products of, as some may suspect, a Westernized middle class. She describes them as:

> In their 20s, mostly under 25; ... cleaners, students from religious families who have for the first time entered higher education; from secular families, whose parents were revolutionaries; whose parents are right wing; who live in rented accommodation with their parents; with no income; the majority from the provinces, with a different first language and ethnicity and perspectives on forms of Islam; settled in the capital since the Iran–Iraq war; who support the current theocratic regime. (Honarbin-Holliday, personal communication)

The always present 'West'

But there are dangers in trying to draw distinctions too simplistically. My purpose is not to define modernity or the West. That would be to risk another essentialism. The important point to make is that these concepts are too easily employed in the politics of Othering. The notion of the 'West' is abhorred, revered, played with, and sometimes all of these at the same time. One of the reasons may well be that its influence, as an economic reality or as an idea, is far-reaching and implicated in everyday lives almost everywhere.

In the West itself the idea of the West is also constructed, as has already been noted, in an idealized individualism. An example of this is the 19th-century beginnings of the Olympic movement, where an association between an idealized Anglo-Saxon heritage and an idealized ancient Greek Hellenism was forged to represent an 'advanced' 'Western' modernity with which to 'improve' the world through sport (Chatziefstathiou and Henry, 2007). A major irony here is that Greece sits firmly within the collectivist domain according to current essentialist theory, as described in Chapter 1.

Outside the West the idea of the West generates deep ambivalence where its freedoms are thought both liberating and corrupt. In this section there are no clear distinctions, but examples of confusion and tension, but with, I think, a clear impression of why concepts of modernity can never really escape this confusion with the West. The East's imagination of the West is depicted in Al Aswany's (2007: 73) satirical account of his fictional character Dr Hassan Rasheed, a 1940s Egyptian 'intellectual' who was intent on 'applying' 'the great Western values – democracy, freedom, justice, hard work and equality' – in his 'contempt' for Egyptian 'backwardness'. A similar characterization can also be found in Kiran Desai's (2007: 176) fictional Judge Jemubhai, who, though having experienced extreme racism during legal training in Britain in the 1940s, surrounded himself with artefacts of the West on his return and 'ate, even his *chapatis*, his *puris* and *parathas*, with knife and fork', and rejected his wife, who had found English face powder in his private belongings (ibid.: 166), because 'an Indian girl could never be as beautiful as an English one' (ibid.: 168).

Rostami-Povey's study of Afghan women struggling under the pressure of political oppression culminating in the US invasion of 2001 reports how they associate 'Western culture' with pornography and night clubs (2007: 73) and Islamophobia since 9/11 (ibid.: 91). She places this in contrast to an unexpected account of the non-Western modernity of resistance to political oppression: '"During the Taliban's period they [men] supported women's activities. They also helped us with the housework although it's not in their culture"' (ibid.: 108, citing interview). Darkly lighthearted is Khaled Hosseini's fictional account of ordinary people's resistance through invoking a major media image of the West, risking severe punishment to engage with the film *Titanic* under Taliban rule:

That summer [2000], *Titanic* fever gripped Kabul. People smuggled pirated copies of the film from Pakistan – sometimes in their underwear. After curfew, everyone locked their doors, turned out the lights, turned down the volume, and reaped tears for Jack and Rose and the passengers of the doomed ship. If there was electrical power, Mariam, Laila, and the children watched it too. A dozen times or more, they unearthed the TV from behind the toolshed, late at night, with the lights out and quilts pinned over the windows. At the Kabul River, vendors moved into the parched riverbed. Soon, from the river's sunbaked hollows, it was possible to buy *Titanic* carpets, and *Titanic* cloth, from bolts arranged in wheelbarrows. There was *Titanic* deodorant, *Titanic* toothpaste, *Titanic* perfume, *Titanic pakora*, even *Titanic* burqas. (2007: 296)

The manner in which the idea of 'Western culture' can be created in situations such as cultural or political confrontation is demonstrated in Orhan Pamuk's fictional description of an encounter between a Turkish Islamicist activist, Blue, and a Turkish journalist, Ka:

'But that's how it is', said Blue. ... 'There is, after all, only one West and only one Western point of view. And we take the opposite point of view.'

'The fact remains that they don't live that way in the West', said Ka. 'It's not as it is here – they don't like everyone thinking the same way. Everyone, even the most ordinary grocer, feels compelled to boast of having his own personal views. So if we said "Western democrats" instead of "the West", you'd have a better chance of pricking people's consciences'. (2004: 233)

Nevertheless, even though Blue, perhaps like Zhang above, may be imagining a simplistic 'one West', it is still real in his mind. Elsewhere in Pamuk's narrative, this common everyday under-standing of an opposition between the West and Islam persists, following the common view of modernity as in conflict with religion described earlier. We therefore see the association of 'the West' and anyone associated with it as 'atheist'. When Pamuk writes about Istanbul and his childhood, he presents a range of contradictory but interlocking images – telling thick description. On the one hand, he describes the common belief among the middle class that 'Westernization', marked by glass cabinets instead of cushions and divans, was a positive, though ambivalent 'freedom from the laws of Islam' (Pamuk, 2005: 10). However, his account of how students react to American teachers indicates a resentment of implications of superiority associated with the West – and, moreover, evidence of the critical thinking which the essentialists deny anyone from a 'collectivist culture' like Turkey:

> The Americans were mostly younger, in their zeal to teach their Turkish students, taking us to be far more innocent and wide-eyed than we were. Their almost religious fervour when explicating the wonders of Western civilization would leave us caught between laughter and despair. Some had come to Turkey hoping to teach the illiterate children of the impoverished third world ... who had taken the wrong path. ... Our veiled resentment of our American teacher was acknowledged amongst us. (Pamuk, 2005: 281)

Neither these students' resentment nor the modernity of the Afghan husbands necessarily means that they are finding other cultural resources than from the West. It could also mean that they really *do* want to be Western but that they resent the indignity of the process of becoming so. This further complexity is expressed by Al-Sheykh's story about the fascination of a Lebanese woman, Samr, with the West, to the extent that she rejects her English husband's fascination with the East:

> When she was in her teens Samr had loved anything that came from the West: language, fashion, food, music, films, (medicaments), names, magazines and countless other things. She adored Western singers and movie actors, and even believed that she was in love with their neighbor, a Frenchman twenty years her senior, because his smile reminded her of Yves Montand's. She waited for him every morning and evening at the entrance to the building where he lived, just to hear him say, '*Bonjour, ma petite fille*' ... She threw herself into all aspects of European life, including home décor. During his stay in Beirut her husband had acquired some pieces of Oriental

furniture: brass trays, a mother-of-pearl table, a patterned rug. But Samr had left them wrapped up in cardboard boxes, dismissing his requests that they be allowed to see the light of day, always with the same reply: 'They remind me of my grandparents' house'. She didn't share his passion for Arab music, a subject in which he had become an expert, and was not remotely interested in studying books on Arab architecture. She would even make fun of him, 'Who's the Arab? you or me?'. (Al-Sheykh 1998: 169–70)

Then, when she does eventually become drawn to her roots, Samr begins to realize that her husband's image of her roots is very different from hers:

Her husband welcomed her return [to liking her roots] since he had been attracted to her mainly because she was an Arab. He liked saying her name, and liked what it meant: the beautiful and convivial and exciting side of night. He liked the way she spoke and the color of her skin, which, according to him, meant that human beings had really existed for thousands and thousands of years, and were born from the soil and colored by the sun. … Although he was able to understand this culture and had studied it in depth, his heart remained immune to it, as if it were mummified like a pharaoh, protected from life and even from death. (ibid.: 172–3)

What begins to become evident here is that it is not so much an actuality of whether someone is or is not 'Westernized', but the intentions behind labelling someone as such. The term itself seems to have no particular substance without the connotations people put on it. The manner in which Samr's husband exoticizes her resonates with the discussion of Othering in Chapter 4.

Who is more cosmopolitan?

Yet, in the Egyptian novel, *The Eye of the Sun*, by Ahdaf Soueif, written in English, it is the Egyptian research student, Asya, newly arrived in Britain to study, who expresses surprise at the lack of the sophistication she expects of modernity in the British university.[10] She is driven to hide away what she considers a very low-grade rug and bedspread in her student room at Lancaster University:

On the floor there is a brown rug of the same texture as the bedspread, only thicker. … She looks at the room again, then she takes two paces and bends down. Using the tips of her fingers she folds up the rug and pushes it under the bed. She lifts the bedspread a tiny bit and peeps: white cotton sheets and a beige blanket. She peels back the bedspread, folds it up and pushes it under the bed next to the rug. (Soueif, 1992: 324–5)

And modernity itself seems low grade when comparing her British tutor's office with that of her Egyptian professor at Cairo University:

A room with modern furniture. Teak effect. But then, she was silly to expect anything else here. To expect deep leather armchairs, an enormous nineteenth-century desk, books piled up on the floor, a silver tray with drinks and biscuits, a window-seat looking out over the white sunny quad – with cloisters. (ibid.: 39)

Her rejection of the rug and bedspread, her being 'silly to expect anything else here', is put into context by this account of Asya and her uncle in Cairo:

They sit on the balcony looking silently at the sky. A warm, moon-lit, July night. Rod Stewart is on the record-player and a supper of cheeses, cold roast beef, salads and yoghurt. ... Mint tea is brewing in the teapot and three small glasses stand ready for it. ... Hamid Mursi, wrapped in his woollen cloak with his beige shooting cap still on his head, sits in a woven armchair and longs for a brandy. (ibid.: 9)

There is a total integration of Egyptian (salads, yoghurt, mint tea, woollen cloak) and what might be considered Western (Rod Stewart and brandy) cultural artefacts. Asya's society is far from the Othering stereotype of the non-West. 'Leather armchairs', 'quads' and 'cloisters' normally associated with the West depict it as many-faceted and complex. It could be argued that these are essentially British residues embedded artificially in a 'pure' Egyptian culture through colonialism or Western-oriented globalization. I would instead maintain that such influences are a normal part of the complexity of any society.

'The West' and the critical periphery voice

The always present West, there, waiting in the wings to hijack any attempt at criticality – *as soon as you are critical or modern you have become Westernized* – thus makes everyone nervous. The battle to dis-associate critical modernity from Westernization is crucial for the non-West to claim the world. The stakes are high and often impos-sible, perhaps as reflected in the statement on the wall of the former American Embassy in Tehran, 'On that day when United States of America [*sic*] will praise us we should mourn.'

This struggle for a recognition which is not attributed to the West is evident in the statements from three Turkish university students in their twenties, when I asked them directly about whether it was possible to be modern without being Western. On one level it was straightforward 'yes'. They all agree with Helen, above, about modernity being the freedom of thought, action and dress; but that was by no means the end of the matter as there were huge pressures to associate modernity with the West:

> We sit in the students' work room at a large table. There are a few other students sitting around with laptops and their books. They tell me that there is a powerful stereotype that everything which is modern comes from the West. Because they are living in Western Turkey they feel stuck in the middle of this idea of the West and what they consider their values. Deniz lives alone in her own flat and she is trusted by her family. Hazel says her family believe in education and are tolerant and democratic about family affairs, but that other people don't think they are modern. When I ask them what these 'values' which they talk about are they refer to not drinking alcohol, boys and girls not living together and no sex before marriage. The stereotype of the West is that all these things happen. Hazel says she hasn't been to Europe. When I ask what she means, when we are actually sitting in the European part of Turkey, she says she means Western Europe. They tell me that a lot of people think that students at our university are modern, and Deniz says that she comes from a very modern city, by which she means that nobody minds what you wear there, whereas in the city where she studies everyone is looking at you. People look at you if you wear a headscarf or 'revealing clothes' (strappy tops, cleavage and shorts). Deniz says she personally does not like to wear revealing clothes. Hazel says that she knows women who have had their headscarves pulled at in her home town. Their ideal of total modernity is for people to be allowed to wear what they want with no one looking at you. They both have gay and lesbian friends and have no problem with this but do not think it is modern when they are persuaded to take on other people's values. Hazel says it is a problem when people think she is not supposed to be modern because of her headscarf. She is prepared not to wear it for her job so that she does not miss out on these opportunities; but they both said that a society which does not allow freedom to wear a hijab for people who want to is not modern. Deniz said that she prays and fasts and does not wear the hijab, and that these are personal issues. (Interview notes)

Powerful discourses about the West and Western Europe are very evident here; and are resonant with the statements about culture which dominate neo-essentialism and are also found in many of the interactions discussed throughout this book. Nevertheless, Deniz and Hazel manage to maintain their struggle for self-determined, non-aligned, personal modernity against all these pressures. There is a sharp irony in Hazel being forced to not wear the hijab in order to take part in the dominant notion of modern society (i.e. no hijab) when she herself feels that the mark of modernity is being able to choose to wear it. The experience of Deniz and Hazel indicates the struggle between dominant discourses and personal action which runs through this book.

I talked to Emine in a Starbucks café, reminded of all the issues raised by Ming, Zhang and Caroline above, with the added factor of directly overlooking the Bosporus, the exact and iconic border between Europe and Asia:

> Emine said that there is freedom for boyfriends and girlfriends to live together in Turkey, but this is not something that many people do. She said that these are personal choices but that traditions are a major factor. Nevertheless, her parents do not interfere in what she does. I asked how far this freedom was considered to be a process of Westernization and she said that most people seemed to believe this to be the case. However, she was very concerned that some people seemed to think that being modern was just imitating the West, whereas she thought people should *take* Western things and adopt them in their own terms.
>
> We talked about Orientalism. She said she had the same imagination about Iran as people in the West had. I suggested that there was in fact a geographical positioning going on, but Emine replied that 'the West' was an idea. I asked her if people considered it a negative or a positive thing to be Westernized. She said that this was to do with what was in people's minds when they used the term, and also with who used the term. (Interview notes)

What Emine has to say indicates a complex ambivalence within which she is both aware of and takes part in the shifting discourses concerning 'being modern', the West and 'tradition'. There is a glimmer of Emine herself falling into the same traps as other people when she looks beyond Turkey further east.

Nafisi's (2004) autobiographical novel, *Reading Lolita in Tehran*, has become popular in the West as a window on its imagination of 'real Iran'. I personally found elements of the novel excellent in the way in which a group of young women were described with detailed ethnographic skill, which contrasted with popular depictions in the Western media – in the sense that the women became complex and cosmopolitan, similarly to the women in Honarbin-Holliday (2009). However, critics such as Khosrowjah (2008) seek to disqualify Nafisi's perception by pointing out that while she purports to be writing a personal story she is in fact creating a national narrative of Iran as a failed theocracy with a failed cultural history, and that she and her

students can only be saved by Western literature – once again projecting the modern-West versus religion discourse. Khosrowjah thus
believes that Nafisi casts the West as culturally as well as politically
superior. On the other side, in a television interview with Nafisi about
her novel,[11] she is keen to state that the women in the story were carrying out their own analysis of the West through its own literature
and that they were definitely not Westernized. Another case is Yin's
(2008: 137) suggestion that the film, *The Joy Luck Club*,[12] presents
an Orientalist depiction of Chinese culture as 'sexist, oppressive,
mysterious, inscrutable, exotic, and savage', even though it claims
the opposite by employing Asian actors and director.

Connected with the issues faced by these two media items is
the issue faced by Periphery academics. I have already referred, in
Chapter 1, to the academy's adopting of neo-essentialist theories
to help build careers. Asante (2008) notes concern that so many
African academics adopt 'Eurocentric' concepts, thus compromising the possibility of expressing the alternative truth of 'Afrocentric'
thought. Asante et al. (2008: 3) suggest that a 'communication imperialism' makes it hard to break away from the boundaries set by
Western academic structures. Asante (ibid: 49) does, however, also
concede that both capitalist and Marxist concepts are European in
origin and can have their uses. It is not so much the adoption of
ideas that concerns me here, however, if they are not essentialist
and Othering. Ideas have always been carried and exchanged across
civilizations, just as have commercial innovations, as suggested by
Ming in the narrative about latte cafés above. Yin's anti-Orientalist
critique of *The Joy Luck Club* above makes use of Stuart Hall's analytical framework, which may or may not be considered Western.

At a deeper level Asante's argument raises another issue perhaps
more central to the concept of self-marginalization (which was looked
at concerning the silence of Kayvan in Chapter 2 and will be dealt
with further in a discussion of discourse strategies in Chapter 7). In
order to establish a discoursal opposition to 'Eurocentric' thought,
Asante may be falling into the trap of essentializing 'Afrocentric'
thought, and produces the very restrictive statement – implying all
Africans, in opposition to all Europeans and all Asians – that:

> Afrocentricity makes no sharp distinction between the ego and the
> world, subject and object. … 'Centred on the self, every experi-
> ence and reality itself is personal.' … Even a term like 'person' or
> 'human' means something different to a European and Asian than
> it does to an African. (Asante, 2008: 47, citing Ruch and Anyanwu)

This invokes the structural-functionalist notion of entire continental
systems in which philosophy, values and everything else neatly govern each other, as discussed in Chapter 3.[13]

Geography

While 'the West' has a powerful rhetorical presence which impacts on the identity claims of the Periphery, there is also a geographical aspect which cannot be denied. Its relationship with the concept of individualism in the minds of neo-essentialists is certainly there. Triandis (2004: x), as described in Chapter 1, transports into the consciousness of interculturalists 'people from individualist cultures' as 'North Americans of European backgrounds, North and West Europeans, Australians, New Zealanders'. Hazel, above, has a view about the 'real' West beginning in Western Europe; and Emine has a vision of places further east which she might not like the West to have of her. The physical reality of the modern coming from a particular location, if it can be accepted as comprising high-profile cataloguing, straightening, planning and bringing technology and efficiency, is evident in these pieces extracted from Ivo Andrić's (1995) account of the arrival of the Austro-Hungarian Empire in the small town of Višegrad in eastern Bosnia and Herzegovina in the late 19th century, in his novel, *The Bridge over the Drina*:

> At the same time officials began to arrive, civil servants with their families and, after them, artisans and craftsmen for all those trades which up till then had not existed in the town. Among them were Czechs, Poles, Croats, Hungarians and Austrians. ... They measured out the waste land, numbered the trees in the forest, inspected lavatories and drains, looked at the teeth of horses and cows, asked about the illnesses of the people, noted the number and types of fruit-trees and of different kinds of sheep and poultry. ... In the third year of the occupation ... the town changed rapidly in appearance, for the newcomers cut down trees, planted new ones in other places, repaired the streets, cut new ones, dug drainage canals, built public buildings. In the first few years they pulled down in the market-place. ... those old and dilapidated shops which were out of line. ... The market-place was levelled and widened. ... The older inhabitants could not understand, and wondered. ..... Had it been left to them the town would have gone on looking as any other little oriental town. ... The new authorities had introduced permanent lighting in the town. There was still one more novelty which the occupation and the newcomers brought with them; the women began to come to the *kapia* [meeting place on the bridge] for the first time in its existence. (Andrić, 1995: 135–41)

Notable is the modernity of the movement and mixing of people, and the emancipation of women to the extent that they can suddenly promenade in places once reserved for men.

One can imagine a continuum of experience from the Far East to North America. There may also be similar lines from South to North America and from the Far East down to Australia and New Zealand. Constructions on this geography are also connected to the particular political histories of different countries – who was colonized by whom, movements to modernize, the origins of these movements, the varying degrees of state structures or economies to support these movements.[13] How nations, peoples, individuals are or feel positioned within global political circumstances thus becomes a major factor in the cultural realities of individuals in their perceived relations with the West and with modernity.

Europe and the US *are* the West; but how far modernity is thought to correspond only with these locations is political and is also constructed by the manner in which individuals position themselves in the global order. It must also be acknowledged that people located physically within the US may consider their own modernity to be associated with a 'European' rather than an 'American' ideal. It may indeed be argued that the Starbucks enterprise imported European, Italian notions of coffee drinking before transporting its Americanness across the globe. One must also not ignore the modernity of the 1960s revolution in the West which brought philosophical ideas from the East. I surprise my Chinese students and colleagues when I tell them that I read the ancient Chinese philosophies of Confucius and Lao Tzu as a teenager. There are Europeans living long term in the West who are not modern, in their adherence to confining tradition; and there are people living far away from the West, in Asia and the East and South, who are modern in their own terms.

Much of this chapter has been about complexities of everyday experience which defy the cultural definitions established by the Centre-West. Common notions such as 'Western' and 'modernity' become difficult to pin down in any reassuring way. Even when juxtaposed with the drawable geography of the West, people from the Periphery can be sometimes there and sometimes not, with movable opinions depending on when, where and how they position themselves and are positioned. These struggles are well known within the Periphery. For the West, there has to be a coming to terms with and an appreciation of the details of this complexity.

Summary

The points made in this chapter are as follows:

* People who feel misrepresented by the common images within Western media and political institutions need to struggle to claim recognition for heir own emergent cultural potentials and proficiency.

- The ability to establish one's own cultural realities which can transcend nationality implies that one can be modern in one's own terms without being Westernized, and that one can travel culturally, with multiple identities.
- Whether or not someone can be said to be Westernized is nevertheless a complex matter, meaning different things to different people. If someone believes themselves or others to be Westernized or not, it is part of their own cultural reality and cannot be questioned. What is at issue is the intention with which people are labelled as such when it implies a superior cultural gain or an inferior cultural loss.
- Geography nevertheless plays an important role. People globally position themselves and also feel positioned on a continuum from East to West, which carries with it subtle senses of inferiority and superiority.
- Periphery expressions of cultural reality are rooted in the complex details of their everyday lives.

Investigation

The following tasks interrogate the principles of Periphery realities claiming the world in the face of always present Western hegemony. It will be useful to carry them out with someone from a different cultural background.

1 Holliday (2005: 95, 107) encounters some of his Hong Kong Chinese language students first in a phonology lecture in their home university, and then talking about their interest in Expressionist paintings in one of his tutorials. On both occasions he says they suddenly appeared to him more 'adult'. He says that thinking of them only as language students had framed them as foreigners with problematic linguistic and cultural skills and had infantilized them.

(a) *If you are able to read his account,* note the precise forms of *bracketing* he had to employ. Use Figure 2 in Chapter 2 above as a model and plot the *thick description* he employs.

(b) *Whether or not you are able to read his account*, reconstruct a similar breakthrough in understanding when an event or piece of information about either you or a person you know suddenly made them become less limitedly 'foreign'.

(c) What were the events and situations which enabled you to do this? Use Figure 2 as a model and reconstruct them as a *thick description*.

2 Describe things which you wish other people knew about you to make you appear a fuller person in their eyes. What sort of *thick description* and *bracketing* would *they* need to employ to be able to do this?

3 Consider other international cultural phenomena similar to the latte café. Sport, music and fashion are possible areas.
   (a) Research their histories.
   (b) What are the arguments for them being Western or otherwise in their development?
   (c) What do you need to do to *make the familiar strange* sufficiently to carry out this task effectively?
4 Carry out a small piece of research in which you interview people about what they mean by 'Westernized' and 'modern'.
   (a) What disciplines do you need to employ in designing the questions you will ask – to encourage *them* to *make the familiar strange* and to produce *thick description* about themselves? Use the research project in Chapter 3 as a model if this helps.
   (b) Employ *critical reading* to work out the probable ideological positions regarding superiority and inferiority behind their statements.
5 Imagine that 'being Western' is like belonging to a club. What could be the gains and losses of belonging to such a club? Use the sequence of steps characterizing the Othering process near the beginning of Chapter 4 as a starting point if this helps.
6 Consider what you have heard about the 2009 popular demonstrations against the outcome of the presidential elections in Iran, with specific reference to Western influence.
   (a) Construct a table similar to Table 6 to represent essentialist and critical cosmopolitan views.
   (b) Do the same for another political event, e.g. the invasion of Iraq, the banning of religious symbolism in France, the issue of minarets in Switzerland, or the state abduction/rescuing of Aboriginal children in Australia.
7 Consider the examples from fiction in this chapter.
   (a) In what sense do they go beyond the stereotypes, and what enables them to do this? Does this have anything to do with the interpretive disciplines, or with those employed in ethnographic writing (describing only what you saw or heard, or what you know from what one of the characters has told you, not expressing your own opinions or judgements, not imposing any descriptions of national, ethnic or religious cultures)?
   (b) Explain how pieces of fiction you have read succeed in moving beyond national stereotypes.
8 Apply or adapt the *categories of cultural action* to the interaction between Samr and her husband, and then write an analysis.
9 Plan an orientation session for people in some sort of social or cultural role with people from other societies. Consider appropriate participants, presenters, texts and activities to ensure the following:
   (a) an understanding that people from different cultural backgrounds are not confined to expressing themselves through idealized forms of 'cultural heritage';
   (b) how to withdraw from interfering in other people's personal space.

Notes

1 Resistance against the Western image of who they are has driven a number of Iranian and other Middle Eastern writers (e.g. Alavi, 2005; Alsanea, 2008; Satrapi, 2003).

2 Figure 7 and taken from 'Art education, identity and gender at Tehran and al Zahra Universities', unpublished PhD thesis by Mehri Honarbin-Holliday, Art and Design, Canterbury Christ Church University, reprinted with permission from the author. Extracts from *Becoming Visible in Iran: Women in Contemporary Iranian Society* (2009) by Mehri Honarbin-Holliday. Reprinted with permission from I.B. Tauris.

3 The photograph is taken from Honarbin-Holliday (2005: 10) and also discussed in Holliday (2004b: 284) as an example of visual ethnography used to reveal hidden or counter cultures. There is a further discussion of a similar photograph from the same source in Holliday (2007: 112).

4 BBC News broadcast, June 2009.

5 Transcribed from a recording of her conference paper. See a further discussion of Kamal (2003) in Holliday (2005: 36, 177).

6 Ming has already appeared in Chapter 3. Zhang and Ming have already appeared in another narrative in Holliday et al. (2004: 11).

7 The Ken Russell (2008) film, originally shown in 1962, on the young British artists of the day who were pioneering the Pop Art movement features the works of four friends and colleagues.

8 See King's (1991a: 8) cautious suggestion that modernity can be associated with complexity, with the implication that the immensely diverse 'third world' is in effect the 'first world'.

9 See also Gellner's (1994) discussion of modernity and fundamentalism.

10 There is further discussion of these extracts in Holliday (2000).

11 Newsnight Review, BBC 2, 2 July 2009.

12 *The Joy Luck Club* (Wang, 1994) is based on the Amy Tan (1989) novel of the same name, about Chinese American women.

13 A discussion of potentially essentialist 'Asiacentric research objectives' can be found in Miike (2008).

14 Note Kamali's (2007) discussion of 'different forms of modernity' appearing in different parts of the world through Europeanization in the South and Americanization in the North, and a diversity of resistance to this by different Muslim governments, simultaneous with their own modernity movements.

6

A Grammar of Culture

The discussion so far raises the basic question of how far 'culture' is social reality or illusion. To answer this question it is necessary to explore the continuum between what we create, imagine, construct and project about culture, on the one hand, and what might be considered real, on the other. The impression given so far is that any notion of a national culture which can be described and stereotyped is the product of chauvinistic imaginations which are based on ideological forces and sophisticated, seductive discourses which draw us in and invade our minds. The implication is that anything cultural is deeply complex and hard to pin down. Yet at the same time it has been suggested that there is something Other which has been misunderstood. If this also cannot be pinned down, is the solution simply not to describe at all, and that we should withdraw completely from notions of culture with any sense of solidity or certainty? The analysis of interviews with my informants has been used to demonstrate this complexity. Is that therefore where the analysis should be left, or is there something, though complex, which can be established on some sort of factual basis?

It is therefore necessary to look again at the basics of how culture works and then to take this understanding back to the issue of the Centre and Periphery. The purpose of this exploration will not be to look at cultural difference *per se*, but at how culture operates as a basic social entity. I shall begin by looking at more of my informants' views about how they negotiate a sense of culture.

Negotiating Culture

Following the narratives of complexity in Chapter 3, and references to cultural realities being carried by individuals and changing as they move through different social circumstances, the following accounts from my informants reflect particularly on the reality of national culture from a phenomenological point of view, in that nothing is taken for granted, but in response to the group they found themselves in and to how they responded to the people around them.

The group one inhabits

Beth's stated 'circular approach' refrains from stating what might be expected to be the 'content' of her culture in terms of 'identifiable features':

> First of all, what is my cultural identity? The concept itself must be seen as important within a particular cultural tradition to which I can relate or I would not be able to answer this question. I suppose it is defined according to a set of identifiable features that I share with others who belong to the world I most frequently inhabit. These features can only be described in terms that I am familiar with and that I consider important because of where I come from culturally. This sounds a rather circular approach: I define my cultural identity according to factors which are recognized as important for the group I see myself as part of. (Beth)

She does not say that these 'identifiable features' do not exist. As expected, what these features are depends on the specific 'world' she 'most frequently' inhabits. An important implication here is that this 'world' could change. She is not confined to or bound by it; but when she inhabits it she engages with the cultural features that it generates. By not stating what they are, Beth seems to be making the point that at least part of this relationship with her world is a universal matter – a cultural process shared by everyone which is at least equally as important as the content.

She then goes on to talk about the 'defining factors' in this process. Here I include her comments on some of these. Others were seen in her comments in Chapter 3:

> Defining factors seem to be language, education, ancestry, religion, profession.
>
> *Language.* I'm not sure how to explain the role of an English native speaker as part of my cultural identity. If I think about cultural identity as a set of features I share with others, language is too broad, or maybe it's that English is too widely spoken to indicate a particular culture. If I spoke Catalan, or Welsh, for example, I would have strong reasons for asserting the importance of language but I can only claim English as part of my cultural identity when I say what aspects of English are important to me – English literature for example, familiarity with Beowulf, Chaucer, Shakespeare, the thrill of a performance at the Globe or indeed, a West End performance by a noteworthy playwright. ... Reading? Much of the most vibrant literature in English today is written by Indian, Malaysian, Sri Lankan, Canadian, African or Australian writers. English, then, allows me to cross cultural boundaries.

... *Education*. Education must also include culture with a big C – but with a strong western influence to start with – the traditions of renaissance painting, the glories of gothic architecture for instance, but I have selected from the background that I was presented with from an early age. Hence, while I may remember being fascinated by descriptions of ancient Rome in my year 4 history book, others who attended the same classes may have forgotten about them and remember coming first in arithmetic instead. Thus, 'cultural identity' seems to involve making choices from what we were provided with initially and taking these choices in certain directions. (There is a lot more to be said about education but this is getting a bit long!)

... I had no choice over language, religion and ancestry and they have left their marks, influencing my later professional choice. Having been given certain structures, I then had to make sense of them and adjust my thinking as I gathered knowledge. (Beth)

These elements of what could certainly be referred to as 'national culture' are clearly formative. They relate to the notion of cultural universe introduced in Chapter 3; and Beth communicates the sense of 'bathing' in them. Her experience of language is as engaging as that of Salim with Arabic in Chapter 3; but she is conscious that its global position carries her beyond national boundaries. Her statement that there is 'no choice' seems at first sight in conflict with the sense of openness she expresses earlier. The important point must surely be, though, that once she finds herself with the education, ancestry, and so on that she has been awarded through birth, she *then* has to 'make sense of them' and 'adjust' her thinking.

With reference to other groups

Mario and Helen both talk about how they discovered aspects of their national culture as they compared themselves to people who they perceived to be different from them. Mario gains this perspective through living outside Italy:

I am increasingly becoming aware of some of the features of my cultural identity that can be associated with my being Italian. In other words, there are traits of my behaviour which I'd probably not even notice if I had been living in Italy and that I now notice, or I am induced to notice, because I can see them from an external point of view, so to speak. So, others may define my identity in a direct way (e.g. 'as an Italian, you tend to ...') or in an indirect way (e.g. through the observation of their behaviour). (Mario)

Helen provides a detailed reflection of discoveries through encounters with childhood friends from different backgrounds and from her sojourn in Japan. This is taken from an email response to notes I sent her regarding our face-to-face interview:

> Whilst reading it back, I remembered a deep sense of what it had felt like in Japan to be 'the alien' if you like. ... I suppose that yes, I had grown up in a culturally diverse society, despite not being particularly aware of this fact – that's not to say I was not aware of cultural differences around me, but more so that I *was* aware, but simply accepting of the fact. And indeed interested in and keen to learn about other 'cultures' around me. For example, it didn't really ever occur or matter to me that a my best friend at secondary school was a Jewish girl called Clara. She was my best friend. She just happened to be Jewish! I would often go to Clara's house on a Friday after school, and would share in Sabbath/Shabbat dinner with her and her family. And then some Friday's, she would some to *my* house, where we would have 'fish-n'-chips'! (Friday was *always* 'fish' day in my house, because of the 'traditional' Christian meal of fish on a Friday ... and my mother, at that time, was particularly religious!) And that's all I thought about it at that time I suppose. (Helen)

This awareness of culture growing out of experiences of diversity is then heightened by defining Self in juxtaposition to a majority Other – which seems significantly different from demonizing the Other in opposition to an idealized Self as discussed in Chapter 4:

> Whilst in Japan, I gained a sense of what it felt like to be in a minority – to be one of the people that was treated with curiosity! And it was a fascinating time for me, and perhaps it is that which had made me really focus on 'my' culture – because as a foreigner (or 'gaijin' as some Japanese would refer to us westerners) you would start to question what exactly 'my' culture was, and why these people were so fascinated by me?! (Helen)

At the same time there is an interesting engagement with the dominant discourse of the opposition between modernity (i.e. being Americanized, 'independent and self-sufficient') and tradition (i.e. being family oriented), as discussed in Chapter 5:

> In Japan, there appears to remain a great deal of 'tradition' still with regard to the family. Whilst technological advances seemed great, and younger generations embraced a very Americanized and modern culture through clothes and music, at the *other* end of the scale, there was still a huge focus on the importance of marriage, on the importance of family, tradition etc. ... Many of my students were housewives, and came to learn English because they would not

have jobs to go to, but rather an 'allowance' that their business-men husbands would give to them. To me – as a young lady who had grown to be independent and self-sufficient, almost stubbornly so! – this seemed quite strange, fascinating and 'alien'. (Helen)

But seeing examples of the modern in the unfamiliar leads to a turning round of the discourse by reflecting on how the expected foreign traditional is also present in the familiar modern:

But then, I did wonder that had I had the opportunity to sit with housewives from wealthy backgrounds in England and discuss their sense of duty to 'family', that similarities would have become apparent – perhaps? I could not honestly say, as I have never been a housewife in this country, nor Japan or anywhere else! (Helen)

This reference to the foreign in the Self sits interestingly with John's perhaps playful, yet serious, reflection on what he would be prepared to defend with regard to cultural identity. He refers to a range of aspects of what others might associate with him: 'British' student behaviour and architecture, contrasted with social class, ethnicity, regionality and gender. These are then set against what some might consider to be a common 'British' trait of taking pride in being thought of as *not* British.

If a non-Brit were to say to me 'The trouble with you Brits is that you ...' I would take it personally to some extent, while being happy to disown my nation and say 'the Brits' rather than 'we'. At one level I don't like it when Sonia (my Italian wife) complains about British student drunkenness and laziness when compared with Italian students, say, or the ugliness of British cityscapes, and although I know she is right I like to find counter examples of good things to say about my countrymen. Sometimes I tell people about my Huguenot background, mostly when explaining my unusual name, and once in Inverness in the (long ago) days when I used to wear a beret I was quite pleased when I was called a froggie in the street. Somebody once said I had a French-shaped head (!), which rather pleased me too because it made me feel kind of different and spe-cial (it's not much, I know!). I don't think I'd mind if I was accused of being *so middle class, so white, so southern,* but I would mind if I was called *so male* and *so English* – depending perhaps on how I was being accused of being. I think I might want to defend *being English* more than *being male*. But on the whole I don't think I *am* defined explicitly by others in terms of a cultural identity – more in terms of personality or moral character perhaps. If I was called a *lying Englishman* I'd be upset about being called a liar but I'd hear it more as *lying like all the English,* so I'd be upset about being cast as a member of a lying nation. (John; his emphasis)

The 'reality' in this account is less in how others might imagine him than in John's feelings about how he is depicted. In this sense there is some further indication regarding the relative importance and layering relating to national versus other categories, which again relates back to the complexities in the interviews in Chapter 3.

Dialogue of necessity

Moving from statements to observation of behaviour, a detailed example of how cultural complexity can form against a backdrop and influence of national institutions is presented here in Honarbin-Holliday's description of the dress code of Iranian women outside the office of the Director of the Tehran Museum of Contemporary Art. On the one hand, there are political imperatives that cannot be overcome, and may be seen as confining individual expression. However, on the other hand, there is immense individuality in how these imperatives are negotiated.

First she describes two women who, because of their official posts, need to conform strictly to the government-imposed dress code:

> One notes two ladies behind large desks. They are in well tailored but austere roopoosh [a woman's coat designed to cover the body according to Islamic rules of modesty] and scarves, probably mass-produced. Black, brown or dark navy blue are often favoured in governmental offices such as this, cream and other neutral tones might be tolerated during the hot season at private institutions. These ladies wear absolutely no makeup, and their fitted maghna'eh headscarves are in a single colour well secured under the chin, not exposing their hair above their foreheads. Because they represent the senior management team, their status requires strict observation of the dress code, and though courteous and accommodating they do not act in a familiar manner.
>
> The Director's personal assistant in particular seems to have great authority, evident in the polite, knowledgeable, and firm manner of her speech. There is a sense of urgency in her actions. ... She is fluent in English and highly articulate in her observations on art and socio-political issues. At a later stage of my visit she tells me she was trained at art school at the time of the Revolution, studying dance. I do not believe she has got used to observing the dress code; rather, she tolerates it with exactitude because of her professionalism and the need to remain employed. (Honarbin-Holliday, 2009: 55)

The reference to the revolution, which took place in 1979, indicates the time at which the dress code was imposed. There is a sense here that conformity to a code which outsiders may consider a statement of national culture, does not indicate a lack of personal authority and dynamism, and that the will of the individual can be in dialogue with it. This is more evident in women who have opportunities to be more independent of the government and are not dependent on employment. The second woman, in contrast, has a job which is less visible in the office and is able to be more 'herself', 'rather than signifying institutionalized identities' in the way she dresses. She 'occasionally comes out with a faxed or emailed message' and wears 'a long black roopoosh which is discreetly and subtly styled and waisted with well-considered darts and fine buttons and pockets' and 'stylish dark blue jeans' (ibid.: 55–6). A third woman, who does not work for the Museum but is curating a particular show, is able to take this self-expression further:

> She is in a very light cinnamon coloured trouser suit fitted at the waist; the jacket falls to about ten inches above the knees. Her headscarf, a wide band of loosely woven soft linen-silk mix, is a radiant apricot cream in colour. It lightly rests at the back of her head with most of her hair and neck visible; each end of the headscarf crossing very loosely well below her chin, falling over her shoulders to the back. Her neck shows off her gold chain. (ibid.: 56)

Honarbin-Holliday is careful to point out that this woman is a lecturer at a university that is less associated with the discourses of the 1979 revolution than Tehran University, where lecturers 'wear the chador', the full, black, head-to-toe covering, 'as a mark of support for the hard-line factions in the government' (ibid.: 57).

Another woman, who displays another facet of dress, is the 'tea lady'. Like the 'front of office' women,

> She is also in a black headscarf, trousers, and well-worn slightly crumpled cotton roopoosh; but this is more like a working uniform which has been washed often. ... The tea lady's headscarf is worn with a casual air, knotted thinly under her chin, and it does not seem to matter how she wears it. It is highly likely that the tea lady comes to work wearing a chador as an outer and unifying garment, removing it during the tea-serving period. It is also possible that she is not at all religious and wears her hijab to demonstrate her sociocultural allegiances with a residential neighbourhood. (ibid.: 56)

The significance of this is the note of caution that this form of dress, which conforms to more traditional urban communities, and which may not have changed at all as a result of the 1979 revolution – although having the appearance of the expected Muslim women's covering – may not mean that the woman herself is particularly religious and thus represents a further complexity in the dialogue between the individual, national, community and religious requirements. Honarbin-Holliday argues that these diverse forms of dress 'highlight the individual's cultural competencies, economic privilege, resistance and gendered solidarity'. She connects this with her broader thesis about Iranian women's 'perseverance with education, looking for means to become economically independent, and learning to explore, articulate, and gather pace in the discussion of civil society', which is 'related to the desire to become visible as a social as well as political force, even at the cost of being arrested' (ibid.: 58). This example from Iran represents, for at least two of the women, resistance against a dominant national order – which is interesting to contrast with the resistance against dominant Centre-Western discourses explored in Chapter 5. In other locations there may be no need for resistance, as may be evident from my informants.

Particular Content and Universal Process

What might therefore be gleaned usefully from these informant extracts and the descriptions of women's clothing, put together with the categories of cultural action that have been used to make sense of narratives in each chapter, are three aspects of cultural reality, which are represented in Figure 8. Important here is the dialogue between these three elements. The figure does not represent the enclosed system preferred by structural-functionalism expressed in Figure 3, but rather a strong sense of negotiation and movement as indicated by the broad arrows at top and bottom of the figure, which is implicit in the looser social action theory represented in Figure 4. The relationships are complex. There are no easy explanations in this model. I shall explain each of the three main parts of the figure in turn, starting with the areas of particularity because they are more familiar, and then spending more time on the underlying universal cultural processes.

Particular Social and Political Structures

This is the area, on the left of Figure 8, which has drawn most discussion in the neo-essentialist view of things. These structures are particular to cultural locations, which may be nation, but also other macro-forces such as religion and ideology [i]. They are also particular to global position and politics [ii]. These structures are implicit

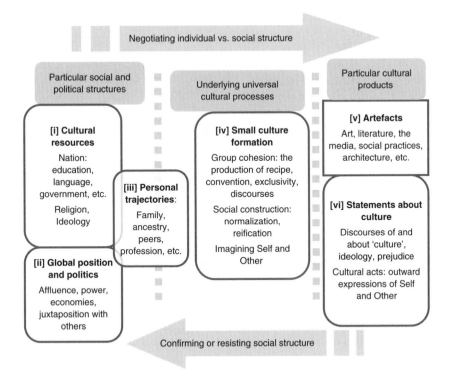

Figure 8 Aspects of cultural reality

in Beth's reference to education and language above. They are also implicit in the national government and religious regulations governing the dress of the women outside the Museum Director's office. However, they are also concerned with the structures that go beyond nation; and in several cases there is an indication of realities being formed through positioning against cultural Others. These particularities are central to each person's sense of well-being; but they do not have to be confined to 'a culture'. On the one hand, everyone has a hunger for them because of the way in which we are all wired as cultural animals. On the other hand, their particular meaning will depend on a person's particular cultural universe, which will be dependent on their particular cultural trajectory through life.

Cultural resources

Cultural resources [i] provide a backdrop, colouring, flavour and texture for the underlying universal cultural processes. They can be a positive influence, as in the case of Beth, or something to resist, as in the case of the women outside the Director's office. It is important to note here that I do not want to make too much of the nationality of these women. They are a particular group of women whom Honarbin-Holliday encounters by chance, with a complex of individual perspectives. Once again, my informants provide important insights into this process.

Miriam, perhaps in opposition to the divisive politics which have caused her exile from Zimbabwe, feels close to a particular aspect of her nation which she constructs as respect for others; while Sabina very consciously selects the aspect of her religion which opens the door to a particular appreciation of art:

> A big feature of my cultural identity is not so much African traditions, ceremonies, festivals, and language, but it is about attitudes towards, and respect for, each other. What has changed in terms of my cultural identity is that although I still identify myself as a Zimbabwean, I'm now a *white* Zimbabwean, and with *British* heritage, which makes me less welcome by the government, and makes me feel like although *I am* a *Zimbabwean* in my heart, I am no longer a Zimbabwean on paper – I have lost my citizenship (birthright?) because I was living abroad for more than one year without returning. (Miriam, email interview)

> Perhaps the best word to define the major feature of my cultural identity is 'education'. To make an example, I was brought up as a Catholic. I am by no means a practicing Catholic, and I positively disagree with the Church on many issues. And yet, there is a part of me that will always be Catholic and that I am loath to discard. I know that this is going to sound ridiculous, and I'm only mentioning it because it is a gut reaction, but being a Catholic puts me in a position to understand and appreciate so many wonderful works of art, and I am grateful for that. I'd never 'get' Caravaggio, otherwise! (Sabina)

Several informants are open about romanticizing aspects of their national or regional 'culture' in response to particular issues, associations or memories. Victoria invokes 'British fairness' when faced with things that annoy her in France, while Sabina invokes Neapolitan passions for life, and Helen recovers nostalgic ideas from a past before she was born:

> However, I always feel more British in difficult or hostile situations, for instance at the prefecture in France or when I have to deal with insurance companies or banks. And when I disagree with something I am aware that my opinions are often a reflection of a set of values shared by a number of British people (I am thinking here

of a law introduced in France forbidding the wearing of religious headwear in public institutions). I remember thinking that the law was unfair, intolerant and discriminatory (since, for example, Muslim women who wore the veil would not be able to get jobs in public institutions or attend public universities thus alienating Muslims even more in France) and I remember mentioning to friends, rather smugly (the UK being the most tolerant nation in the world!!!) about how in the UK Sikh policeman are allowed to wear the traditional turban. Secularism in the UK, for me anyway, was definitely not the same as *laïcité* in France. (Victoria)

I really identify with (an ideal?) Neapolitan culture, with its cult of hospitality, its passion for food, its vibrancy and 'cheekiness', its pleasure in the small things in life, its organized chaos, and even its mood swings, from a sunny temperament to an occasional outlook on life that borders on the Greek tragedy. (Sabina)

I asked Helen what she felt about national culture. She began by talking about nostalgia and referred to World War II which she knew about through her grandparents. There was a sense that something had been lost. When I asked her about values she began by once again talking about loss – things like 'stiff upper lip' (I suggested being calm under pressure and she seemed to agree). It was not that she necessarily believed that this 'value' was a good thing, but that it had been there, again belonging to the past. (Helen, interview notes)

The influences referred to by Ulysses are a complex interface between a national media and US icons which drove him to learn English.

Greek television in the 70s and 80s is another of the greatest influences of my cultural identity. Not sure how much to say about it here but it was a monopoly of state controlled channels (one, and later two), and it was the main source of information and entertainment in my pre-teen and teen years. Overflowing with western, mainly US, programs, it also played a role towards me liking English enough to want to learn it beyond FCE level which was the norm for children of my age. The cultural hegemony argument was to remain unexplored territory for many years (good!), so I liked the Dukes of Hazzard and still think Cathy Bach was really cute. Same for Farah Fawcett (then Farah Fawcett-Majors) from Charlie's Angels. (Ulysses)

What is especially significant in these accounts is the manner in which individuals *select*, albeit tacitly in many cases, the resources important to them. The notion of calm in the face of difficulty, which may connect with Helen's reference to 'stiff upper lip' above, can be connected with the Western narratives of the small rational English person winning against the despotic East, enhanced by the tourist commodification of the essentially collectivist tribal Other, as discussed in Chapter 4. Within a globalized world of widely accessible media and internet images it may be argued that this ability to select is a new phenomenon.[1] I would like to argue that choices are always there and are organized and resonated with according to whatever a person's narrative and trajectory of Self may turn out to be. Khorsandi (2009: 9, 65) recounts how she, as a four-year-old child, with experience only of her immediate surroundings in Iran and Britain, begins to piece together meaningful references from the resources of both Iranian and English children's songs.

Global position and politics

Stuart Hall (1991a: 20) makes the point that even though globalization is changing its position, 'at a certain moment in history' the cultural identity of the English has been built around their 'position as a leading commercial world power' to the extent that they feel that 'they can command, within their own discourses, the discourse of almost everybody else' within 'an all-encompassing "English eye"'. This is consonant with the long-standing Centre-Western narratives of chauvinism described in Chapter 4. Indeed, I maintain, following the discussion of critical cosmopolitanism in Chapter 1, that some form of global positioning and politics is an undeniable influence in all intercultural settings and drives the particular imaginations of Self and Other which feed the underlying universal cultural processes of how people see each other [vi].

Particular Cultural Products

These products, on the right of Figure 8, are the result of the negotiation between the particular social and political structures and the underlying universal cultural processes.

Artefacts

These are the visible aspects of society which relate to many people's popular view of culture, and which have been the superficial focus of liberal multiculturalism discussed in Chapter 4. The various dress codes of the women outside the Museum Director's office are an excellent example of artefacts. The list in [v] just scratches the surface of what artefacts might include – so many aspects of the appearance of a society and what people do in it, from how buses and streets look to how animals are killed and where screws are sold. As time moves on they become the resources in [i].

These cultural artefacts are very physical (as indicated by the box in the figure). What they actually comprise will result from the particular outcome of the discoursal factory [iv] of small culture formation within the domain of *underlying universal cultural processes*. They will also be empty references until they are set against the ideologically driven statements about culture [vi].

Statements about culture

This category is built on the principle that what people say or otherwise project consciously about their 'culture' are not descriptions of what their cultural group is actually like – except that there are people who wish to project themselves in this manner. Thus, while such statements are cultural acts, they are also artefacts of the culture. At another level, they indicate cultural agendas. Thus when someone, like John in Chapter 2, states that his culture is individualist and is marked by self-determination, it does not necessarily mean that self-determination is a defining characteristic of his, or of that group, but that this is the ideal with which he wishes to be associated. Helen's statement about being modern and free in Chapter 5 is certainly based on what she sees around her; but her statement that it is more likely to be the case in Britain does not hold up to her subsequent observation of other places, and is driven by an idealization. The statement that 'all British people like football' does not mean that all British people like football. One would need to look at the conditions within which the statement is made to begin to understand its deeper meanings.

Underlying Universal Cultural Processes

These processes, in the centre of Figure 8, concern more personal trajectories and the basic fabric of small culture formation, which are key to the dialogic nature of culture. They are common across national boundaries. They involve skills and strategies through which all parties, regardless of background, negotiate their individuality.

Personal cultural trajectories

While this category is placed across the boundary with, and largely within, the domain of particular social and political structures, I describe it here because it is an important bridge between these structures and underlying universal cultural processes. Such trajectories are described in some detail by my informants in Chapter 3. While particular to specific cultural realities, they are also personal. Together with underlying universal cultural processes, they form the basis for social action which is in dialogue with but not confined by social structure.

Small culture formation

Underlying universal cultural processes become especially visible in small culture formation (Figure 8 [iv]), where there is an 'intermediate level of social structuring' in which there are identifiable discourses (Fairclough, 1995: 37). Small cultures are also referred to by some of my informants in Chapter 3. They could be a wide range of social groupings from neighbourhoods or communities to work, friendship or leisure groups (e.g. Beales et al., 1967: 8), and even forming around people by vending machines or on other momentary occasions (Spradley, 1980: 54, citing Monsey). The women outside the Museum Director's office referred to above would certainly qualify as a small culture. Small culture could also be the very visible aspects of culture which an individual is conscious of in her or his vicinity.

It is at the small culture level that there is the most visible dialogue between the particularity of nation and the universality of personal social action. By this I mean that we can actually see, among the women outside the Museum Director's office, physical representations of this dialogue in the details of their clothing. The universal manner in which the women negotiate dress interacts with *which* forms of dress and *which* circumstances are determined by the particularities of national politics and conventions.

The negotiated nature of individual social action in small culture is particularly well illustrated in Baumann's ethnography of the cosmopolitan mélange of the Southall suburb of London. A major observation is the variety of ways in which 'culture' is perceived and dealt with, to refer to different entities at different times:

> The vast majority of all adult Southallians [each] saw themselves as members of several *communities*, each with its own *culture*. The same person could speak and act as a member of the Muslim *community*

in one context, in another take sides against other Muslims as a member of the Pakistani *community*, and in a third count himself part of the Punjabi *community* that excluded other Muslims but included Hindus, Sikhs, and even Christians. (1996: 5; his emphasis)

These 'renegotiations of *culture* and *community*' comprise 'what anthropologists conceive culture to be in the first place: a process of making and remaking collective sense of changing social facts' (ibid: 189; his emphasis). Culture will thus mean different things to different people:

There is a different culture of the activity for each set of role per-formers. These differences form a part of the cultural makeup of the overall group of people who perform the activity, but there is no one culture of that activity for the group as a whole, one that all its mem-bers share. ... The cultural makeup of a society is thus to be seen not as a monolithic entity determining the behaviour of its mem-bers, but a mélange of understandings and expectations regarding a variety of activities that serve as guides to their conduct and interpretation. (Goodenough, 1994: 266–7)

Culture is thus 'in process; it moves' (Beales et al., 1967: 5), 'the sum total of all the processes, happenings, or activities in which a given set or several sets of people habitually engage' (ibid.: 9), a social 'tool-kit' which emerges to 'solve problems' when required, an underlying competence in which people are 'active, often skilled users' (Crane, 1994: 11). Small culture formation also relates to Wenger's notion of community of practice, where, for example, 'boundary objects' involve discourses, routines and artefacts which are a microcosm of larger cultural processes (2000: 236ff.).

I shall elaborate on this universal process of moving, making and remaking culture by looking in more detail at aspects of Figure 8 through the medium of a reconstructed narrative concerning a mul-tinational MA group which I had the pleasure to be associated with some years ago. The significance of the group is that its entire life was only 12 months, in which time it demonstrated visible and rapid features of culture formation to which each individual applied their own underlying universal abilities to build culture while taking from a range of particularities from their diverse national backgrounds. The narrative is, however, taken beyond my experience of this particular group to a broader experience of similar groups.

MA group formation

The group comprised a number of nationalities – Japanese, Indonesian, Brazilian, Black South African, US, and Dutch – who came together and formed a very visible cultural character, starting from scratch, over the 12-month period of the full-time programme. A major feature of this was holding birthday parties for each of the members and inviting their tutors.

I shall also refer to Honarbin-Holliday's descriptions of the clothing of the women outside the Museum Director's office above, for the analysis of which I take full responsibility. At the risk of clumsiness, and where I feel I can, I will try and indicate in parentheses where particular and universal aspects of culture are predominant.

Cohesion and continuity

Bubble [iv] in Figure 8 represents the basic social and psychological function of culture as a process. This is a largely *universal* set of processes with *particular* outcomes:

> For the MA group, the birthday parties (particular) help to forge a cohesive identity and enable group expression and exclusivity (universal). They create a convention or recipe for holding the parties, thus reducing the need for ongoing negotiation (universal), by clearly defining who can come, always using the classroom as a venue, inviting tutors at short notice, and providing inexpensive soft drinks and decorative 'party food' (particular).

In a similar manner, the women outside the Museum Director's office display shared, often unspoken discourses, recipes and conventions (universal) regarding how to dress well in resistance to government restrictions (particular). They also gain cohesion from exclusivity (universal) to this politics of nation (particular).

The particularity of resources in bubble [i] in the figure is employed by the universal need for group cohesion to provide social continuity. It needs to be remembered that although small culture may be formed rapidly,

> Cultures, even in their most individualised practices, result also from validations of a past. Culture-making is not an *ex tempore* improvisation, but a project of social continuity placed within, and contending with, moments of social change. (Baumann, 1996: 31)

Thus, in the case of an aeroplane crew, 'the men in the crew form the group or society and the airplane constitutes a sort of combined environment' which provides a wider tradition and history (Beales et al., 1967: 10). Something similar can be seen in the MA group:

In the newly forming culture of the MA group, each member will bring culture residues (universal) from other educational, classroom, collegial and peer experiences (particular). They draw on the combined influence (universal) of various 'national' cuisines in the food provided, dominated perhaps by a Japanese orientation to tidy minimalism, a British academic informality in the fairly casual way in which tutors were invited, a definite collegiality which might have derived from notions of both close-knit studentship, evident in several of the societies represented, and a professional bond – for all were language teachers – and influence of the local institution arrangement which enabled almost all classes for this group to be held in the same room (particular). In university departments made up of a range of nationalities, cultural residues will be brought from different 'national' experiences; but commonalities of educational, collegial and peer experience from all these contexts will be the building blocks for the new culture (particular).

Among the women outside the Museum Director's office there is an interaction between Islamic, traditional and European residues and influences (particular). These carry notions of class, community and sophistication (universal), and histories of (particular) religious, class and community associations.

The social construction of reality

Put in very simple terms, social construction, in bubble [iv] in Figure 8, means made by people rather than having an existence of its own. This notion becomes acute when it is related to right or wrong, to the findings of science, or to God. Indeed, it means that 'we can no longer return to the comfortable assumptions of traditional scholarly and scientific work, and a host of related institutions such as mental health, education, the justice system, organizational life and politics' (Gergen, 2001: 1). This construction by people is bound up with a series of complex group processes such as discourses and ideologies, so that what becomes 'taken-for-granted', or 'thinking-as-usual' may begin to appear 'real' or as established 'knowledge' when it is not.

The process of normalization, sometimes referred to as naturalization, or routinization, is where behaviour which is socially constructed for the sake of group cohesion becomes routine:

In the master's group the normalization of the birthday parties takes the form of an almost automatic routine in which there is no need to explicitly plan and negotiate whether or not and how the parties will be held each time. People take on regular roles for carrying out the tasks for organizing the parties as taken-for-granted. The parties thus quickly become an institution in their own right which is embedded in the deeper fabric of the MA group to the extent that it becomes as 'normal' a constituent as class timetables, assignments and grading.

Among the women outside the Museum Director's office, some of the forms of dress will become normalized to the extent that their significance as a process of resistance may become so embedded in the taken-for-granted that it becomes tacit rather than conscious. This is why it might take the discipline of *making the familiar strange*, as described in Chapter 2, to notice it, and why people, might talk about it in focused interview when they have not thought about it for a long time. Thus, forms of resistance, aspects of critical-ity and explicit demonstrations of autonomy may go underground for long periods. Hence, we need to be very careful about generalized statements about how certain people, or indeed whole 'cultures', are uncritical or 'passive'. This will be looked at in more detail in Chapter 8.

The idea of the social construction of reality can be traced to Berger and Luckmann's (1979) classic text, first published in 1966. It means that what is considered 'real' is constructed by people, instead of existing independently of people. An example of this is the notion that it is wrong for a man to have more than one wife. This can be said to be socially constructed because whether or not it is true is decided by people. This can be confirmed by the fact that people in some societies believe that a man can have more than one wife. The implication is that this truth does not exist outside a par-ticular society.

Social construction can, however, work in different ways: either we construct as individual people or as a group, or we are con-structed, and determined, by the group and by the ideologies that govern the group; and if the latter is true, then my thesis falls down because we would be inescapably conditioned by chauvinistic dis-courses and probably by cultures. This dilemma is evident in the ambivalence in the manner in which Berger and Luckmann com-bine both social action theory, which supports the agency of the individual, and structural-functionalism, which supports determi-nation and domination by the functions of society (1979: 207). This dilemma leads Berger and Luckmann to 'a dialectic of individual and society, of personal identity and social structure' (ibid.: 208). Thus, 'Berger and Luckmann's account shows how the world can be socially constructed by the social practices of people, but at the same time be experienced by them as if the nature of their world is pre-given and fixed' (Burr, 1995: 10).

A newcomer to the MA group, six months into its life, felt intimidated by the birthday party routine. Her resistance was a complex matter. She stated to everyone that she did not like birthday parties; but what became apparent to the more observant members of the group was that she really wanted a role in organizing them and felt frustrated that there wasn't a way in because the roles had become routinized. In the rapid hurly burly of MA life, fed by the huge pressures of assignments, there was actually a loss of memory, among at least some the other members of the group, of how they used to meet and talk about whether or not and how to organize the parties. Not having such meetings had become an unquestioned reality of the culture. The details of the routinization of roles had become forgotten; and they had become reified.

Reification

Reification works in a similar way to normalization. However, whereas normalization involves *making* a social construction 'normal' and taken-for-granted, reification involves *forgetting* the 'unreal' nature of social construction altogether. Ideas taking on a life of their own become more 'real' and influential than the original idea – the process of making the unreal appear real and of making the ideological appear neutral.

Reification is a central characteristic of the development of academic and professional thought and the rise and fall of scientific revolutions described by Kuhn (1970). The structural-functionalist picture of society (Chapter 3) and the apparent science of Hofstede (Chapter 1) gives the impression that cultural descriptions are neutral. What has been forgotten in the enthusiastic detail of everyday science and professionalism is the possibility that definitions of culture or society may be heuristic devices – temporary models created as rough, unreal measures against which to look at a messy, real set of phenomena. The modernist desire for certainty and the subsequent denial of ideology are particularly prevalent in professions, which need to project themselves as owning certainty that their work is efficient and accountable. The temporary models have been reified, and their systemic inadequacies transformed into rationales for chauvinism. These are all examples of reification which are revealed by the postmodern acknowledgement of the pervasiveness of ideology.[2] Most interculturalists would not deny that collectivism is only an idea – a heuristic. The question is: how powerful is the idea of collectivism and how far does it carry chauvinism – to make it dangerous, so that the tacit, or 'understood' nature of this knowledge increases until it is completely overlooked, and how easy is it to prevent collectivism from being reified into something that is imagined to really exist? As such, it would mean that societies really are collectivist. At the same time it has to be understood that 'just' ideas are also real things. This will be explored in Chapter 9. Reification will be looked at again in Chapter 7.

The case of the women outside the Director's office cuts to the heart of political reification – as a deliberate statement of resistance against allowing forms of dress that are imposed by politics to take on the appearance of the *only* forms of dress in a 'normal' world. In many ways, however, reification is an innocent process. Like Othering, reification is just the natural thing that people do as part of a basic force in social life. Berger and Luckmann remind us that it is not a 'perversion' or 'a sort of cognitive fall from grace', but a natural social process common in theoretical and non-theoretical thought (1979: 107). What is 'real' or 'not real' is also hard to pin down. An irony in the struggle for dress is thus my Iranian niece, who was born at the moment of the imposition of the dress, telling me that it is actually not the issue that I imagine it to be because it is not 'political' or 'religious', but simply 'everyday outdoor clothing' – perhaps one form of reification being used to combat another.

Discourse

Discourse is evident in two of the bubbles in Figure 8. In bubble [iv] discourse as a regulator goes along with the need for recipe and convention. In bubble [vi] it is one of the products of culture, which in turn has a return influence on [iv] in that pride of cultural product encourages cohesion.[3] There are several uses of the term 'discourse'. Perhaps the most popular is discourse as a formal discussion or debate. It can also be a stretch of language, especially for the purpose of study, for example classroom discourse as what teachers and students say to each other. The use with which I am concerned here is at a more macro level[4] – 'the concrete expression of the language–culture relationship because it is discourse that "creates, recreates, focuses, modifies, and transmits both culture and language and their interaction"' (Sarangi, 1994: 414, citing Sherzer). Fairclough (2006: 26) suggests that discourses play a powerful role in the process of reification as 'imaginary representations of how the world will be or should be within strategies for change which, if they achieve hegemony, can be operationalized to transform these imaginaries into realities'.

As an applied linguist my own focus is more on the language element. One could argue that discourses provide small cultures with the systems of language or concepts necessary for shared understanding. The women outside the Museum Director's office in Honarbin-Holliday's description above display a strong sense of their dress norms through the established meanings of 'hijab', 'chador', 'roopoosh' and 'maghna'eh' which represent a core knowledge from which to be creative and against which to measure resistance, and also of what is appropriate in specific settings and occupations, and what is a tolerable balance between conformity and resistance.

The presence and power of such a discourse becomes evident when one is with a group of people whose views, and indeed ideology, is evident from the manner in which they use language. The experience can be quite threatening because one can be forced into a position of either compliance or alienation. If the discourse of the group is racist, the 'way of talking' can be so powerful that one must either join with it, remain silent or get into very difficult and perhaps impossible confrontation. This is because to communicate easily with the group one must use their way of talking. There does, however, not have to be a sinister agenda for the power of discourse to be evident:

> The initial aversion of the newcomer to the MA group to the birthday parties was partly due to a feeling of being alienated by the insider language (universal) which had built up around the birthday parties (particular). The other members made reference to dates, 'the guests', 'shopping' and so on without explanation of exactly what they were talking about. This equipped the original members with an esoteric knowledge which automatically excluded outsiders (universal). The newcomer observed that when the MA group were together amongst other students, this insider discourse was displayed in front of the students in an annoying manner, especially when it extended into first name references to tutors in such a manner that they gave the impression of an intimate relationship (particular).

It is highly likely that the MA insiders could have been unaware of this exclusionary strategy, and that, as above, it takes an outsider to see what is going on.

Successful confrontation will require the development of an equally powerful discourse. Associating discourses with power and confrontation gives rise to the concepts of dominant and counter- or hidden discourses. So, if the dominant discourse is racist, to successfully overthrow it there has to be a counter-discourse; and if the counter-discourse is insufficiently strong it may have to go underground and become a hidden discourse. At a more innocent level, but equally powerful:

> The newcomer eventually found an ally among the original members of the group, who also did not really enjoy the birthday parties because she suspected they were a means for gaining favour

with the tutors. Together they were able to begin to undermine the dominant, reified birthday party discourse, by setting up a counter-discourse which had a sort of pincer strategy. On the one hand they openly spoke against the events; on the other they questioned the arrangements in such a way that they managed to turn the dominant discourse into a less reified form.

The formation and development of discourses is thus implicit in the process of reification. Discourses tend to collect around iconic terms and phrases, of which 'collectivism' and 'individualism' are excellent examples, especially when they are associated with an attractive set of associations or 'spin'. The 'spin doctors' of late modern politics are therefore the engineers of ideological change, with discourses as their major tools.[5] I define a technical discourse as a particularly powerful way of talking or writing which is built around the iconic technical terminology which contributes to the identity of the profession, academic discipline or other specialist group. The approaches to cultural description of theorists such as Hofstede or Trompenaars are rife with iconic technical terms that carry and sustain specific thinking about the social world, such as 'uncertainty avoidance', 'power distance', 'universalism' and 'particularism'.[6] This then becomes the core of normalization, if not reification, when new practice becomes an established routine, and what were once contested ideas become real things. I recall that at a university staff meeting in the mid 1990s colleagues voiced resistance to a suggestion that students should be considered as 'customers'. Within two years these same colleagues, along with everyone else, were using the term as an everyday part of their professional discourse when talking about students. This is part of a widespread process within late modern society whereby the state sector institutions are being 'invaded' by commercial discourses which can be traced back to Thatcherism in the UK and Reaganism in the US, resulting in the commodification of health and education.[7]

An important aspect of bubble [vi] is therefore that group members' statements *about* 'culture' or 'their culture' should be seen as products or artefacts *of* the culture, expressing how they socially construct their image of their own culture, rather than a direct description of their culture. In doing this they may play up and exaggerate various aspects of cultural resources available to them (bubble [i]). For example, Tong (2002) suggests that Chinese teachers' statements about the influence of Confucianism on their students' behaviour represent not so much a Confucian Chinese national culture, but the way in which the cultural source of Confucianism is *used* to explain student behaviour within the teachers' professional culture. Hence Baumann's (1996) ethnographic interest in what Southallians *say about* and *do with* 'culture' as evidence of how 'culture' is constructed within the culture he is investigating. Seeing projected images of 'culture' as artefact and cultural product in this way tells us something about the way in which notions of culture are reified, and dominant discourses of culture are set up:

> It was quite common for MA group members to make statements about how open and friendly they were as a group. They made explicit references to the birthday parties as evidence of a tension-free relationship with their tutors and welcoming new members. The newcomer and her ally felt that these statement bore little relationship to what was actually going on – their own alienation and the tensions that collected around individual members sometimes quite frantically 'buttering up' tutors during the parties.

It may also be common for the women outside the Museum Director's office to make statements about how the political restrictions in their society made individualistic expression impossible – quite different from Honarbin-Holliday's observations, above, of creative dressing. This does not, however, necessarily mean that the statements about the culture are less accurate than the observations of behaviour. These outward expressions of Self and Other in [vi] relate back to the core universal process of imagining Self and Other [iv]. Getting to the bottom of what is going on between and within these various discourses requires a special type of disciplined rigour, as described in Chapter 2.

Ideology

Ideology is present in bubbles [i] and [vi] in Figure 8. It is closely related to the social constructions of reality, normalization and discourses, which are in many ways the building blocks of ideology as the higher-order belief systems. Hence, it could indeed be said that the manner in which the MA group construct birthday parties generates and represents an ideology of friendliness and inclusivity as a product of their small culture. The women outside the Director's office might also be said to be producing an ideology of self-determined professionalism. Ideologies are, however, normally thought of as being large things, underpinning recognized political movements with a capitalized name such as Communism, or Orientalism, as discussed in Chapter 4. The ideologies of essentialism, structural-functionalism and cosmopolitanism, which are the major concerns of this book, are not capitalized because they have not achieved the same degree of popular recognition; but they are still large things.

Within the small cultural formation what may therefore be happening is that ideology as cultural product in bubble [vi] is associated with wider movements. Thus, just as cultural residues from nation, and, indeed, ideology, are drawn on as residues and influences in bubble [i], they are reinforced in small culture formation in [iv] and do indeed feed back to either confirm or resist the social structures of nation (bottom of Figure 8). Hence, there may well be larger influences at play with the MA group, to do perhaps with ideologies of democracy and socialism brought in as residues by various of the members of the group. There must be caution, however, against making any association between the creativity in dress of the women outside the Director's office and the Muslim Kossaibati's negotiation of British high street fashion in Chapter 5. While there are clearly influences, the ideology produced by the women outside the Director's office is *that* theirs is a modernity that is not Western. The relationship with reification is complex in that ideologies do not generally deny social construction. They decree the superiority of some constructions over others. Hence, the notion that women and men should have equal rights is a socially constructed reality preferred by the ideology of feminism.

Language

It is important here to say something about language as this is commonly thought to be a central feature of cultural reality and has been referred to as such by my informants Salim and Beth and above in Chapter 3. In Figure 8 language is thus located in bubble [i] as a cultural resource – as the major feature of the cultural universe and 'major player' within which Salim situates a large part of his cultural identity. There is however a strong connection with discourse in bubbles [iv–vi] as discussed in detail above; and in this respect it is possible to begin to deconstruct how elements of language might work in a little more detail.

In a major sense language as a body of words and phrases is the location of the expressive, creative aspects of culture found in [i] and in the artefacts of culture in [v] in Figure 8. Literatures, the media and everyday talk carry this expression, bringing together and dividing in the multiplicity of settings, regionalities and small cultures of complex society. Phrases like 'crazy golf' and 'the Dunkirk spirit' are examples of this. They are iconic expressions that relate back to very specific histories and associations within a particular society.

However, at another level, language is a mathematically coded form of communication with neutral grammars and vocabularies, which is instrumental, responds to the need to survive in any particular setting, can adapt to be a lingua franca, and is multi-attachable to diverse cultural settings. Hence, English can be an international code for air-traffic control, stretched and refined for international commerce, and can express the literatures of a dozen different societies.

At the level more related to discourse in small culture location as described above, language is marshalled to fulfil very specific functions of institutional projections and idealized descriptions. A particular and very telling example of this is the English language textbook, which purports to teach, for example, 'British English', but in fact projects an idealized, refined code of designer English that suits a particular educational profession at a particular time (Holliday, 2008: 128).

English, because of its particular world history, has become a conduit of intercultural communication rather than the representation of a particular national culture. Many readers will complain that the entire argument in this book is flawed because it is based on interviews with informants only through the medium of English – and that what they have to say is skewed by the power of English as a cultural force. I strongly feel, in my defence, that the opposite is the case. That all my informants are remarkably articulate in English means that they are able to express their diverse cultural realities competently through English as a neutral medium. When our Syrian friend Safa comes to visit we engage with her particular brand of English which is rich in Syrian cultural references and expressions, including Arabic phrases that have crept into it to perfect the enrichment.

Imagining Self in relation to Other

Imagining Self in relation to Other in bubble [iv] is at the heart of the issue of cultural chauvinism. Much has been said about the idealization of the Western Self and the demonization of the non-Western Other in previous chapters. Placing it within the domain of underlying universal cultural processes makes it appear a natural part of creating social cohesion within small cultural groups, particularly within intercultural communication scenarios where each actor tries to make sense of the other – as a normal everyday process for everyone. It is to do with any social group establishing an image of strength and superiority in the face of other groups. Businesses, professional groups, families, football teams and so on may emphasize efficiency, specialism, ideology or morality. The cult of the 'mission statement' is part of this. Equivalent negative attributes about competing groups will also be projected. The degree to which these projections are based on reality, or really are imagined, may be hard to establish. It has been noted above that there are residues of individualism in John's society, but insufficient to make his claim to total individualism accurate.

However, placing this core of cultural chauvinism within the universality of what we all do also indicates that responsibility has to be taken for it by everybody at every level. It underlies everything that takes on the presence of neutrality in cultural difference, and attempts to solve this difference. It is at the core of what is denied within neo-essentialism.

Summary

The following points have been made in this chapter:

- Three significant aspects of cultural reality are (a) social and political structures of nation, which provide a backdrop against which (b) underlying personal cultural processes interact within the personal membership of small cultures to produce (c) the cultural products both of artefacts such as art and literature, and discourses and ideologies of Self and Other.
- Another significant distinction is between the particularities and universalities, each of which exist along a cline, with nation being more to do with particularity, and underlying personal processes being more universal.
- Within small culture formation the interaction between national and personal realities, between the particular and the universal, the social construction of reality, and the workings of discourse and ideology are particularly visible.
- Imagining Self in relation to Other is an underlying universal cultural process and thus is always present in the intercultural communication which is claimed to be neutral within neo-essentialism. It is at the heart of the ideology that is denied.

Investigation

The following activities engage with the complexities of cultural formation raised in this chapter. Carry them out with someone from a different cultural background if you can.

1 Consider Helen's experience in Japan. Recall times when you observed unfamiliar cultural behaviour which made you more aware of familiar behaviour.
   (a) Reconstruct the experience using *thick description*.
   (b) Describe what you learnt and why.
   (c) In what way was this unexpected?
   (d) What prejudices did you therefore uncover about the way in which you looked at culture?
2 Consider John's statement. Can cultural behaviour include not taking culture seriously, taking it too seriously, saying or imagining things about it which are not true, or denying it?
3 How far is the content and opinion expressed in this book of a particular cultural nature?

4 Consider the women outside the Museum Director's office.
   (a) Use Figure 2 in Chapter 2 as a model and plot the *thick description* Honarbin-Holliday employs.
   (b) Note where the cultural behaviour of the women is stretched, negotiated or changed. What are the boundaries to this?
   (c) Reconstruct examples of this from your own experience. Use *thick description* to get to the roots of how stretching cultural reality is possible and what the complex reasons for it might be.
5 When you go to a strange place:
   (a) How do you discern whether what you see is imposed, pretence, an artificial or instrumental display, 'real', 'false', a form of resistance, and so on?
   (b) What universal strategies do you use? What experience from your own cultural universe do you need to invoke?
   (c) Reconstruct a specific example. Describe what you need to do to *make the familiar strange* to enable you to do this – to become conscious of what you may normally do unconsciously – to make tacit cultural knowledge explicit.
6 Considering all of the above, when someone comes back from travel and says 'I experienced a foreign culture', what exactly do they mean? What are they projecting or denying about themselves?
7 Consider the narrative about the MA group and the surrounding text in which it is discussed.
   (a) Write a detailed *thick description* of a series of events in which a small culture was created. Place this in one column of a two-column table.
   (b) In the other column note the details of how reality was socially constructed, reification, and the creation of discourses and ideology.
8 Reconstruct a cultural problem which you have encountered employing *thick description*.
   (a) Parts of the China narrative in Chapter 3 may help you here; as might plotting the *thick description* in a diagrammatic form like Figure 5 in Chapter 2.
   (b) Apply or adapt the categories of cultural action.
   (c) Determine the degree to which the problem had to do with underlying universal cultural processes, and how these related to particular cultural aspects.
   (d) What did you therefore learn, and what did you need to learn?
9 Plan an orientation session for people who are going to be in multinational groups. Consider appropriate participants, presenters, texts and activities to ensure the following:
   (a) an understanding of the universals of group behaviour which transcend and are meaningful to people from different cultural backgrounds;
   (b) a withdrawal from an ethnocentric stance on how to organize.

Notes

1 See Mathews's (2000: 93) discussion of the 'supermarket' of cultural resources available to those who have access to it.

2 Discussion of the relationship between reification and Othering, and legislating over truth, can be found in Keesing (1994: 302), Sarangi (1995: 59, citing Bauman) and Holliday (2005: 22).

3 This complex discourse role is described in a somewhat similar way in Lankshear et al. (1997: 18–20).

4 Gee (1997: xv) labels discourse as a stretch of language and as a way of being as 'small "d"' and 'big "d" discourse', respectively.

5 Examples of discourses as ideological tools are discussed in Silberstein (2004) on the slide towards a 'war on terror' in the US after 9/11, and Fairclough (2000) on the political discourse of 'New Labour' in Britain.

6 Elsewhere I describe the manner in which the Centre-Western chauvinistic discourse of English language education is built around such iconic terms as 'learner-centredness', 'learner training', 'autonomy' and 'skills' (Holliday, 2005).

7 Examples of commodifying discourses are discussed in Fairclough (1995).

7

Discourses of Cultural Disbelief

In Chapter 6 I suggested that ideology is deeply embedded within the discourses of culture formation within the everyday statements about and constructions of culture (Figure 8 [iv, vi]) which produce the sustained cultural disbelief discussed in Chapter 4. This chapter will look more closely at the discourses of disbelief and demonstrate that while there is a perceived, uncrossable intercultural line between 'our' culture and 'their' culture it will be impossible to move to a critical cosmopolitan position. I will focus on Delanty et al.'s suggestion that Othering in Western liberal society has become normalized to the extent that it is 'domesticated' and submerged beneath 'ordinary prejudice' (2008a: 1–2). It thus becomes implied that 'we have racism but apparently no racists' (ibid.: 11).

Penetrating Professional Discourses

The following narrative describes a conference workshop given by an intercultural communication trainer about how to minimize culture shock when working in a 'non-Western' organization. As with the other ethnographic reconstructions, it is a composite of several observed events. The subsequent analysis derives from being told, in a number of conversations with intercultural trainers, that they face the dilemma of having to present cultural difference in definite terms to satisfy clients who want a straightforward product, and also from my own experience of the building of certainty in the parallel profession of English language teaching.[1]

The dilemma of training

The presenter sets out to demonstrate how Western teachers can be prepared for work in Greece. He suggests that culture shock can be addressed by 'recognising the difference between your own culture and the host culture'. First we are asked to consider the following 'basic values of Western culture':

Individualism, self-reliance/independence, equality, competition, material wealth, hard work, personal control over the environment, change, time and its control, future orientation, action orientation, informality and directness.

Then we are given questions to ask about the other culture, and then answers are provided with respect to a Greek language school where the presenter had recently worked. There was no exploratory discussion. The questions and answers are simply presented in a handout as follows:

Questions about the 'other culture'	Answers regarding a Greek language school
Is there great respect for the teacher in the classroom? Would the teacher ever be challenged? How close is the relationship between students and teacher? Are students expected to be modest and polite? Are students expected to participate in discussions with the teacher?	Respect, no challenging, distant relationship, modesty and politeness, no discussion expected
What is the attitude to timing and punctuality in the culture? How traditional is the society? How past-oriented is the society? How important is conformity? What is the cultural attitude to history?	Poor timing and punctuality, very traditional and past-oriented, high conformity, history important
How formally do your colleagues dress? Are shoulders/legs covered? Are pants worn? Are jeans worn?	Formal, covered, few pants or jeans
How competitive and assertive are your colleagues/students? How are conflicts confronted? How direct is the communication style? Is negotiation valued? How is criticism handled? How important is face-saving?	Low competition and assertiveness, conflicts not confronted, indirect, poor handling of negotiation and criticism, a lot of face-saving
Are there any topics which should be avoided in classroom discussion? Are there any gestures which could be misinterpreted?	Topics avoided, foreign gestures
How computer-literate are your colleagues/students? What are attitudes towards plagiarism and cheating?	Not very computer-literate, significant cheating and plagiarism

The presenter concluded the session by asked the participants to say whether or not they would arrive for a dinner appointment at a friend's house late or on time. She was visibly wrong-footed when several of the British participants said that they would be late. The 'right answer' that she had in mind was that the British, being individualist, would always be on time.

While this presentation appears a naïve and over-simplistic version of the positivist sequence described near the beginning of Chapter 2, which moves from an *a priori* description of 'Western values' to a 'useful' comparison with the 'other culture', I wish to place it within the context of a professional strategy for meeting customer training needs. The following sequence describes this strategy as moving from a cautious handling of concepts to reification.

Sequence of reification in intercultural training

1 The need for a saleable professional product with accessible, dependable, measurable specialist concepts.
2 Established descriptions of cultures with generalizations and exceptions that can be used to generate discussion and catchy technical terms.
3 Routine use of descriptions and technical terms.
4 Deintellectualization in which critiques are either forgotten or 'understood'.
5 The descriptions and technical terms become the everyday language for the profession and customers.

The process of reification – forgetting the 'unreal' nature of social construction altogether – is described in Chapter 6 as a basic feature of culture formation. It happens everywhere as an underlying universal cultural process. Here it is central in sustaining an illusion about foreigners in a Greek language school under the guise of professional practice.

In the workshop the saleable product (step 1) is 'Western values' contrasted with the foreign culture. The concept of Western values is sufficiently specialist to show the trainer as expert; but to make the concept accessible to clients it has become a simplification of the definition of individualism. It forces an equally simplistic and exaggerated characterization of the 'foreign culture' as collectivist. It represents a positive norm by which the 'other culture' can be 'checked out' against the questions in the handout as either conforming or underperforming. There could certainly be discussion of these features (step 2), but there is not time; and it would have been seriously led by the force of the division. The resulting overgeneralized description of the 'Greek culture' is simple and seductive; and technical terms such as 'individualism', 'traditional', 'past-oriented', 'formality' and 'face' are presented as routine and unproblematic as suggested in steps 3 and 4 in the sequence. There is a strong sense in the workshop that the presenter does not herself consider these concepts to be problematic. They have become the routine tools of her trade; and the reification is complete.

The resulting deintellectualization (step 5) is represented by the lack of exploratory discussion in the conference presentation, even when the models set up by the presenter backfire in the final stage. The simplification papers over complexity. There is no discussion of whether it is really such an easy matter to suggest that Greece is 'non-Western', or of the clear irony of suggesting that Greece is collectivist when it is the symbol of 'individualist' resistance against the 'despotic' East in Western history. (See the discussion of the geographical positioning of 'the West' and the construction of Greece in the Olympic movement in Chapter 5.) Neither is there discussion of the presumption that respect for authority, formality and preoccupation with history are higher or lower in different societies. It is hard to imagine that any society could exist without such features of social cohesion. They are universals that are displayed differently at different times and in different places. It needs to be considered that 'pants and jeans', presented as non-traditional and informal, may themselves have become traditional and have acquired a degree of formality in Western society. The wearing of jeans has in my experience becomes widespread in a great many locations across the world, though mediated by fashion in different ways in different places. The outcome is therefore a successful reification of 'individualist Western values' in contrast with a 'non-Western Greek culture'. They have become solid, unproblematic, established concepts which can be used as a matter of routine in the training session. The outcome is an unquestioned Othering of the Greek institution.

Sustained Disbelief

There are important questions to be asked with regard to reification and the power of discourses that create the illusions which it sustains. It is easy to get the impression that the professionals in step 5 of the sequence of professional reification above are completely taken in by technical terminologies. Can it really be the case that intercultural trainers really do 'forget' the criticisms of the theories they are using just because they become routine or 'understood'? It is the profound disbelief that the Other can really be as proficient as the Self which is the hardest to shake. The widespread nature of this disbelief and the powerful narratives which underpin it have been looked at in Chapter 4. A seemingly innocent set of such perceptions concerning what newcomers from the Periphery have to offer is implicit in this recent experience:

Personal hygiene

Paul and Richard were talking about Richard's experience of taking part in orientation sessions for Middle Eastern students travelling to the US to study. Richard asked Paul if he didn't think it was insulting to tell the students that they needed to learn about personal hygiene. Paul said that, as a university lecturer, he had been on the receiving end and heard the complaints from the American families with whom some of the students had stayed. They said that the students just didn't know how to use the bathroom. They spilled water everywhere so that it damaged the carpets and even came through the ceiling. They even tried to wash their feet in the toilet bowl before praying.

Richard suggested this wasn't really to do with the concept of personal hygiene. Instead it was to do with how to use unfamiliar bathroom equipment, and that it was wrong and demeaning to suggest that the students needed to learn about personal hygiene before they went to the US, when they had perfectly good standards of personal hygiene in their own society.

Paul said that Richard was overreacting as everyone, including the students, knew that no one was assuming they did not have perfectly good personal hygiene according to the standards of their own culture.

The key phrase here is 'according to the standards of their own culture'. This conversation between Richard and Paul on one level represents a sincere attempt to make sense and to be fair. However, as implicit in the liberal multiculturalism described in Chapter 4, the outcome is to acknowledge 'their' rights to be who they are in 'their culture', until they want to come and mix with 'us'. This is a neo-racist point of view because it implies a blanket definition of what a particular set of people can or cannot do, with a strong undercurrent of deficiency. The indisputable point is that Paul and Richard should realize where this conversation is leading, and also where it comes from.

Levels of awareness

In the case of Paul and Richard, and the people involved in orienting newcomers who share their beliefs, whether or not they might at any other time consider the statement 'according to the standards of their own culture' to be Othering, they have forgotten this because it has become a routine assumption in the professional process of, perhaps, considering the needs of the American families who are their

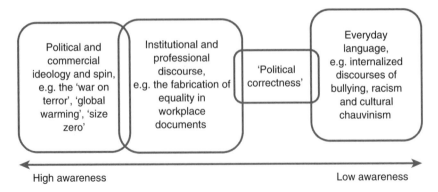

Figure 9 Levels of reification

customers. The degree to which we are all aware of reification will vary considerably. Figure 9 presents a very rough continuum from high to low awareness over a range of types of social location. The levels of awareness indicated will be different for different people in different circumstances; and the areas do overlap. Within high awareness of reification I have placed political ideology. Much of the British public, and I think people everywhere, are aware of political spin and its equivalent in commercial advertising; and this has been heightened since 9/11. Whether or not they approve of the US and British invasion of Iraq, there is awareness of the contestation of 'weapons of mass destruction' and also of the discoursal power of the phrase itself. While the terminology of 'discourse' might remain academic, the manipulative power of 'rhetoric' is well understood so that even the traditional authority 'research' and 'statistics' are contested.

Moving right in the figure, what takes place in institutions and professions may involve less awareness. Here, with the massive and subtle invasion of such areas as education and health by consumerist and managerialist discourses (e.g. Fairclough, 1989: 35; 1995: 89), we know that institutional processes like learning objectives and patient charters are not really sound mechanisms for fairness, quality and democracy; but we still design them, write them, use them and talk about them in meetings as though they are sound mechanisms because they have become an embedded part of the fabric of our professional and workaday lives. At this level we may thus be initially aware but are gradually taken in. I remember myself and colleagues being acutely resistant to the discourse of quality assurance when it first arrived more than ten years ago; but with the necessity to use and be involved with its technology, although resistant to a degree, we now conform to it as we daily speak its language. Being sucked into a workplace discourse simply by the nature of engagement with it may therefore go part way towards explaining the attitudes evident in Paul's reaction to Richard in the above narrative. The powerful liberal discourse in Western multi-cultural society, described in Chapter 4, would also actually make it quite hard for Richard to persist in his questioning and suggest to Paul that he is being racist.

The most problematic of all is the level at the far right of the low awareness spectrum in Figure 9, where it is easy for us to be 'stand-ardly unaware' of how ideology has become naturalized in our own everyday language (Fairclough, 1995: 36). This is where we are rac-ist or sexist without knowing, at the frontier of political correctness.

Political correctness

I place political correctness between this level and the previous one because in one respect there is considerable awareness that is evidenced by the considerable intellectualized resistance to the reification of what is perceived to be a superficial sanitization of vocabulary. The problematic notion of 'political correctness' becomes a major battleground in the struggle between discourse and freedom of thought. One of my informants has the following to say about British society and it resonates with a number of other conversa-tions I have had:

> People who are not racist are frightened of being racist because we have to apologize for our past all the time – the silly end of political correctness. Young women get annoyed by sexist language, but it isn't such a big deal. (Summary of interview with Helen)

I have political correctness in inverted commas because the phrase itself has become a discoursal icon. 'Political correctness', or 'PC' is the suppression of words and phrases that are considered chauvinistic, and the adoption of new terms to replace them.[2] The most common kinds of examples are perhaps: 'he or she' instead of 'he' or 'she', and 'chairperson' or 'postperson' instead of 'chairman' or 'postman', to equalize the gender reference in gender-neutral statements; and 'black' instead of 'negro' or 'nigger', and the removal of 'gollywog' from the children's *Noddy* stories to neutralize terms which are considered to have particular racist connotations.

The complexity of this phenomenon is demonstrated by an event which took place on the 2007 British television reality show, *Big Brother*, where a young white woman used the word 'nigger' to refer to black friends. The white woman was immediately removed from the programme despite her claims that she was not racist (BBC,

2007; *Mirror,* 2007). This was considered a racist act because, as a black woman in a television discussion group later said, 'nigger' has a history of racism when used by white people. One of the news reports says the following about what the white woman thought had happened:

> When asked to explain what happened, she said … [they], together with fellow housemates …, had been joking around. She said it [nigger] was 'a friendly term' where she came from, 'not a hurtful word' and that she had not meant it in an offensive way. (BBC, 2007)

In a transcript of the exchange we hear, just after the word was uttered:

> 2nd white woman: (shocked laughter) Me, I can't believe you said that.
>
> Black woman: You are in trouble.
>
> White woman: Don't make a big thing out of it then. I was joking.
>
> Black woman: I know you were … but that's some serious shit, sorry.
>
> (*Mirror,* 2007; names removed)

There is a multiplicity of possible interpretations of what is going on here; but one of them may certainly be that the white woman is failing to understand a well-established but complex discourse in which she thinks she has become an insider but in fact may still have an outsider status. The bald on-record manner in which the black woman responds makes one wonder if she is in fact commenting on what is allowed in the discourse itself. The white woman can therefore be said, though unwittingly, to have stepped outside the discourse in such a way that others are also forced to step outside the discourse to respond, often causing discomfort.

The white woman is nevertheless projecting another discourse which claims not to be racist but in which others recognize a racism which she is unaware of. Indeed, she may well be party to a denial of racism by claiming that there is not a problem by a 'discursive disclaimer' through her own 'self-presentation' as familiar with the world of race (Wodak, 2008: 65). Another example of this can be seen in a previous series of *Big Brother*, this time for celebrities, in which three white women were thought by many viewers to be racist in the manner in which they spoke to an Indian co-contestant. Here the verdict was far less clear because it was not dependent simply on the utterance of particular vocabulary. The event attracted considerable attention within days of the broadcast, ranging from the media regulator Ofcom, which received 3500 complaints about 'alleged racism', along with another 1000 to Channel 4, and the

Commission for Racial Equality (Holmwood and Brook, 2007). The Indian woman was referred to as 'the Indian' by one of the white women, who also explicitly refused to pronounce her name correctly, within the context of other people referring to her as 'cunt' and 'fucking Paki' – referred to by some of the contestants and others as the 'c' and 'p' words. While most participants in a *Guardian* newspaper chat column (Brook, 2007) acknowledged that this was abusive language, there was extended discussion about whether or not this was actually racist and indeed bullying. The arguments which were put forward for and against the behaviour being racist are represented in Table 7, based on the chat comments in Brook (2007).

Table 7   For and against acknowledgements of racism

'It *isn't* racism'	'It *is* racism'
Class and education: The working-class white women (albeit successful media celebrities) are responding to being intimidated by the middle-class, elegant, well-spoken, articulate Bollywood film star	Othering: There are references to an imagined 'uncleanness', inferiority or backwardness of food, health and habits
'Teaching her a lesson': They are responding to the Indian woman's arrogant, spoilt behaviour	There is distaste for a darker skin colour
Resistance to superficial political correctness: No one complained when, e.g., the American contestant was referred to in the same manner or imitated (implying harmless banter or ribbing, which she should learn to put up with)	There is hatred in the face of at least one of the white women
There is no such thing as race	
Shared Otherness: One of the white women is 'mixed race'	
The Indian woman is playing 'the race card' if she accuses the others of racism	
Conclusion This is just a particular case of retaliation, rudeness or teasing which should not be generalized into racism	Racializing: The behaviour is directed towards a real or imagined group of people who suffer from long-term derision

Overreacting versus frames of disbelief

The argument that it is not racism is strong and certainly in the interests of a society that prides itself on sensitivity and liberalism, within the concept of multiculturalism discussed in Chapter 4. While it is recognized that unpleasantness has occurred, it is explained away as being against an individual rather than a group, and not part of a deeper narrative of Othering. Hence, if indeed the incident *was* racist, the rationalizations that it was not, on the left of Table 7, become excuses. On the other hand, these excuses are the basis of the thinking-as-usual discourse. Unless a social group explicitly bases its sense of cohesion on antagonism towards another group, for example in war, racism would be considered dysfunctional and pushed underground.

The argument that it *is* racism, on the right of Table 7, relates to the manner in which the aggressive behaviour is sustained hatred towards a whole group of people. The references to 'they', 'over there' and 'wherever *they* live' emphasized in the *Guardian* chat items, indicate this:[3]

> when complaining that the Indian woman had undercooked the chicken suggesting that in India that is how all chicken is cooked, which in turn makes 'them' ill, which in turn makes 'them' stay slim. And one of the white women saying she didn't know where the Indian woman's hands had been was accompanied by such a disgusted curl of the lip that it smacked of racism. (Brook, 2007: comment)

This was not a white girl objecting to having someone touch her food, it was a white girl objecting to a specific type of person touching her food, as can be seen from the subsequent comments to the effect of 'urgh is that how *they* eat their food *over there* in China or India or wherever *they* live' (ibid.; their emphasis).

In this respect the people at whom derision is levelled can be said to be *racialized*, or constructed as a racial group.[4] Racializing does not always result in racism: people can racialize themselves for the purpose of constructing an ethos of political resistance. Racializing another group does, however, build a capital of Otherness which is fertile ground for excluding hatred. Food and hygiene are common foci, as in the conversation between Paul and Richard above, as well as sexual behaviour and the treatment of women. The difficulty which the 'is not racist' discourse has in understanding the 'is racist' discourse, and the rationalization against the possibility of racism or cultural chauvinism, is exemplified in the following incident, also based on ethnographic notes, where the thinking-as-usual discourse recategorizes an event to avoid confronting the possibility of racism:

> At a dinner party Aisha was talking about the price of a house she had been looking at. Alan felt that she was exaggerating and remarked that Aisha didn't have a head for figures.

On a later date Aisha complained to Alan that he had seriously insulted her in front of their friends by saying she had a problem with numbers. Alan disagreed, saying that it was just innocent teasing – nothing significant about it. An argument ensued. Alan maintained that he ought to be the one to know that he really hadn't meant anything because it was he who had made the comment. Aisha sustained her insistence that there had been an insult. She said that there was an implication that she was fabricating a false argument, and that this was part of the way in which his society characterized people who came from her society – as 'cheating' foreigners – and that it wasn't just him: it happened again and again and again.

When Alan thought about this again he realized that she was right. He had to recall the entire incident. He had to excavate something deeper in his thinking; and indeed it *was* all to do with a deeper, long-standing prejudice. The important point was that, even if Aisha had been exaggerating, his interpretation of her behaviour was framed in a cultural disbelief that preceded and framed it.

This might be compared with this composite of stereotypical comments about British people from the *Yahoo! Answers* website:

They have bad hygiene, bad food, good manners, scruffy hair, 'fitted' clothing and great comedy and an oblique way of speaking. They drink beer, ride bikes, drink tea, swear, get in huge hooligan fights, complain about everything, and are very concerned about rankings and who's to blame for 'failures'. They are artistic, rude, 'fashionable', deep thinking, sweater-wearing, intelligent, boastful, polite, a bit snobbish and formal, calm under pressure, witty, and quite cold. Their men are gay. They fail to understand the impacts of their actions on other people.

One could argue that this collection of adjectives is not an example of Othering because it balances the negative with the positive. That may be the case; but a more important difference is that the target population is not positioned as culturally inferior by the instigators of the description and has not been subjected to continued damage, traces of deeper hatred and long-standing disbelief in the same way as the Indian woman in *Big Brother* or Aisha in the above example have been. There is a deep inequality between these groups of people.

The lack of awareness which Alan displays in his interaction with Aisha above represents a general lack of awareness of complicity in Othering in everyday talk. Lansley (1994: 52–3) provides examples of this among teachers talking about their students. They are heard to say 'He's really thick. He's not worth bothering about', or 'Arab students always have terrible spelling problems, don't they?' Other teachers collude silently. Even if they disagree, they do not wish to confront the speaker over 'such a small issue' and 'reflect' or 'mirror' her or his statement to show solidarity. Though the second statement approaches racism, it might seem admissible while 'only' talking about students. It is 'only' staffroom talk. However, it gets more serious when colleagues are allowed to say 'women are terrible drivers, aren't they?' and then 'Pakistanis are taking over the area, aren't they?' Nevertheless, collusion is still easier than disagreeing. The use of the question tag helps make it sound as though the obvious is being stated and that disagreement is all the more inappropriate. Lansley (ibid.) labels this type of talk 'moral illiteracy', and considers it to be one of the building blocks of prejudice.

The subtleties of Othering can easily be lost between the lines in a wide variety of texts. Returning to the apparent neutrality of intercultural communication studies discussed in Chapter 1, while accepting that such instances will also be present between the lines of my own text,[5] one can note that Scollon and Scollon's (2001: 1) explanation of why a Chinese businessman fails to communicate with a 'Western' listener, because 'it is not quite clear what the speaker's main point is', does give the impression that the problem is with the 'Asian speaker'. This impression is continued as they locate their discussion in the individualism–collectivism dimension:

> The idea of 'self' which underlies western studies of communication is highly individualistic, self-motivated, and open to ongoing negotiation. ... We believe that this concept of the 'self' is not entirely appropriate as the basis for Asian communication. There is a reason to believe that the 'self' projected by Asians is more collectivist. (ibid.: 46)

The sustained focus on categories of difference within the dominant neo-essentialist paradigm has the effect of superimposing on all intercultural interactions a sense of there being a 'problem' for the Self which is based on difference with the Other. Because the categories continue to be associated with particular parts of the world, the sense of 'problem' cannot avoid taking on an 'us'–'them' tenor which is one small step from a cultural chauvinism in which a somehow more efficient 'West' looks out over a less efficient, and indeed less civil, non-'Western' Other. The neo-essentialist discourse thus becomes the modernist successor of the colonialist paradigm.

Back to training and orientation

Readers may feel that I have ventured too far into areas of racism for a book on intercultural communication. That the two are inextricably bound together within a liberal multiculturalism in which race is hidden beneath the smokescreen of culture has already been argued in Chapter 4. More specifically, much can be learnt regarding claims of innocence in the intercultural communication training scenario and John and Paul's conversation about orienting newcomers to the US earlier in this chapter, and indeed from the eChina Programme scenario depicted in the positivist sequence near the beginning of Chapter 2. To make this point, Table 8 is a repeat of Table 7, this time with reference to the intercultural scenarios already described. The excuses in the second column fall very much within the liberal multiculturalist viewpoint. The third column tends to point out the ideology within this viewpoint by laying bare the hidden facts of Othering and the powerful systemic discourses which set up frames of cultural disbelief.

The undoing of cultural disbelief requires a deep appreciation of the potential for newcomers to go further than a third space and to contribute to and indeed enrich the unfamiliar cultural practices in the place in which they arrive. The irony is that this has

Table 8   For and against acknowledgements of cultural chauvinism

Conclusions about 'other cultures'	'It *isn't* culturally chauvinistic'	'It *is* culturally chauvinistic'
Not getting to the bottom of the statement that 'the processes of articulating what you are thinking and why you're thinking it, is not generally practised in China' (Chapter 2) Thinking that people who work in Greek language schools are non-Western, conformist, formal, non-confrontational, etc. (this chapter) Middle Eastern students have different standards of hygiene (this chapter) Middle Eastern people exaggerate about money (this chapter)	Just different cultures and values We are not judging, just describing them so that we can understand how to behave with them The people themselves agree with these descriptions Talking about culture has nothing to do with prejudice and has nothing to do with race Shared Otherness: we have lots of friends from other cultures and we respect and celebrate their values and traditions It would be wrong to expect them to be like us	Othering: There are references to an imagined, implied cultural deficiency associated with particular groups of people, constituting either lack of articulation, lack of individual assertiveness, 'uncleanness' or dishonesty There is a suspicion with regard to these deficiencies before the event in *a priori* frames of disbelief This systemic disbelief is hidden beneath discourses of professionalism, tolerance and cultural equality and celebration Opposition from members of Othered groups may be unspoken and unheard because of discoursal strategies of withdrawal

often been the veiled intention of travellers from the Centre to the Periphery in their missions to improve the deficient cultures of the non-Western Other under the cover of the morality of 'helping' described in Chapter 4. The narrative in the next section demonstrates how, with a bit of perseverance, this happens in the other direction.

The Intercultural Line and the Third Space

At the heart of the discourse of cultural disbelief is an indelible line between Self and Other. In the middle column of Table 8 this line maintains a separation between types of people collected around the statement 'it would be wrong to expect them to be like us'. On the surface it may appear to represent respect for difference, but at a deeper level it divides how 'we' do things from the problem of how 'they' do things. This line, drawn thickly in the left half of Figure 10, in the neo-essentialist paradigm, cuts off the possibility of the shared underlying universal cultural processes evident in the critical cosmopolitan picture on the right of the figure.

The less definite critical cosmopolitan picture on the right of Figure 10 still has two national cultural domains, but they are

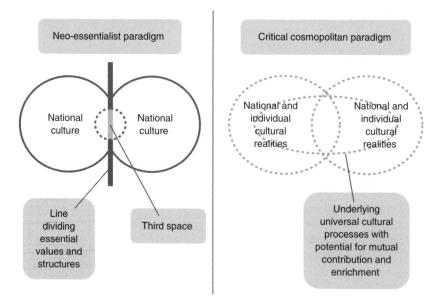

Figure 10 Removing the line

relatively blurred and they are places where the individual is in dialogue with the particularities of the respective national structures
by which they are influenced. In both domains there are underlying universal cultural processes, shared across the domains, which
enable this dialogue. The major point of this book is that it is these
underlying universal cultural processes which provide everyone with
equal cultural proficiency which has the potential to be applied in
every other national cultural domain.

An important aspect of the intercultural line, in the left half of
Figure 10, is the third space, in which it is possible for intercultural travellers to negotiate their position with regard to the new
culture. It is important to be cautious in a critique of the notion of
a third space. It is employed by a number of intercultural researchers who have genuinely and critically tried to come to terms with
the problems of an essentialist view of culture; and the related
concept of hybridity, where someone at the same time maintains
the attributes of their own culture while taking on in a limited way
those of another, has also been adopted by critical postcolonialist
theorists as a space 'that entertains difference without an assumed
or imposed hierarchy' (Bhabha, 1994: 5).[6] It cannot be denied that
the possibility of 'crossing' a harder intercultural line and creating
third spaces, in-between places, has massive potential for theorizing cultural creativity. For example, Fay (1996: 55ff.) talks about
'permeable' and 'rearranged' cultural boundaries with 'interplay
and exchange'; but there is nevertheless a strong sense that the
'deeper cultural rhythms', to do with time, space and, of course,
politically loaded 'agency', are still mutually exclusive. The concept
of the intercultural line remains, and is often used to indicate a
division of values which in turn indicate a division in what people are prepared to do or are capable of doing. Byram (2008) also
provides an extensive account of creative cultural struggle around
the notion of hybridity; but it also is framed in terms of the indel-
ibility of the intercultural line, where ethnic groups are mutually
exclusive and 'tolerate poorly the presence of "hybrids"' (ibid.: 62),
and the values of the other culture can be 'incompatible with one's
own' (ibid.: 69).

The notion of a third space or hybridity thus has at least the potential of denying the possibility of complexly diverse cultural ownership expressed by many of my informants and the Iranian students
represented in Chapters 3 and 5. The concept of cultural realities
that can transcend national cultural boundaries and be carried with
individuals as they travel from place to place is counter to the concept of hybridity. One does not have to be in-between. People have
the power to be completely several things at once. Kumaravadivelu
puts this well:

> Proponents of cultural hybridity would expect me to create a 'third culture,' or a 'third space', without allowing either my inherited Indian culture or my learned American culture to fully determine my values and beliefs … a state of ambivalence … in-betweenness that is supposed to result when individuals … displace themselves from one national/cultural context … into another … I do not believe I am dangling in cultural limbo. Instead, I believe I live in several cultural domains at the same time – jumping in and out of them, sometimes with ease and sometimes with unease. … In fact one does not even have to cross one's national borders to experience cultural complexity. If we, as we must, go beyond the traditional approach to culture that narrowly associates cultural identity with national identity … then we easily realize that human communities are not monocultural cocoons but rather multicultural mosaics. (2007a: 5)

Kumaravadivelu goes on to suggest that the concept of hybridity 'wrongly places the margin at the centre and, in doing so, it conflates the distinction between the oppressed and the oppressor' (ibid.: 112), and that cultural identity is 'fragmented, not unified; multiple, not singular; expansive, not bounded' (ibid.: 142–3).

It is not for me to suggest that writers for whom these concepts are instrumental in undoing the cultural hegemony of the Centre are mistaken. I have already said that my purpose is not to speak for the Periphery but to try to unravel the thinking of the Centre. My problem is that while there is a concept of a line between 'our culture' and 'their culture', it cannot remain at a level of mutual respectfulness. It cannot help but lead to the neo-essentialist discourse, which I have critiqued throughout, of 'us' and 'them' and Self and Other which has to imply an imagined inequality. Hofstede's (2001: 28) statement that most people are in fact hybrid because they do not fit exactly his national categories is simply working down from an essentialist position.

I am not suggesting that intercultural behaviour is not an immense struggle. While I speak throughout about people's ability to carry their cultural realities and transfer their basic cultural skills from one place to another to build new realities and to contribute to and enrich the cultural practices that they find, I do not suggest that this is an easy matter. Kayvan in Chapter 2, Lamis in Chapter 4, Samr in Chapter 5 and Aisha in this chapter, all have to struggle to be understood in the face of disbelief. I will describe in Chapter 8 how Qing has to struggle to engage with the strange British university seminar. The question is not whether or not there is misunderstanding or miscommunication when people travel and encounter cultural strangeness. The question is how this struggle is interpreted and what its causes are supposed to be. Byram (2008) provides a detailed account of the intercultural struggle of a range of individuals including Eva Hoffman's (1998: 105) discomfort with the annoying English rendering of her Polish name (Byram, 2008: 65), and Paulston talking about conflicting values and mental break-down (ibid: 67) and what nationality people feel after long-term residence in another country (ibid.: 63). These are all valid 'statements about culture' but, as in the reconstructed narratives throughout this book, these statements are cultural texts which can be read in different ways. My own reading of Hoffman's (1998) *Lost in Translation* did not begin from my own preoccupation with an indelible intercultural line and therefore inspired me with accounts of someone struggling to write herself into and taking ownership of a new and strange cultural universe. This struggle to take ownership is the topic of the next chapter.

Summary

The following points have been made in this chapter:

- The process of reifying products and processes for client consumption is particularly powerful in professional discourses, of which intercultural communication training is an example. It results in a deintellectualization of issues which move from being 'understood' to forgotten. Disbelief in the cultural proficiencies of the foreign Other thus becomes strengthened.
- While there is considerable awareness of the false reality of many public and professional discourse forms within Western society, this false reality it can be considerably reduced in the everyday detail of workplace discourses, especially with the common cynicism directed at 'political correctness' and the belief in 'fairness' upon which professional discourses depend.
- Like instances of racism, instances of cultural chauvinism can therefore easily be explained away as isolated cases of non-aligned interpersonal aggression or misunderstanding.
- The crucial factor in admitting cultural chauvinism, as with racism, is excavating personal beliefs in the cultural deficiency of whole groups of people, to which dominant cultural descriptions contribute.
- Critical to removing disbelief in the cultural Other is thus the removal of the intercultural line between Self and Other which has been sustained in a neo-essentialist approach. The alternative is a critical cosmopolitan recognition of underlying universal cultural processes that transcend the national structures with which they are in dialogue.

Investigation

The following tasks are designed to get to the bottom of and undo everyday discourses of disbelief. It will be helpful to carry them out with someone from a different cultural background.

1 Use or adapt the *categories of cultural action* to deconstruct the intercultural communication training, the personal hygiene and the Aisha and Alan narratives.

2 Use the discussion of the intercultural communication training event to reconstruct a professional event you regularly take part in which is connected with cultural or related social relations.

3 Use or adapt the professional reification sequence at the beginning of the chapter to help you *make the familiar strange* by trying to recognize the discourse and to stand outside it. You will need to *bracket* any professional loyalty you have to the event.

   (a) *Thick description* will help you to uncover all the relevant elements of the event.

   (b) Use the professional reification sequence at the beginning of the chapter again to help you to work out (i) what issues are left as 'understood' and therefore not pursued, and for what professional reasons, and (ii) what technical terms or concepts are problematic and yet used as a matter of routine and therefore got used to.

   (c) Use or adapt the *categories of cultural action* to analyze the narrative.

   (d) Evaluate the professional reification sequence.

4 Carry out a small piece of research in which you interview people about what they think about third spaces and hybridity.

   (a) What disciplines do you need to employ in designing the questions you will ask? Use the research project in Chapter 3 as a model if this helps. You will need to consider the following:

       (i)   How can you encourage *them* to *make the familiar strange* and to produce *thick description* about themselves?

       (ii) They may not be familiar with the terms 'third space' and 'hybridity'.

       (iii) The concepts 'third space' and 'hybridity' are quite seductive and may constitute 'easy answers'.

   (b) Employ *critical reading* to work out the probable ideological positions regarding superiority and inferiority behind their statements.

5 Plan an orientation session for preventing people from arriving in Alan's position. Consider appropriate participants, presenters, texts and activities to ensure the following:

   (a) an excavation of personal deep prejudices about other people's societies which pervade everyday interaction;

   (b) withdrawal from offence without being patronizing.

Notes

1   See the discussion of the construction of the professional discourse of English language teaching in Holliday (2005: 39–61) and Holliday and Aboshiha (2009).

2   For a full discussion of the politics of political correctness see Lea (2009), and with reference to prejudice against 'non-native speakers' see the discussion between myself and Alan Waters (Holliday, 2007c; Waters, 2007a, 2007b).

3   I have replaced real names with either 'white woman' or 'Indian woman'.

4   A discussion of racialization can be found in several places (Kubota and Lin, 2006, 2009; Rich and Troudi, 2006; Spears, 1999).

5   There is a discussion in Holliday (2007: 177; 2005: 31) of how I discovered instances of Self–Other chauvinism in my own ethnographic description of the behaviour of Chinese students.

6   There are various discussions of the third space as a critical concept (e.g. Guilherme, 2002: 167; Zhu, 2008; Kramsch, 1993), and of different views of hybridity as a postcolonial concept and also its relationship with critical cosmopolitanism (Canagarajah, 1999: 208; Delanty, 2006: 33; Young, 2006: 159).

8

Creative Cultural Engagement

This chapter will present the other side of the coin to Chapter 7. The major example will demonstrate the critical cosmopolitanism image of culture on the right-hand side of Figure 10 and generate a discussion of the detail of how newcomers from the non-West are able to take ownership of and indeed contribute to and enrich the cultural practices that they find. I say 'removal of the intercultural line' with caution because its concept is very strongly there in the mind of the Centre-West. Newcomers therefore have to face the deep discourses of disbelief described in Chapter 7 and the pervading ideology of a demonized, deficient Other. This is not a simple matter. Once again, the purpose is not to speak for the newcomer but to make it clear to the Centre-Western vision that the commonly perceived behaviour of newcomers is *not* an indication of their deficiency, but rather an indication of their struggle to take very proficient ownership.

Qing and the Seminar

The following narrative is about Qing's experience with seminars in a British university. The narrative is based on conversations with students from a range of national backgrounds, including about their experiences with seminars and academic life in Britain.[1]

> Qing and her Chinese friend Tom were talking about their experience of British university seminars. Qing was anxious because she felt that everyone was always watching her, wondering why she didn't talk. Tom said that she shouldn't worry so much because they weren't expected to speak because of their culture. Qing wasn't happy with this excuse – that 'East Asian' students had some sort of issue with 'face', and weren't prepared to make mistakes and be criticized in front of other students. Their lecturers also seemed to use this culture thing as a way of labelling people that they disapproved of. They were constructed as those 'problem students' who didn't speak and therefore were 'passive' and didn't think.

She later had coffee with her Romanian friend, Lara, who had a completely different opinion. She said that she had read in her social science course before she came to Britain that face was a universal thing that different people dealt with in different ways. She said that there was a particularly annoying student in one of *her* seminars who just wouldn't stop talking – and that that was *his* way of saving face. The irony was that he was also Chinese. Everyone knew that some people, from whatever society, covered up their deeper anxieties with extroverted behaviour.

Qing went back to Tom and said it was about time they took some action. She convinced him to help her to do some research about how to succeed in seminars. She had also done social science at university before she came to Britain and knew how to do this sort of research. They agreed to use their 'quiet' times to observe and note. They laughed because the British lecturers and the other students would never imagine what they were doing beneath the 'silence'.

After two weeks they met again and shared notes. It wasn't easy. Tom said that Qing was still clinging to stereotypes when she suggested that the British were just more assertive. Eventually they came up with the following types of student behaviour: (a) not attending the seminars at all; (b) trying to hide lack of preparation by talking off the point, avoiding eye contact, or not speaking; (c) posturing – sitting in certain places or in a certain way – to try and *appear* 'academic'; (d) being quiet a lot of the time, but, when they did speak, showing they clearly *had* done the reading and knew what they were talking about, and responding to other students and also listening. There was quite a revelation here, and there were some strategies that some of the quieter British students were using which both Qing and Tom could identify with.

Qing met Lara again and said that the research had been useful in helping to demystify some of the things that were going on in seminars and had shown a way through for a quiet student who was prepared to work hard. However, when she told Lara that she still felt very inadequate, she could see that that Lara was immediately thinking this was because of her culture. She was therefore very careful to point out that if she was going to be one of those students who said little but clearly had done the work and knew what she was talking about, it was her knowledge of the language, not her culture, that got in the way. She said someone had to know a lot of English to transform what they had read into something to say about it in a short space of time – and also to actually break into a conversation that was dominated by noisy show-offs. Then she was shocked when Lara, who she thought had perfect English, said that she too struggled with all of these things, and she just hoped for a tutor who would shut up the so-called extroverts and help her find some space to speak. However, there *were* times when there were spaces for her to perform well – when she was asked questions directly, and when she was given the opportunity to give a short presentation.

Qing was very pleased when Lara offered to give her some tips on how to do this effectively. It was all to do with preparation. She was also pleased that she had used her Chinese university social science. She had always felt that the British, and her English teachers before she came to the university, had never shown any recognition that she might have any academic knowledge before she came to their classes. The research she had carried out with Tom, and the further conversations with Lara, even made her begin to believe that she had important skills to bring to the seminar issue, and that hard-working 'international' students like her might even begin to change the expectations of what was normal in British university seminars.

Table 9 applies categories of cultural action to the narrative. As with narratives in previous chapters, this is not a straightforward analysis. While there is one column for each of the characters, the information available in the narrative does not allow every cell to be filled. The column furthest to the right does not represent a particular person or set of people, but what the three characters between them say of their experience of British lecturers and students.

A number of things are revealed. The statements about culture from the three characters, Qing, Tom and Lara, all represent some form of ambivalence with regard to the stereotype which is imposed by British lecturers and students – discomfort or opposition from Qing and Lara, and perhaps reluctant compliance on the part of Tom. The statements in the table are of course initial ones, and may change as a result of the experience in the narrative, at least for Qing and Tom.

The global position and politics cells indicate Lara's apparent ambivalence in her positioning partially with a Centre and partially with a Periphery discourse. There is some evidence elsewhere for this sort of behaviour. Petrić (2009) describes how Central and Eastern European English language teachers realign their cultural identities in different ways depending on their particular backgrounds when dealing with a profession dominated by teachers who have English as a first language. This also resonates with my discussion in Chapter 5 of how people from certain geographical locations can construct different Others depending on whether they are looking East or West. Hence, her 'natural' expectation that education and science is 'Western', in the cell above, is sufficient for her to be for a moment surprised at Qing's ability as a researcher.

Table 9 Explaining Qing and seminars

Categories of cultural action	Qing	Tom	Lara	Experienced attitudes of British lecturers and students
Statements about culture	'I am uncomfortable when everyone is watching me because I don't talk in seminars. It is an excuse to say that Chinese students are expected to behave like this'	'We can live with the convenient stereotype of "silence" imposed on us'	'Everyone has some sort of problem with face. Being quiet or noisy isn't necessarily a national cultural thing, but just another way of protecting face'	'Students from South East Asian cultures are not expected to speak in seminars because of "face" issues'
Global position and politics	Experience of having one's behaviour defined by confining cultural stereotypes. Experience of being stereotyped as problematic because of being 'quiet', and of being referred to as 'a culture'		Sometimes 'Western' when comparing herself with Qing and Tom	Belief in providing a superior Western education
Cultural resources	An ethos of hard work flavoured by a collaborative spirit. A social science education		A social science education. Expectation that social science education is Western	Expectation that social science education and creative autonomy is Western and not 'silent'
Underlying universal processes	Establishing the relationship between Self and Other through an analytical process of observation. Imagining the Other as equally problematic or academically skilled as Self. Demystification of the Other. Learning deeper aspects of Self by experiencing the Other. Resistance against a dominant Centre discourse			

The cultural resources cells speak less than expected about Confucianism – though this may possibly have some connection with Qing's propensity for collaborative hard work. What is more significant is the references to social science education for all three characters. This in no way means that their respective societies are marked for their social science education, but that they have social science education just like Western societies. This may seem a statement of the obvious until juxtaposed with the British lecturers' and students' expectation that they do not, where 'silence' implies lack of knowledge.[2] The cultural resources she brings with her will influence her actions, but as part of the process of cultural extension and enrichment involved in engaging with new cultural realities. It thus may be the case that Qing has never before behaved in the way she does in British university seminars.

Her behaviour in the seminar is thus not a straightforward representation of her national culture, but a product of cultural realities which are expanded as she travels from familiar to less familiar scenarios and which provide her with an enriched competence in strategically applying underlying universal cultural skills. This is indicated on the left of Figure 11. It would therefore be wrong to say that Qing is learning the host culture as a distant object, but instead expanding her existing cultural abilities creatively to accommodate it, so that she may be developing a broader set of cultural abilities than people who have not travelled. Indeed, she

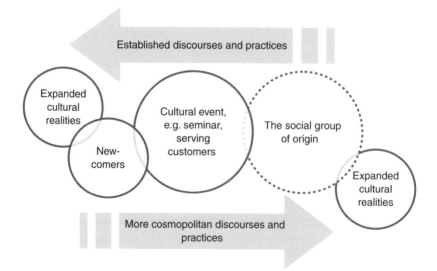

Figure 11 The cosmopolitanizing of culture [3]

learns much to demystify the seminar in discovering the issues that everyone has with it; and then realizes that she possesses perfectly adequate mechanisms for doing the same. As with communicative competence, with language itself, with discourse competence and so on, there must be an underlying potential to grow and expand in response to new situations, scenarios and small cultures. This does not have to be the result of travelling abroad, but of moving through different discourses and small cultures within the everyday complexity of society.[4] Qing's actions may not be possible for everyone. They depend perhaps on self-confidence and persistence (which I emphasize as personal rather than cultural attributes); but they are nevertheless based on universal principles. Her engagement with the seminar enables her to find herself and show her skills and subsequently benefit and be appreciated.

Contributing and enriching

Qing's newcomer engagement also causes the British university seminar to grow culturally to accommodate people like her. The movement from the left to the right of Figure 11 indicates that the seminar and the people engaging with it will become more cosmopolitan as she contributes to and enriches their practices. The process of newcomers engaging creatively with cultural events such as British university seminars in effect brings a positive expansion of indigenous cultural realities. The social group receiving the newcomers should really also engage creatively, effecting more cosmopolitan discourses and practices. One example, from the Qing narrative, might be that the personal research she carries out could be recognized by British lecturers and students and eventually British students could be encouraged to carry out similar research. The same might apply to seminar behaviour, where British students who are less capable of speaking out in a focused manner learn from newcomers like Qing how to mark personal spaces and prepare content about which to speak in the seminar. The answer to the often heard question of whether or not British – or indeed any other – universities should change their academic requirements to accommodate foreign students should be that newcomers can strengthen existing standards. Their engagement means that they are buying into the existing system, but in such a way that the modes of meeting these standards are diversified.

This cosmopolitanizing process (bottom of Figure 11) takes place where expanded cultural realities on the part of the newcomer engaging with found events and practices eventually lead to the expansion of those found realities. This process of becoming more cosmopolitan through contact with foreign cultural realities should be familiar to many of us. It is certainly in the spirit of Beth's experience of being a 'cultural catholic' reported in Chapter 3. This small event is an example:

> I bought bread from the supermarket that really no one liked and hardly anyone wanted to eat. I nevertheless continued to eat it until there was just a small amount left and threw it away. Throughout I had in my head images of small pieces of dried bread left on the tops of walls and window ledges in the Middle Eastern countries where I had lived. This was explained to me when I was in my 20s – that bread was considered sacred and must not be thrown away. Unwanted bread was therefore left in places where others could find it. Of course this blends with my Protestant thrift that makes me eke out the very last of the toothpaste; but it also means that I have imbibed a cultural practice from elsewhere and taken it away with me.

Things might, however, not always be so unproblematic. The event which gave me the idea of learning from newcomers is as follows:

> I recently encountered a shop assistant who appeared non-British in that she acknowledged my eye contact and then answered my question about the availability of a product while she was still serving her current customer. I say non-British because, while this practice is common in many parts of the world, I believe that in Britain shop assistants are for the most part expected not to engage with another customer, even with eye contact, until they have finished serving the current one, even in the most culturally diverse settings.
>
> On the one hand, I certainly welcomed what I felt was an improvement in practice. On the other hand, other customers, especially 'British culture' hardliners, might find it odd and even distasteful; and her employer might reprimand her for bad customer practice.

This is an example of the cultural contestation referred to by Delanty (2008: 92–3) in Chapter 1. If the newcomer shop assistant did eventually succeed in sustaining her 'foreign' practice, it would be through her skilful application to the extent that it would be considered more effective by onlookers and begin to catch on. There are many new, unfamiliar cultural practices that catch on rapidly – for example, keeping a long space between you and the person in front of you in a queue to preserve their privacy in entering PIN numbers. It is a contest between skill and the power of established discourses and practices (see the top of Figure 11). Opposition to cultural innovation does not have to be between people from different countries. Goodman (2007) provides a detailed account of how a young Algerian Berber female activist, supported by fellow male 'project of society' activists, applied discoursal strategies to establish equal footing for men and women in public spaces.

Qing is able to move, adopt and change because, while many cultural practices are more common in some societies than others, she is able to work with new ones because of the natural potential for individuals to transcend the structures of their societies, or to carry cultural practices with them from one society to another.

Complex perceptions

While I would like to argue that Qing's actions represent the newcomer's innate ability, given the appropriate opportunity, circumstances and desire, to engage with and contribute to the unfamiliar cultural practices which they encounter, how this is perceived by the social group in which the practice originates is far from a straightforward matter.

One possibility is that Qing's actions, despite their individualistic attributes, may *still* be perceived negatively as contributing to a collectivist stereotype. Her silence would continue to be the attribute most noticed. As Qing observes in the narrative, the British lecturers and the other students would never imagine that she was actively carrying out research beneath the silence. The power of the narrative connecting 'silence', 'collectivism' and 'passivity' is so great that it would lead to a sociological blindness, in that, whatever is happening before their eyes, they will see something different because they are ideologically and discoursally wired to see things in a particular way for all the reasons described above.

Another possibility is that Qing's eventual success in the seminar would be explained away as cultural assimilation. This is defined by Kumaravadivelu in the following way: 'To adopt the behaviours, values, beliefs, and lifestyles of the dominant cultural community and become absorbed in it, losing my own in the process ... to have metamorphosed into a somebody with a totally different cultural persona' (2007a: 4). Kumaravadivelu goes on to critique this concept of assimilation as a Centre-West construction which pretends integration but has a chauvinistic intention to make an imagined inferior Other the same as 'us' (ibid.: 68). The action which Qing takes is not going to make her 'like' British students. Qing's creative and innovative agency would therefore not be recognized and would in effect add to the chauvinistic stereotype of someone coming from a collectivist culture – that they would have to become 'like us' to succeed because they do not possess the ability to succeed in their own culture.

What would not help a deeper understanding of Qing's action is the students who do not appear to take the sort of action that she does and therefore appear to conform to the collectivist stereotype of passivity. This would come under the heading of what Kumaravadivelu (2006: 22; 2008: 17, citing Alvarez) defines as self-marginalization or self-Othering – where the Periphery consciously or unconsciously 'surrenders' to and therefore 'legitimizes' the Othering discourses of the Centre. Examples of this would be people claiming that they come from collectivist cultures and therefore do not have the background to participate in educational or work activities which require critical thinking, or that people where they come from are not used to thinking critically. Within my own field of English language education there has been a spate in the last decade of teachers coming on master's courses in British universities and saying 'in my context' – i.e. in my entire country – 'teachers don't allow their students to ask questions'. In these cases it would appear that they have bought into a simplistic definition of who they are and where they come from which has been constructed by the Centre and denies complexity. Such self-Othering acts are further legitimized by their lecturers who allow such comments to pass without analysis in their assignments. This becomes a vicious circle because the lecturers have presumably also bought into the same illusion of a non-complex Other and believe that they are allowing their students to voice their identities.[5] In Marxist terms there would appear to be a degree of false consciousness on both sides, which I will pick up in Chapter 9.

However, I say 'would' because I am not sure that these are always cases of self-Othering. There has already been a reference in Chapter 2 to Kumaravadivelu's suspicion that Kayvan's silence in the face of John's accusation that he lacks self-determination is such a case, whereas it may instead be an active discoursal strategy in the face of a dominant discourse.

Understanding strategic discoursal withdrawal

A strategy of discoursal withdrawal may be at the centre of much behaviour where cultural newcomers appear to be passively submitting where in fact they may be actively engaging. Such withdrawal is described in a piece of research on Japanese student classroom behaviour carried out some time ago. The students found the regime of the language classroom too difficult to engage with and remained silent. The silence itself, though derived from available cultural resources, was uncharacteristic when compared to Japanese students' behaviour in Japanese secondary school classrooms. The British teachers exercised control over when and for what reason the students could speak, whereas the Japanese teachers observed allowed their students to speak when they wanted beneath the formal structure of the lesson (Holliday, 2002: 20).[6] This silence nevertheless served to strengthen the negative stereotype of silent Japanese students.

Similar observations can be made of Iranian students of technical English at a British university who, on the one hand, 'fail' to carry out group activities effectively but, on the other hand, effect a revolution and succeed in imposing their own classroom structure (Holliday, 2005: 102–3); Taiwanese students whose teachers think are slow to learn on a British study skills programme when in fact they are getting the input they need elsewhere because the teachers seem unapproachable and the instructions too complicated (ibid., citing Chang); and high school students in Hong Kong whose teachers say are too bound by Confucianism to be 'active' in the classroom and yet are very 'active' out of sight of and in opposition to the teacher (ibid.: 97–8, citing Tong). Rampton and colleagues demonstrate that looking in detail at what is actually going on in multiethnic London secondary schools reveals a complexity that supports unexpected cultural realities (e.g. Rampton, 2007; Rampton et al., 2008). Flam and Bauzamy (2008) describe how marginalized groups suffering the hidden racism and symbolic violence of Western society, despite the common view that they remain unaware and passive, find multiple ways to 'fight back'. Such 'multiple strategies' are also described by Sawyer and Jones (2008: 245, citing Scott): '"foot dragging, false compliance, flight, feigned ignorance, sabotage, theft ... cultural resistance" ... ironic, subversive, double meanings'. The latter refers to the tradition of slave songs in the African-American community.[7] Such strategies are well known on the global scene, for example, Japanese playing back the exotic imagery created by the West to attract tourists and business.[8] At an interpersonal level, it can be strategic to act out the image people have of us in order to gain their approval. An example of this is Chinese students feeding their university tutors with the stereotype that they, the tutors, are familiar with, in order to ease communication. This may be a survival strategy. Khorsandi provides an interesting case in her reconstruction of a memory, as a seven-year-old girl, of strategically tolerating a misunderstanding to escape being punished while at school in Britain:

> 'Don't worry', I heard her say through my fog of panic. 'You are not in trouble because I know you are a very nice little girl but haven't got the confidence the other children have. It's not easy coming from another country is it?'
>
> I had no idea what being Iranian had to do with this but things seemed to be going my way so I was happy to go along with whatever theory Mrs Oliver had come up with if it meant getting out of trouble. (Khorsandi, 2009: 120)

I saw an example of discoursal withdrawal in a role-play activity I carried out with a group of British project managers concerning intercultural awareness: [9]

> The situation was a British aid agency funding a curriculum project in a university in an Asian country. Dr Rustam, the lead person in the university, complained because the aid agency insisted on work plans which ignored the organizational culture of the university and the abilities of its staff. Moreover, the aid agency refused to meet and discuss differences because it felt that the documentation it had produced was sufficient and that the university personnel were simply too lazy to read it.
>
> In the role play the British project managers took the parts of people from the aid agency and the university. Their task was to prepare for a meeting at the British Embassy which I would chair, to try to sort out the differences.
>
> At the meeting I was surprised that Alison, the senior British project manager who played the role of Dr Rustam, kept silent and did not put forward her point of view.
>
> During the discussion after the role play, when I asked Alison why she kept silent during the meeting, she said that she had realized that it was not the time to speak – that meeting at the embassy belonged to the same discourse as the aid agency, and that despite overtures of sympathy from the chair of the meeting, she realized that whatever she said would be ineffective. To make her case successfully she would have to wait and choose another, more appropriate moment.

I felt that this outcome of the role play was very effective – in fact more than I could have expected. At least one of the British project managers had succeeded in placing herself in the position of the non-Western university academic, despite expected cultural differences, to the extent that she could genuinely appreciate her dilemma. It suggests that understanding what it means and also how to act when facing a dominant discourse is present not only in global Periphery–Centre relations, but in all walks of life, in all cultural settings at different times in different circumstances. Hence, the British project manager was able to recognize the predicament of the non-Western academic.

This resonates with what Jacob (1996: 2) refers to as 'intermediate actions of resistance' for 'counteracting imperialism'. These actions are considered 'intermediate' because they appreciate the immense power of the dominant discourse against which more direct action would be unsuccessful. These are applied in Holliday (2005: 170) to a group of language students visiting Britain from Hong Kong who appeared 'quiet' in British university classrooms, but asserted themselves in a number of other locations and events in a mixture of strategies of non-compliance and space marking (ibid.: 90–6). The following are the specific strategies suggested by Jacob, with examples from Qing's engagement with the seminar:

- *Marking territories*: working towards establishing her own space in seminars, establishing a personal position as a social researcher.
- *Reconciling with the past*: recognizing her educational capital as a social researcher.
- *Speaking against the grain*: resisting the dominant cultural stereotype and taking strategic action.
- *Moving to centre stage from the periphery*: asserting her presence within her peer group of students and planning to do the same within the larger community through the seminars.
- *Holding back technology*: speaking in seminars only at times within her own control.
- *Breaking silences*: orchestrating a discussion about the dominant cultural stereotype and planning how to continue the discussion through meetings with her peer group.

These strategies bring to mind my personal reading of Eva Hoffman's struggle as a Polish person coming to an American society, referred to in Chapter 7:

> I've developed a certain kind of worldly knowledge, and a public self to go with it. That self is the most American thing about me; after all I acquired it here. 'Don't let them spit on your kasha', my mother advises me defiantly, meaning, roughly, 'Don't let the bastards grind

you down'. In an American way, I don't: I've learnt how to tough it out and stand my ground, cut my losses and choose my fights and talk back to tall men. (Hoffman, 1998: 251)

As Qing notes that her own anxieties about the seminar may also be shared by some British students, one does not have to be nationally foreign to feel foreign in relation to cultural practices in the society one inhabits.

Learning from the Margins

In this chapter I have looked at the experiences of newcomers establishing their presence and their skills and discrediting the imagined intercultural line between 'us' and 'them'. Following Stuart Hall's (1991a: 34) statement in Chapter 1, this truer picture of culture comes from the margins which are often hidden by this line. This sort of shaking out of the normal perception of things is important in the discipline of making the familiar strange. A good example of this is Alison, earlier in the chapter, being able to step into the shoes of Dr Rustam. This is a long way from being worried about the 'values' on the other side of the line being different from one's own. Here, my informant, Beth, pieces together a thick description of foreign street and familiar professional life through which she is able to reassess her 'own culture':

> I felt suddenly enlightened when I heard that Mexicans, walking down a street in Guanajuato, would have to stop and acknowledge greetings as it was the height of ill manners not to do so but such behaviour conflicted with the Anglo-Saxon (allegedly) insistence on students being punctual for class. I found the greater importance attached to human interaction an attractive excuse – raising questions about the 'virtue' of punctuality! Without the professional dimension, I would not have found other ways of viewing these aspects of my own culture. (Beth)

The outcome is significantly not an understanding of why Mexican students may not come to class on time, but just possibly a fresh look at the icon of punctuality. Relaxing punctuality would not mean a loss of culture. It is, after all, just one of the many cultural resources people like Beth draw on, and is very often mediated more than we might imagine.

Summary

- Newcomers from foreign cultural backgrounds possess the underlying universal cultural skills to have the potential to contribute to and enrich cultural practices which they engage with, resulting in a cosmopolitanizing of such practices.
- The newcomers expand their own cultural realities through travel between familiar and unfamiliar systems and may cause a cosmopolitanizing expansion of the practices they find. Newcomers may, however, have to face resistance from established discourses and practices.
- Newcomers' discoursal strategies in the face of resistance to their engagement, such as silence or withdrawal, may still be interpreted as cultural deficiency.
- Cultural engagement is different from the established notion of assimilation.

Investigation

These tasks are designed around the principle of newcomer cultural engagement. It is preferable to carry them out with someone from a different cultural background,

1 Reconstruct an event where you or someone you know brought cultural practices and experience from elsewhere and used them to engage with an unfamiliar cultural practice.
   (a) Describe in discoursal terms (referring to Figure 11), in the form of a *thick description*:
        (i)   evidence that this resulted in contribution to or enrichment of the practice;
        (ii) the cultural resources employed;
        (iii) resistance from the social group within which the practice originated;
        (iv) strategies used to deal with the resistance (referring to Jacob's intermediate actions of resistance);
        (v)   expanded cultural realities on the part of the newcomer;
        (vi) expanded cultural realities within the social group of origin.
   (b) Apply or adapt the *categories of cultural action* to the reconstruction.
2 Consider the example of preserving bread.
   (a) Reconstruct a similar example from your experience.
   (b) What cultural resources came into play?

3 An Iranian art student told Honarbin-Holliday (personal communication) that she went through the motions of painting in a traditional Persian style when some French visitors came to her university because this is what they would expect.

(a) Write a *thick description* of a similar instance you have been a participant in or witnessed.

(b) What were the apparent, surface reasons or accusations or judgements made at the time?

(c) What deeper discoursal strategies might have been taking place? Use the examples of Jacob's intermediate actions of resistance to help you. You will need to try hard to *make the familiar strange* because the surface reasons will be the 'easy answer'.

(d) Apply or adapt *categories of cultural action* to the description.

4 Trace other instances of everyday cultural change to their possible sources. Again, *thick description* and *making the familiar strange* will be crucial here to separate 'easy' from unrecognized assumptions.

5 Apply or adapt the *categories of cultural action* to the shop assistant example.

(a) Imagine that there is opposition from the employer and customers.

(b) Construct a *thick description* of all the factors which might bear on the incident.

6 Apply or adapt the *categories of cultural action* to the role-play example.

(a) Construct one column each for (i) the real person of Alison and for (ii) the expectation of the role-play designer that she would use the role to put forward her case.

(b) Construct a *thick description* of all the factors which might bear on the incident.

7 Reconstruct a *thick description* of a scenario when someone has been misunderstood as not participating when in fact they were actively engaging with private strategies.

(a) Relate this to instances where you would misunderstand the potential with which foreign colleagues or students can also engage.

(b) Discuss the politics of allowing space which might apply to these instances. This is a sensitive area because almost all actions on the part of the Centre will be considered an imposition by the Periphery.

8 Carry out a small piece of research in which you ask cultural newcomers to recount examples of where they have contributed to and enriched cultural practices that they have encountered.

(a) What disciplines do you need to employ in designing the questions you will ask – to encourage *them* to *make the familiar strange* and to produce *thick description* about themselves? Use the research project in Chapter 3 as a model if this helps.

(b) Employ *critical reading* to work out the probable ideological positions regarding superiority and inferiority behind their statements.

9 Debate the arguments, citing evidence, for:
   (a) the validity of the concept of underlying universal cultural processes;
   (b) the validity of the concept of cultural assimilation.
   Trace the arguments to cosmopolitanism, critical cosmopolitanism, essentialism or neo-essentialism.
10 Plan an orientation session for people in work or similar settings which employ people from different cultural backgrounds. Consider appropriate participants, presenters, texts and activities to ensure the following:
   (a) an understanding of the potential of culturally diverse ways of working which may enhance existing standards – an appreciation of what people with experience of other systems can contribute;
   (b) a withdrawal from partisan cultural attitudes to good practice.

Notes

1 There is a substantial literature regarding Chinese students in British universities and elsewhere concerning their cultural ability to take part in educational activities, gathered around the issues of 'individualism' versus 'collectivism' cultural stereotypes (e.g. Atkinson, 1999; Cheng, 2000; Clark and Gieve, 2006; Flowerdew et al., 2000; Grimshaw, 2007; Quach et al., 2009; Rastall, 2006).

2 See Holliday (2005: 96) for a discussion of prior academic and cultural knowledge of Hong Kong Chinese students, and Holliday and Aboshiha (2009) for a reference to British English language teachers imagining that Japanese students have little access to knowledge of the world in their own education system.

3 Source for Figure 11: adapted and developed from Holliday (2002: 20).

4 See Lankshear et al.'s (1997: 21) description of expanding the 'field-of-possibles'. See also Angouri and Harwood's (2008) discussion of how people co-construct multiple writing genres in response to different communities of practice.

5 I have been particularly implicated in this deception by promoting simplistic descriptions of other people's 'contexts' in order to 'solve' the 'problems' implicit in them (Holliday, 1994).

6 See further discussion of Japanese students and British classrooms in Holliday (2005: 90–1, citing Hayagoshi).

7 See also the discussion of hidden curriculum and the hidden strategies of women in school and the workplace (e.g. Anyon, 1980, 1983; Benjamin and Walters, 1994; Griffiths, 1995).

8   Further discussion of the Periphery using Centre-defined stereotypes can be found in a number of places (Keesing, 1994: 306–7; Kubota, 1999: 9; Moeran, 1996; Sakamoto, 1996: 113; Sarangi, 1994: 416).

9   This role play is based on the curriculum project scenario described in Holliday (2005: 120–8).

9

Culture, Real or Imagined?

The driving force of the discussion throughout has been a critical cosmopolitan approach in which it is perceived that dominant pictures of culture, which are still largely neo-essentialist in nature, are manufactured by a Centre-Western ideology. This picture is, however, far too simplistic. As discussed in Chapter 1, Hall and his colleagues (King, 1991b) consider culture to be politically constructed everywhere – presumably, therefore, both in the Centre *and* in the margins, the major difference being that the former is well established and the latter struggling for recognition. It would be extremely naïve to assume that the Periphery is not also in the business of constructing discourses of culture, as is evident in the conflict of awarenesses in the Ming–Zhang narrative in Chapter 5. To make sense of this in this epilogue, I will revisit the nature of culture and its relationship with social construction in trying to sort out how far it is real or really imagined.

The Centrality of Ideology

The suggestion, in Chapter 6, that ideology is firmly placed within the underlying universal cultural processes in the formation of small culture ([iv] in Figure 8) seems to contradict my critique of structural-functionalism in Chapter 3 for positivistically placing ideology within the structure of society but denying that ideology is also in the perception of the researcher. I defend my position in this matter by saying that ideology is everywhere, *both* in the fabric of all cultural formation *and* in the manner in which social scientists look at culture.

This ubiquity of ideology implies that the chauvinism which it potentially produces is also everywhere. If this is the case – which is the postmodern dilemma – both the Centre-West and the Periphery must own up to their fair share of ideology and of imagining the Other. Indeed, the claim that only the Centre-West is chauvinistic can easily be accused of being essentialist.[1] I have also critiqued the neo-essentialist position that all cultures, as described in Hofstedian

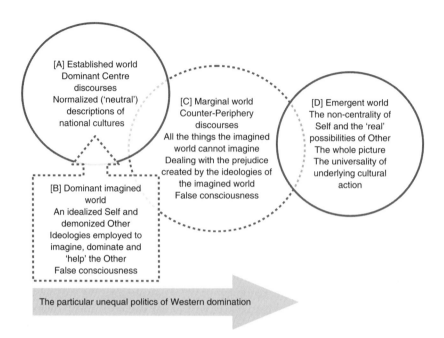

Figure 12 Competing worlds

terms, are equal but different. At the same time, in Chapter 6 I seem to be contradicting this critique by suggesting that culture formation has a large universal component. Indeed, my description of culture formation does resonate somewhat with structural-functionalist models of society such as Parsons's (1951) *The Social System*. Figure 12 tries to make sense of these dilemmas by trying to make sense of what are in effect competing worlds. I will deal with each part in turn.

The established and the dominant imagined worlds

The relationship between an established world and a dominant imagined world which influences it, on the left of Figure 12, comprises the complex of construction, ideology and politics which by its nature invents cultural images of the foreign Other and the denial of ideology discussed in Chapter 1. The established world [A] comprises the normalized research and literature which appears neutral and scientific and forms the basis of the dominant neo-essentialist paradigm in intercultural communication studies. However, the established world is an illusion in that its basis is the dominant imagined world [B] of underlying, unspoken and denied ideology and prejudice which constitutes the long-standing narratives of Othering described in Chapter 4. These two worlds are Centre *because* of the manner in which they always define the Other.

Deeply implicit in this complex of perception is the *false consciousness* of the dominant imagined world. Berger and Luckmann (1979: 18) relate a particularly aggressive notion of ideology as 'ideas serving as weapons for social interest' to the Marxist notion of false consciousness, which they define as 'thought that is alienated from the real social being of the thinker'. The implication here is that social construction produces a deceptive reality which hides something truer and more honourable for the people involved, and that there are agents of this deception. This fits the Marxist narrative in which it is the oppressed proletariat who are falsely conscious if they remain deferential to an order constructed and imposed by the ruling class. I would like, however, to think that false consciousness could be everywhere – implicit in thought itself. This is implied by Engels, who is thought to have coined the term, also connecting it with ideology:

> Ideology is a process which of course is carried on with the consciousness of the so-called thinker but with a false consciousness. The real driving forces which move him, he remains unaware of, otherwise it would not be an ideological process. He therefore imagines false or apparent driving forces. Because it is a thought process, he derives both its content and form from pure thought, either his own or that of his predecessors. He works with purely conceptual material which he unwittingly takes over as the product of thought and therefore does not investigate its relations to a process further removed from and independent of thought. Indeed this seems to him self-evident, for it appears to him that since all activity is *mediated* by thought, it is ultimately *grounded* in thought. (Engels, 1934: 81; his emphasis)

Thus, false consciousness is fed by a confidence in an arrogance of thought – which has been described in the discussion of the denial of ideology in Chapter 1.

The only hope of undoing this false consciousness is for the established world to appreciate the degree to which it is based upon the ideologies and prejudices of the dominant imagined world and to become open to the counter-discourses of the marginal world [C].

The marginal world

The marginal world represents the Periphery, or the vernacular, struggling for recognition as suggested in the critical cosmopolitanist arguments in Chapter 1. The marginal world remains half hidden by the established and dominant imagined worlds, but is positioned, ironically, in the centre of Figure 12 because it is in effect the most solid of all the worlds – a set of unrecognized truths. The counter-discourses of the marginal world are nevertheless also ideologically constructed and therefore no more 'real' or true than the Centre discourses. In some cases they will themselves suffer from a false consciousness associated with the self-marginalizing adoption of Centre discourses. However, this also is far from a simple matter. I have argued in Chapter 7 that what may appear to be a self-marginalizing adoption of Centre discourses may at least sometimes arise from discoursal strategies of resistance.

It needs to be noted that the whole relationship between these competing worlds is itself universal to any cultural formation, small or large, whether a football team psyching up against another team or a university developing a mission statement, and in effect comprises the underlying universal cultural process of imagining Self and Other in Figure 8 [iv]. What is specific to the focus of this book is the particular unequal politics of Western domination, at the bottom of the Figure 12, which drives a particular chauvinism with regard to non-Western societies.

The emergent world

What may happen, which it is the aim of this book to encourage, is that these counter-discourses will sufficiently shake the certainties of the Centre to open up the possibility of seeing something else – an emergent cultural world [D] on the right of Figure 12. This would be not so much true descriptions of 'other cultures' – because that would be just another naïvely positivist, essentialist exercise. Instead this would be a realization of the inadequacy of the Centre picture of the world, a recognition of the potentials of the Periphery, and of the manner in which cultural descriptions are mediated by ideology.

The Fact of Ideology

The ubiquity of ideology itself, in all four worlds in Figure 12, gives rise to a series of sociological facts. Such facts are often associated with Emile Durkheim, who defines them as 'ways of acting, thinking and feeling which possess the remarkable property of existing outside the consciousness of the individual ... which are invested with a coercive power by virtue of which they exercise control over him' (1982: 50). While Durkheim has been critiqued in Chapter 3 for his structural-functionalist view of culture, it is nevertheless possible to consider his notion of sociological facts as applicable to what has been learnt from postmodernism – that traditional truths are mediated by ideology. Whilst I do not follow Durkheim's thesis to the extent that individuals are completely determined by these facts, I think they can offer explanations for behaviour. Also, following the discussion in Chapter 3, the facts need to acknowledge the role of ideology as an interactant with individual action and with social structure (as in social action theory) rather than contained within and a product of it (as in structural-functionalism).

What I therefore take from Durkheim is the idea of the social act, rather than the specific social facts he might promote. The sociological facts I would like to propose, as the basis for believing that cultural chauvinism against non-Western cultures is a reality, are as follows:[2]

1 Ideology is always present in social life, and manifests itself within everyday language and behaviour.
2 The established liberal academic, professional and civilizational discourses of 'culture' hide ideology by projecting technical superiority through constructing their beliefs as neutral.
3 In a postcolonial world there continues to be an 'us'–'them' relationship in which a Western Self imagines a culturally deficient foreign Other. This relationship is sustained through cultural and linguistic imperialism and constructions of confining regional, religious and ethnic cultures.

Fact 1 is a universal, about the nature of social life; and facts 2 and 3 are special cases of fact 1, concerning a particular aspect of social life and current global politics, respectively. Facts 1 and 2 are supported by the work of critical discourse analysts such as Fairclough and go back to Foucault, and by the understanding we have of false consciousness from Marxist sociology above. Fact 2 relates specifically to neo-essentialism in intercultural studies and training described in Chapter 1, and liberal multiculturalism in Chapter 4, and is the basis for the liberal–essentialist duality. Fact 3 relates to the narrative of Orientalism described in Chapter 4. The word 'continues' is significant here in that these narratives are in effect a revival of much older narratives.

As social facts these give the impression that there is some degree of clarity about how the world actually is. While it may never be possible completely to capture this reality, once the centrality of ideology has been established, for which we must be thankful to the postmodern turn, some things just begin to fall into place. The following summarizes what has been noted about the nature of culture so far. It needs to be remembered here that I am not claiming this as empirical fact on the basis of extensive quantities of data, but on the basis of what might only be the beginnings of qualitative observation, bringing together a range of impressions from small qualitative studies, a particular set of established social theory and literary observation in fictional works:

- Nation is an important influence on and resource for individual cultural realities through education, media, histories, political structures, language and so on (Figure 8 [i], Chapter 6).
- Individuals are able to draw on, act in dialogue with, or resist national social structure, and ideology, given the right circumstances (Figure 8).
- Basic cultural skills and processes are universal (Figure 8 [iv]).
- There are personal mediations between underlying universal cultural processes and national structures (Figure 8 [iii]).
- Ideology impacts both on the formation of culture and on the manner in which this formation is described (Figure 8 [iv, vi]).
- The dominant Centre-Western imagination of an idealized individualist Self and a demonized collectivist Other is so powerful and normalized that it is difficult to see emergent Periphery cultural realities (Figure 8 [vi]).

There are a number of realities implicit in this list. The first five points are the basics of how culture operates, some of which is particular and some of which is universal; but there are also elements of resistance in the second point which relate to emergent non-Western cultural realities. The sixth point concerns the products of cultural illusions that nevertheless inhabit elements of certainty within Centre-Western discourses of culture. In the third point are the basic elements of culture formation; but in effect this also involves all the others, because this basic culture formation generates all the ideologies and discourses in the other areas. An implication here is that the competing worlds of Figure 12 are interrelated within the broader scope of the underlying universal processes of culture formation indicated in Figure 8. This fact was the starting point in the discussion of methodology in Chapter 2, where it is the underlying universal cultural processes within the established world of the Centre that need to be marshalled to see through the illusion and understand the underlying universal cultural processes of the Periphery in the emergent cultural world.

Cultural Realism

As argued throughout, it is not national culture *per se* that is a problem – simply the way in which it is characterized in the established Centre-Western world. I have cited Kumaravadivelu's important text on culture and language education a number of times throughout. One of his major themes is acknowledging the fact of nation in his rendering of 'cultural realism' (2007a: 143). There is a danger of relativism here, as it may well be argued that all the worlds in Figure 12 are equally real. It is therefore necessary to insert value into the equation, so that it is possible to say that there *is* a reality out there which is tru*er* and more honourable. When talking about culture it is difficult to see what this might be because culture by its nature is always going to be socially constructed, and, as argued above, is every-where. I therefore wish to come out and assert that the realities of the emergent, the margins, the Periphery have more value than the falsely conscious imaginations of the Centre. This is not due to a patronizing liberationism, but, in the words of Berger and Luckmann (1979: 18) above, to recover 'the real social being of the [Centre-Western] thinker'.

Kumaravadivelu (2007a: 143) claims social constructivism in his cultural realism, which it is important to contrast with the more extreme constructionist analysis of society in which everything is constructed and no reality is left. Fairclough (2006: 18) underlines this distinction and also maintains the constructivist position in his engagement with the realism of actual social structures and their fine balance with social agency:

> Human beings engage in social activity in a preconstructed social world which is largely beyond their control. They have to come to terms with it, accept that they can only act within certain parameters and constraints. Yet human beings are agentive, strategic and reflective beings, and the preconstructed social world is a socially, humanly, constructed world, the outcome of past and continuing human agency, strategy and reflexivity. Wherever people engage in social activity, they reflexively produce representations of it and of their own place within it; these representations may (given certain social conditions) be consolidated and stabilized in diverse shared discourses, and they may include imaginaries for possible alternative forms of social activity, and may (always subject to particular social con-ditions) come to be parts of strategies for social change. (ibid.: 163)

The role of discourses in constructing or reifying 'imaginaries' has been dealt with in detail in Chapter 7.

What needs to be defined

One of the impacts of the reassessment of what is considered real is a shifting of attention from trying to define too closely the precise nature of a *particular* culture to describing the more *universal* roles of discourse and ideology in culture formation and the structure of cultural chauvinism. Perhaps one of the problems we have had with the notion of culture in academic and professional discourses is that the technicalization of these discourses has demanded too much definition of particular cultures. This issue became apparent to me during the following incident:

> At the end of a conference presentation, a Chinese research student asked my advice about her research findings. Although she was trying to avoid stereotypes, when she interviewed some Chinese students about their English language learning styles much of what they described did indeed have 'Chinese characteristics'. My response to her was that although the characteristics may certainly conform to her expectations of a Chinese cultural context, this did not mean that they were not also common to other cultural contexts. I put it to her that she was trying to over-categorize what the students said. She then asked me what my definition of culture was. I said that I didn't think that I had to define culture before I could talk about it. I felt she was also trying to over-define what it was to be Chinese. When I asked her if she would always refer to herself as Chinese, she said she would not, and that in fact she sometimes preferred to refer to herself as French. I had to admit that this surprised me because I had fallen into the trap of thinking she was simply Chinese because she looked Chinese, missing the point that she could be French Chinese. This unexpected statement didn't help me to define her more precisely, but instead educated me in how complex she was.

At several points throughout I have drawn attention to the individual nature of the events and people I have referred to – not wishing to 'make too much' of their particular nationalities or social groups. It has been important to focus on people as people. John and Kayvan, Caroline, Ming and Wang, Qing, each of my informants, the women outside the Museum Director's office, the MA group, are all just people who find themselves in certain sets of circumstances.

In my opinion the critical cosmopolitan image of culture does not suggest separate cultures that interact or can be easily recognized and located. If it is to be said that a person has a culture, it is not something to belong to, to pass in or out of, to choose or deny, to make decisions about, or really to describe. While it will be characterized differently according to national and personal trajectories, instead it is something that is always there as a permanent though changing complex of realities experienced through influences and references, and practised in everyday social action. This does not mean that it is not in reality *imagined* to be quantifiable, as in statements and discourses about culture.

Summary

- There are multiple cultural realities across which ideology is a ubiquitous entity and within which imaginations about the nature of culture are a major feature.
- There are four competing or interacting cultural worlds connected with the individual's universal process of orienting Self and Other: (1) an established world of Centre discourses of culture, supported by (2) an imagined world of chauvinistic ideologies; and (3) a partially hidden marginal world of counter-Periphery discourses which generates (4) an emergent world of the unexpected cultural realities of the Other. The particular issues of this book are where these relationships are framed within the unequal politics of Western domination.
- A constructivist approach acknowledges the ideological nature of perceptions of culture and favours the emergent realities of the Periphery because these can help undo the false consciousness inherent in Centre-Western discourses.
- Cultural realism acknowledges the influence of nation, but as a backdrop rather than a confining all-defining essentialist entity.
- By learning from the counter-discourses from the Periphery, the Centre can understand the inaccuracies of the way it describes the foreign Other and the cultural possibilities of the Periphery.

Conclusion

The final investigatory task at the end of each chapter invites the design of an intercultural orientation session which relates in some way to the content of the chapter. Each one is directed at reforming a Centre-Western attitude towards a cultural Other by means of an increased understanding and, in several cases, a withdrawal. These two elements run throughout the book. Increased understanding may not seem problematic at all for a Western civilization that makes understanding its bread and butter; but the understanding that is needed is of complexities which are not part of its normal image of the world. All sorts of Eastern philosopies speak of the need to begin with unlearning. What has to be unlearnt in this case is the many centuries of understanding based on ideologies of world aggression, colonization and 'improvement'. This is a difficult matter because, as I hope this book has reminded us, these ideologies are so far-reaching and deeply rooted as to be invisible to their authors – a surprising thing considering how well known they are to everyone else. Hence the need for withdrawal. The disciplines associated with a critical interpretivism which runs through the investigatory tasks are all to do with this – with stepping back to see what might just be already going on without some sort of imagined moral intervention. The Periphery would then no longer be the Periphery, nor the Centre the Centre.

There is a need to be positive about all of this. On the last afternoon of writing this book I watched a documentary about Derrida near the end of his life (Dick and Kofman, 2002). He said something I really do disagree with, and also something which seems to be the key. It really is not the case that we are all bound by our histories and the narratives we have grown up with. The cataloguing of this sort of thing in Chapter 4 is not there to frighten us so that we all give up and go home. It is referred to as an 'indelible' politics because it cannot be undone. The histories and narratives cannot be undone because they are already there. We are all sexists and racists in our histories and narratives. But making a great struggle to see through them is the work of civilization. The key is that the elements of deconstruction are already there in the corners which make the concentration of the system solid; they are not something to be applied after the event. Human intelligence and autonomy are already there in absolutely everyone and always have been.

Notes

1   See Pennycook's (2000: 14) critique of easy dichotomies of the West and the non-West, especially with reference to my own work (Holliday, 1994).

2   These social acts are adapted from an earlier discussion of cultural chauvinism in English language education (Holliday, 2007c: 364).

Glossary

Bracketing
Putting aside the common prejudices which influence the way researchers look at social phenomena.

Centre
A location or state of economic and political power which defines and imposes meaning on the rest of the world.

Collectivism
A cultural label which implies lack of self-determination, group loyalty, deference to authority, lack of autonomy, inability in planning and organizing, and so on.

Commodification
Treating something as though it has a commercial value and can be bought and sold.

Construction
Presenting something in such a manner that it influences how other people think about it.

Critical cosmopolitanism
A sociological paradigm in which culture has blurred boundaries and is politically constructed, and in which the cultural realities of the Periphery struggle for recognition against the imposed definitions of the Centre.

Critical interpretivism
In social research, an approach which bases evidence on non-aligned observation and allows realities to emerge.

Critical reading
Looking for the hidden ideology in texts.

Cultural chauvinism or culturism
Depicting people as inferior or superior because of imagined cultural traits – parallel to racism and sexism.

Essentialist
Presenting people's individual behaviour as entirely defined and constrained by the cultures in which they live so that the stereotype becomes the essence of who they are

Heuristic
Temporarily imagining something to be of a certain nature for the purpose of investigation.

Ideology
A system of ideas which promote the interests of a particular group of people.

Individualism
A cultural label which implies self-determination, personal responsibility, independence from authority, autonomy, critical thinking, ability to plan and organize, and so on.

Liberal–essentialist duality
A mismatch between Western society's genuine (liberal) desire to oppose cultural chauvinism and its inability to recognize cultural chauvinism within its own structure due to an inherent lack of criticality.

Making the familiar strange
Applying research strategies which enable fresh, non-aligned perception of social phenomena.

Methodological nationalism
Employing the idea of one nation state which coincides with one language and one culture as a basis for social science.

Modernism
In social science, a perception of social reality which can be explained in neutral rational terms.

Neo-essentialism
The dominant approach within the sub-discipline of intercultural communication studies which follows the essentialist and highly influential work of theorists such as Hofstede while claiming a more liberal, non-essentialist vision.

Orientalism
Constructing the non-West as culturally deficient.

Other
A construction of what is different from the Self.

Othering
Applying cultural or another sort of chauvinism to a particular group of people, or to a person as though they are essentially defined by the imagined negative characteristics of that group.

Periphery
A location or state which lacks economic and political power in such a way that it is defined and given meaning by the Centre.

Positivism
In social research, an approach which sees evidence as structured by *a priori* theory.

Postmodernism
In social science, believing that both the subject and the methodology of investigation are ideologically constructed.

Racializing
Treating people as though their defining characteristics are racial.

Reification
Treating something as though it is real to the extent that it becomes believed to be real.

Self
A construction of what is different from the Other.

Self-marginalization, or self-Othering
Accepting the negative characteristics imposed by the Centre.

Social action theory
A social theory which perceives individual action to be in dialogue with social structure.

Social construction of reality
A social presentation of something in such a manner that it influences how other people think about it.

Structural-functionalism
A social theory which perceives social structure to be the major force in defining individual action and which therefore explains social action in terms of how it functions within the whole social structure.

Thick description
A broad interconnection of phenomena with which to underpin understanding and meaning in social research.

References

Afshar, H. (2007) Muslim women and feminisms: illustrations from the Iranian experience. *Social Compass*, 54 (3): 419–34.

Agar, M. (2007) Culture blends. In L. Monaghan and J. E. Goodman (eds), *A Cultural Approach to Interpersonal Communication: Essential Readings*. Oxford: Blackwell, pp. 13–24. (Originally published 1994, *Language Shock: Understanding the Culture of Conversations*, New York: William Morrow, pp. 13–30.)

Ahmed, A. S. and Donnan, H. (1994) Islam in the age of postmodernity. In A. S. Ahmed and H. Donnan (eds), *Islam, Globalization and Postmodernity*. London: Routledge, pp. 1–20.

Al Aswany, A. (2007) *The Yacoubian Building*. London: Harper Perennial.

Al-Sheykh, H. (1998) *I Sweep the Sun off the Rooftops*. London: Bloomsbury.

Al-Sheykh, H. (2002) *Only in London*. London: Bloomsbury.

Alavi, N. (2005) *We are Iran*. London: Portobello Books.

Alibhai-Brown, Y. (2000) *Who Do We Think We Are: Imagining the New Britain*. London: Penguin.

Alsanea, R. (2008) *Girls of Ryadh*. London: Penguin.

Andrić, I. (1995) *Bridge over the Drina* (transl. L. F. Edwards). London: Harvill Press.

Angouri, J. and Harwood, N. (2008) This is too formal for us…: a case study of variation in the written products of a multinational consortium. *Journal of Business and Technical Communication*, 22 (1): 38–64.

Antal, A. B. and Friedman, V. J. (2008) Learning to negotiate reality: a strategy for teaching intercultural competencies. *Journal of Management Education*, 32 (3): 363–86.

Anyon, J. (1980) Social class and the hidden curriculum of work. *Journal of Education*, 162 (1): 67–92.

Anyon, J. (1983) Intersections of gender and class: accommodation and resistance by working-class and affluent females to contradictory sex-role ideologies. In S. Walker and L. Barton (eds), *Gender, Class and Education*. London: Falmer Press, pp. 19–38.

Asad, T. (1973) Introduction. In T. Asad (ed.), *Anthropology and the Colonial Encounter*. London: Ithaca Press.

Asante, M. K. (2008) The ideological significance of Afrocentricity in intercultural communication. In M. K. Asante, Y. Miike and J. Yin (eds), *The Global Intercultural Communication Reader*. New York: Routledge, pp. 47–55.

Asante, M. K., Miike, Y. and Yin, J. (2008) Issues and challenges in intercultural communication scholarship. In M. K. Asante, Y. Miike and J. Yin (eds), *The Global Intercultural Communication Reader*. New York: Routledge, pp. 1–8.

Atkinson, D. (1999) A critical approach to critical thinking. *TESOL Quarterly*, 33 (4): 625–53.

Atkinson, P. and Coffey, A. (1995) Realism and its discontents: on the crisis of cultural representation in ethnographic texts. In B. Adam and S. Allan (eds), *Theorizing Culture: An Interdisciplinary Critique after Postmodernism*. London: UCL Press, pp. 41–57.

Baumann, G. (1996) *Contesting Culture*. Cambridge: Cambridge University Press.

BBC (2007) Racism row housemate apologises. Retrieved from http://news.bbc.co.uk/go/pr/fr/-/1/hi/entertainment/6732873.stm, 21 December 2009.

Beales, A. R., Spindler, G. and Spindler, L. (1967) *Culture in Process*. New York: Holt, Rinehart.

Beaton, S., Dhadda, K., Good, J., Harvey, S. and Taylor, J. (2005) *Soldier, Husband, Daughter, Dad* [documentary]. BBC 1.

Beck, U. and Sznaider, N. (2006) Unpacking cosmopolitanism for the social sciences: a research agenda. *British Journal of Sociology*, 57 (1): 1–23.

Bendix, R. (1966) *Max Weber: An Intellectual Portrait*. London: Methuen.

Benjamin, L. and Walters, S. (1994) Power and Resistance in Gender Training. *Agenda*, 22: 86–91.

Berger, P. and Luckmann, T. (1979) *The Social Construction of Reality*. Harmondsworth: Penguin.

Betsall, A. (1979) Rupert and the ice skates. In *Rupert: The Daily Express Annual*. Express Newspapers, pp. 58–87.

Bhabha, H. (1994) *The Location of Culture*. London: Routledge.

Bond, M. H., Žegarac, V. and Spencer-Oatey, H. (2000) Culture as an explanatory variable: problems and possibilities. In H. Spencer-Oatey (ed.), *Culturally Speaking: Managing Rapport through Talk across Culture*. London: Continuum, pp. 47–69.

Bradford, A. S. (1994) The duplicitous Spartan. In A. Powell and S. Hodkinson (eds), *The Shadow of Sparta*. London: Routledge, pp. 59–86.

Brook, S. (2007) Are the Celeb Big Brother housemates racist? *Guardian Unlimited*. Retrieved from http://www.guardian.co.uk/media/organgrinder/2007/jan/16/arethecbbhousematesbeingr, 21 December 2009.

Burr, V. (1995) *An Introduction to Social Constructionism*. London: Routledge.

Burroughs, E. R. (2007) *A Princess of Mars*. New York: Penguin. (Originally published 1912.)

Byram, M. (2008) *From Foreign Language Education to Education for Intercultural Citizenship: Essays and Reflections*. Clevedon: Multilingual Matters.

Canagarajah, A. S. (1999) On EFL teachers, awareness and agency. *ELT Journal*, 53 (3): 207–14.

Chatziefstathiou, D. and Henry, I. (2007) Hellenism and Olympism: Pierre de Coubertin and the Greek challenge to the early Olympic movement. *Sport in History*, 27 (1): 24–43.

Checkland, P. and Scholes, J. (1990) *Soft Systems Methodology in Action*. Chichester: Wiley.

Cheng, X. (2000) Asian students' reticence revisited. *System*, 28 (3): 435–46.

Clark, R. and Gieve, S. N. (2006) On the discursive construction of 'the Chinese Learner'. *Language, Culture & Curriculum*, 19 (1): 54–73.

Clark, R. and Ivanič, R. (1997) *The Politics of Writing*. London: Routledge.

Clifford, J. (1986a) Introduction: partial truths. In J. Clifford and G. E. Marcus (eds), *Writing Culture: The Poetica of Politics of Ethnography*. Berkeley: University of California Press, pp. 1–26.

Clifford, J. and Marcus, G. E. (eds) (1986b) *Writing Culture: The Poetica of Politics of Ethnography*. Berkeley: University of California Press.

Collier, M. J. (2005) Theorizing cultural identifications: critical updates and continuing evolution. In W. B. Gudykunst (ed.), *Theorizing about Intercultural Communication*. Thousand Oaks, CA: Sage, pp. 235–56.

Comaroff, J. and Comaroff, J. (1992) *Ethnography and the Historical Imagination*. Boulder, CO: Westview Press.

Crane, D. (1994) Introduction: The challenge of the sociology of culture to sociology as discipline. In D. Crane (ed.), *The Sociology of Culture*. Oxford: Blackwell, pp. 1–19.

Delanty, G. (2006) The cosmopolitan imagination: critical cosmopolitanism and social theory. *British Journal of Sociology*, 57 (1): 25–47.

Delanty, G. (2008) Dilemmas of secularism: Europe, religion and the problem of pluralism. In G. Delanty, R. Wodak and P. Jones (eds), *Identity, Belonging and Migration*. Liverpool: Liverpool University Press, pp. 78–97.

Delanty, G., Wodak, R. and Jones, P. (2008a) Introduction: migration, discrimination and belonging in Europe. In G. Delanty, R. Wodak and P. Jones (eds), *Identity, Belonging and Migration*. Liverpool: Liverpool University Press, pp. 1–20.

Delanty, G., Wodak, R. and Jones, P. (eds) (2008b) *Identity, Belonging and Migration*. Liverpool: Liverpool University Press.

Denzin, N. K. (1994) The art and politics of interpretation. In N. K. Denzin, and Y. S. Lincoln (eds), *A Handbook of Qualitative Research*. Thousand Oaks, CA: Sage, pp. 500–15.

Desai, K. (2007) *The Inheritance of Loss*. London: Penguin.

Dick, K. and Kofman, A. Z. (2002) *Derrida* [film]. Los Angeles: Jane Doe Films.

Dobbin, F. R. (1994) Cultural models of organization: the social construction of rational organizing principles. In D. Crane (ed.), *The Sociology of Culture*. Oxford: Blackwell, pp. 117–41.

Durkheim, E. (1964) *The Division of Labour in Society* (transl. G. Simpson). New York: Free Press. (Originally published in 1933.)

Durkheim, E. (1982) *The Rules of Sociological Method* (transl. W. D. Halls). New York: Free Press.

Ellis, D. G. and Moaz, I. (2006) Dialogue and cultural communication codes between Israeli Jews and Palestinians. In L. A. Samovar and R. E. Porter (eds), *Intercultural Communication: A Reader*. Belmont, CA: Wadsworth, pp. 231–7.

Engels, F. (1934) Engels to Franz Mehring. Marx–Engels correspondence, London, 14 July 1893. *New International*, 3: 81–5.

Fairclough, N. (1989) *Language and Power*. London: Addison Wesley Longman.

Fairclough, N. (1995) *Critical Discourse Analysis: The Critical Study of Language*. London: Addison Wesley Longman.

Fairclough, N. (2000) *New Labour, New Language?* London: Routledge.

Fairclough, N. (2006) *Language and Globalization*. London: Routledge.

Faubion, J. D. (2001) Currents of cultural fieldwork. In P. Atkinson, A. Coffey, S. Delamont, J. Lofland and L. Lofland (eds), *Handbook of Ethnography*. London: Sage, pp. 39–59.

Fay, B. (1996) *Contemporary Philosophy of Social Science: A Multicultural Approach*. Oxford: Blackwell.

Flam, H. and Bauzamy, B. (2008) Symbolic violence. In G. Delanty, R. Wodak and P. Jones (eds), *Identity, Belonging and Migration*. Liverpool: Liverpool University Press, pp. 221–40.

Fleming, D. and Søborg, H. (2004) Human resource strategies as a technology of governance in Danish subsidiaries in Southeast Asia. Retrieved from http://geert-hofstede.international-business-center. com/geert_hofstede_contrarian_position.shtml, 21 December 2009.

Florean, D. (2007) East meets West: cultural confrontation and exchange after the First Crusade. *Language & Intercultural Communication*, 7 (2): 144–8.

Flowerdew, J., Miller, L. and Li, D. C. S. (2000) Chinese lecturers' perceptions, problems and strategies in lecturing in English to Chinese-speaking students. *RELC Journal*, 31 (1): 116–38.

Gee, J. P. (1997) A discourse approach to language and literacy. In C. Lankshear, J. P. Gee, M. Knobel and C. Searle, *Changing Literacies*. Buckingham: Open University Press.

Geertz, C. (1993) *The Interpretation of Cultures*. London: Fontana.

Gellner, E. (1994) Foreword. In A. S. Ahmed and H. Donnan (eds), *Islam, Globalization and Postmodernity*. London: Routledge, pp. xi–xiv.

Gellner, E. (2005) *Words and Things*. Oxford: Routledge.

Geoffroy, C. (2007) 'Mobile' contexts/'immobile' cultures. *Language & Intercultural Communication*, 7 (4): 279–90.

Gergen, K. J. (2001) *Social Construction in Context*. London: Sage.

Gérôme, J.-L. (1857). Le Marché d'Esclaves [painting]. Williamstown Massachusetts: Sterling and Francine Clarke Institute. Retrieved from http://commons.wikimedia.org/wiki/File:G%C3%A9r%C3%B4me_Jean-L%C3%A9on_The_Slave_Market.jpg, 22 December 2009.

Giddens, A. (1991) *Modernity and Self-Identity: Self and Society in the Late Modern Age*. Cambridge: Polity.

Goffman, E. (1972) *Relations in Public*. Harmondsworth: Penguin.

Goodenough, W. H. (1994) Toward a working theory of culture. In R. Borofsky (ed.), *Assessing Cultural Anthropology*. New York: McGraw-Hill, pp. 262–75.

Gooderham, P. and Nordhaug, O. (2004) Are cultural differences in Europe on the decline? Retrieved from http://geert-hofstede.international-business-center.com/gooderham.shtml, 21 December 2009.

Goodman, J. E. (2007) 'An association for the 21st century': Performance and social change among Berbers in Paris. In L. Monaghan and J. E. Goodman (eds), *A Cultural Approach to Interpersonal Communication: Essential Readings*. Oxford: Blackwell: pp. 400–12. (Originally published 2005, *Berber Culture on the World Stage*, Bloominghton: Indiana University Press.)

Grande, E. (2006) Cosmopolitan political science. *British Journal of Sociology*, 57 (1): 87–111.

Griffiths, V. (1995) *Adolescent Girls and Their Friends: A Feminist Ethnography*. Aldershot: Avebury.

Grimshaw, T. (2007) Problematizing the construct of 'the Chinese learner': insights from ethnographic research. *Educational Studies*, 33: 299–311.

Guba, E. G. and Lincoln, Y. S. (2005) Paradigmatic controversies, contradictions, and emerging confluences. In N. K. Denzin and Y. S. Lincoln (eds), *Handbook of Qualitative Research*, 3rd edition. Thousand Oaks, CA: Sage, pp. 191–215.

Gubrium, J. F. and Holstein, J. A. (1997) *The New Language of Qualitative Research*. New York: Oxford University Press.

Gudykunst, W. B., Lee, C. M., Nishida, T. and Ogawa, N. (2005) An introduction. In W. B. Gudykunst (ed.), *Theorizing about Intercultural Communication* Thousand Oaks, CA: Sage, pp. 3–32.

Guilherme, M. (2002) *Critical Citizens for an Intercultural World: Foreign Language Education as Cultural Politics*. Clevedon: Multilingual Matters.

Guilherme, M. (2007) English as a global language and education for cosmopolitan citizenship. *Language & Intercultural Communication*, 7 (1): 72–90.

Haggard, H. R. (1985) *King Solomon's Mines*. London: Macmillan. (Originally published 1892.)

Haggard, H. R. (2001) *Nada the Lily*. Holicong, PA: Wildside Press. (Originally published 1892.)

Hall, E. T. (1976) *Beyond Culture*. New York: Doubleday.

Hall, S. (1991a) The local and the global: globalization and ethnicity. In A. D. King (ed.), *Culture, Globalization and the World-System*. New York: Palgrave, pp. 19–39.

Hall, S. (1991b) Old and new identities, old and new ethnicities. In A. D. King (ed.), *Culture, Globalization and the World-System*. New York: Palgrave, pp. 40–68.

Hammersley, M. and Atkinson, P. (1995) *Ethnography, Principles and Practice*, 2nd edition. London: Routledge.

Hannerz, U. (1991) Scenarios of peripheral cultures. In A. D. King (ed.), *Culture, Globalization and the World-System*. New York: Palgrave, pp. 107–28.

Hannerz, U. (1999) Reflections on varieties of culturespeak. *European Journal of Cultural Studies*, 2 (3): 393–407.

Herodotus (1972) *The Histories* (transl. A. de Sélincourt), new edition. Harmondsworth: Penguin.

Hoffman, E. (1998) *Lost in Translation*. London: Vintage.

Hofstede, G. (2001) *Culture's Consequences: Comparing Values, Behaviours, Institutions and Organizations across Cultures*. London: Sage.

Hofstede, G. (2003) *Culture's Consequences: Comparing Values, Behaviours, Institutions and Organizations across Cultures*. 2nd edition. London: Sage.

Holliday, A. R. (1990) A role for soft systems methodology in ELT projects. *System*, 18 (1): 77–84.

Holliday, A. R. (1994) *Appropriate Methodology and Social Context*. Cambridge: Cambridge University Press.

Holliday, A. R. (1999) Small cultures. *Applied Linguistics*, 20 (2): 237–64.

Holliday, A. R. (2000) Exploring other worlds: escaping linguistic parochialism. In J. Davison and J. Moss (eds), *Issues in English Teaching*. London: Routledge, pp. 141–7.

Holliday, A. R. (2002) Japanese fragments: an exploration in cultural perception and duality. *Asia Pacific Journal of Language in Education*, 5 (1): 1–28.

Holliday, A. R. (2004a) Social autonomy: addressing the dangers of culturism in TESOL. In D. Palfreyman and R. Smith (eds), *Autonomy across Cultures*. London: Palgrave, pp. 110–26.

Holliday, A. R. (2004b) The value of reconstruction in revealing hidden or counter cultures. *Journal of Applied Linguistics*, 1 (3): 275–94.

Holliday, A. R. (2005) *The Struggle to Teach English as an International Language*. Oxford: Oxford University Press.

Holliday, A. R. (2007a) Autonomy and cultural chauvinism. *Independence*, 42: 20–2.

Holliday, A. R. (2007b) *Doing and Writing Qualitative Research*, 2nd edition. London: Sage.

Holliday, A. R. (2007c) Response to 'ELT and "the spirit of the times"'. *ELT Journal*, 61 (4): 360–6.

Holliday, A. R. (2008) Standards of English and politics of inclusion. *Language Teaching*, 41 (1): 115–26.

Holliday, A. R. (2009) Interrogating the concept of stereotypes in intercultural communication. In S. Hunston and D. Oakley (eds), *Introducing Applied Linguistics: Concepts and Skills*. London: Routledge, pp. 134–41.

Holliday, A. R. (2010a) Analysing qualitative data. In A. Phakiti and B. Paltridge (eds), *Continuum Companion to Research Methods in Applied Linguistics*. London: Continuum, pp. 98–110.

Holliday, A. R. (2010b) Complexity in cultural identity. *Language & Intercultural Communication*, 10 (2): 1–13.

Holliday, A. R. (2010c) Cultural descriptions as political cultural acts: an exploration. *Language & Intercultural Communication* 10 (3): 259–72.

Holliday, A. R. and Aboshiha, P. A. (2009) The denial of ideology in perceptions of 'nonnative speaker' teachers. *TESOL Quarterly*, 43 (4): 669–89.

Holliday, A. R., Hyde, M. and Kullman, J. (2004) *Intercultural Communication*. London: Routledge.

Holliday, A. R., Hyde, M. and Kullman, J. (2010) *Intercultural Communication: An Advanced Resource Book for Students*, 2nd edition. London: Routledge.

Holmwood, L. and Brook, S. (2007) Big Brother racism complaints soar. *Media Guardian*. Retrieved from http://media.guardian.co.uk/site/story/0,,1991561,00.html, 18 January 2007.

Honarbin-Holliday, M. (2005) Art education, identity and gender at Tehran and al Zahra Universities. Unpublished PhD thesis, Art and Design, Canterbury Christ Church University, Canterbury.

Honarbin-Holliday, M. (2009) *Becoming Visible in Iran: Women in Contemporary Iranian Society*. London: I. B. Tauris.

Hosseini, K. (2007) *A Thousand Splendid Suns*. London: Bloomsbury.

Jack, G. (2009) A critical perspective on teaching intercultural competence in a management department. In A. Feng, M. Byram and M. Fleming (eds), *Education and Training: Becoming Interculturally Competent*. Clevedon: Multilingual Matters, pp. 93–114.

Jacob, P. G. (1996) Coming to terms with imperialism: safeguarding local knowledge and experience in ELT curriculum development. Unpublished paper, Department of English, University of Pune.

Jandt, F. E. (2001) *Intercultural Communication: An Introduction*. Thousand Oaks, CA: Sage.

Jensen, I. (2006) The practice of intercultural communication: reflections for professionals in cultural meetings. In L. A. Samovar and R. E. Porter (eds), *Intercultural Communication: A Reader*. Belmont, CA: Wadsworth, pp. 39–48.

Jordan, G. and Weedon, C. (1995) The celebration of difference and the cultural politics of racism. In B. Adam, and S. Allan (eds), *Theorizing Culture: An Interdisciplinary Critique after Postmodernism*. London: UCL Press, pp. 149–64.

Kabbani, R. (1986) *Europe's Myth of Orient: Devise and Rule*. Basingstoke: Macmillan.

Kamal, A. (2003) Western culture's effects on Gulf students. Paper presented at the 37th Annual TESOL Convention.

Kamali, M. (2007) Multiple modernities and Islamism in Iran. *Social Compass*, 54 (3): 373–87.

Keesing, R. M. (1994) Theories of culture revisited. In R. Borofsky (ed.), *Assessing Cultural Anthropology*. New York: McGraw-Hill, pp. 301–12.

Khorsandi, S. (2009) *A Beginner's Guide to Acting English*. London: Ebury Press.

Khosrowjah, H. (2008) Carried by the wind: Iranian exilic biographical novels. Unpublished Paper, Department of English, Strate University of New York, Brockport.

Kim, M.-S. (2005) Culture-based conversational constraints theory. In W. B. Gudykunst (ed.), *Theorizing about Intercultural Communication*. Thousand Oaks, CA: Sage, pp. 93–117.

Kim, Y. Y. (2005) Association and dissociation: a contextual theory of interethnic communication. In W. B. Gudykunst (ed.), *Theorizing about Intercultural Communication*. Thousand Oaks, CA: Sage, pp. 323–49.

Kim, Y. Y. (2006) Intercultural personhood: an integration of Eastern and Western perspectives. In L. A. Samovar and R. E. Porter (eds), *Intercultural Communication: A Reader*. Belmont, CA: Wadsworth, pp. 408–39.

King, A. D. (1991a) Introduction: Spaces of culture, spaces of knowledge. In A. D. King (ed.), *Culture, Globalization and the World-System*. New York: Palgrave.

King, A. D. (ed.) (1991b) *Culture, Globalization and the World-System*. New York: Palgrave.

Kossaibati, J. (2009) It's a wrap. *The Guardian*. Retrieved from http://www.guardian.co.uk/lifeandstyle/2009/mar/30/fashion-hijab-muslim-women, 21 December 2009.

Kramsch, C. (1993) *Context and Culture in Language Teaching*. Oxford: Oxford University Press.

Kramsch, C. (2005) Post 9/11: foreign languages between knowledge and power. *Applied Linguistics*, 26 (4): 545–67.

Kubota, R. (1999) Japanese culture constructed by discourses: implications for applied linguistics research and ELT. *TESOL Quarterly*, 33 (1): 9–35.

Kubota, R. (2001) Discursive construction of the images of US classrooms. *TESOL Quarterly*, 35 (1): 9–37.

Kubota, R. (2003) Unfinished knowledge: the story of Barbara. *College ESL*, 10 (1–2): 84–92.

Kubota, R. (2004) Critical multiculturalism and second language education. In B. Norton and K. Toohey (eds), *Critical Pedagogies and Language Learning*. Cambridge: Cambridge University Press, pp. 30–52.

Kubota, R. and Lin, A. M. Y. (2006) Race and TESOL: introduction to concepts and theories. *TESOL Quarterly*, 40 (3): 471–93.

Kubota, R. and Lin, A. M. Y. (2009) Race, culture, and identities in second language education: introduction to research and practice. In R. Kubota and A. M. Y. Lin (eds), *Race, Culture, and Identities in Second Language Education: Exploring Critically Engaged Practice*. New York: Routledge, pp. 1–23.

Kuhn, T. (1970) *The Structure of Scientific Revolutions*. Chicago: University of Chicago Press.

Kumaravadivelu, B. (2003) Problematizing cultural stereotypes in TESOL. *TESOL Quarterly*, 37: 709–19.

Kumaravadivelu, B. (2006) Dangerous liaison: globalization, empire and TESOL. In J. Edge (ed.), *(Re)locating TESOL in an Age of Empire: Language and Globalization*. London: Palgrave, pp. 1–26.

Kumaravadivelu, B. (2007a) *Cultural Globalization and Language Education*. New Haven, CT: Yale University Press.

Kumaravadivelu, B. (2007b) Interrogating cultural complexities in the language classroom. Paper presented at the Second International Qualitative Research Conference.

Kumaravadivelu, B. (2008) The other side of Othering. *Independence*, 43: 17–18.

Langan, S. (2004) *Mission Accomplished: Langan in Iraq* [documentary]. BBC 4.

Lankshear, C., Gee, J. P., Knobel, M. and Searle, C. (1997) *Changing Literacies*. Buckingham: Open University Press.

Lansley, C. (1994) 'Collaborative development': an alternative to phatic discourse and the art of co-operative development. *ELT Journal*, 48 (1): 50–6.

Latour, B. (2006) War of the worlds – what about peace? *Matrix, Bridge the Gap*. Retrieved from http://www.btgjapan.org/catalysts/bruno.html, 19 August 2006.

Lea, J. (2009) *Political Correctness and Higher Education: British and American Perspectives*. London: Routledge.

Lentin, A. (2008) Racism, anti-racism and the Western state. In G. Delanty, R. Wodak and P. Jones (eds), *Identity, Belonging and Migration*. Liverpool: Liverpool University Press, pp. 101–19.

Lewis, F. J. (1869). The Seraff – a doubtful coin [painting]. Birmingham: Birmingham Museum and Art Gallery. Retrieved from http://www.bmagic.org.uk/objects/1891P28/images/136155, 22/12/09.

Lincoln, Y. S. and Guba, E. G. (2000) Paradigmatic controversies, contradictions, and emerging confluences. In N. K. Denzin and Y. S. Lincoln (eds), *Handbook of Qualitative Research*, 2nd edition. Thousand Oaks, CA: Sage, pp. 163–88.

MacDonald, S. (2001) British social anthropology. In P. Atkinson, A. Coffey, S. Delamont, J. Lofland and L. Lofland (eds), *Handbook of Ethnography*. London: Sage, pp. 60–79.

Marciano, F. (1998) *Rules of the Wild*. London: Jonathan Cape.

Martindale, D. (1960) *The Nature and Types of Sociological Theory*. London: Routledge & Kegan Paul.

Mathews, G. (2000) *Global Culture/Individual Identity: Searching for Home in the Cultural Supermarket*. London: Routledge.

McCannell, D. (1992) *Empty Meeting Grounds*. London: Routledge.

McSweeny, B. (2002) Hofstede's model of national cultural differences and their consequences: a triumph of faith – a failure of analysis. *Human Relations*, 55 (1): 89–118.

Mernissi, F. (2001) *Scheherazade goes West: Different Cultures, Different Harems*. New York: Washington Square Press.

Miike, Y. (2008) Toward an alternative metatheory of human communication: an Asiatic vision. In M. K. Asante, Y. Miike, and J. Yin (eds), *The Global Intercultural Communication Reader*. New York: Routledge, pp. 57–72.

Mills, C. W. (1970) *The Sociological Imagination*. Harmondsworth: Pelican.

Mirror (2007) Top Stories: New BB race row: what was said. Retrieved from http://www.mirror.co.uk/news/top-stories/2007/06/07/new-bb-race-row-what-was-said-115875–19259968/, 21 December 2009.

Moeran, B. (1996) The Orient strikes back: advertising and imagining in Japan. *Theory, Culture and Society*, 13 (3): 77–112.

Moon, D. G. (2008) Concepts of 'culture': implications for intercultural communication research. In M. K. Asante, Y. Miike, and J. Yin (eds), *The Global Intercultural Communication Reader*. New York: Routledge, pp. 11–26.

Morawska, E. and Spohn W. (1994) 'Cultural pluralism' in historical sociology; recent theoretical directions. In D. Crane (ed.), *The Sociology of Culture*. Oxford: Blackwell, pp. 45–90.

Nafisi, A. (2004) *Reading Lolita in Tehran*. New York: Random House.

Naghibi, N. (2007) *Rethinking Global Sisterhood: Western Feminism and Iran*. Minneapolis: University of Minnesota Press.

Nayar, B. (2002) Ideological binarism in the identities of native and non-native English speakers. In A. Duszac (ed.), *Us and Others: Social Identities across Languages, Discourse and Cultures*. Amsterdam: John Benjamin, pp. 463–80.

Nzimiro, I. (1979) Anthropologists and their terminologies: a critical review. In G. Huizer and B. Mannheim (eds), *Politics of Anthropology: From Colonialism and Sexism towards a View from Below*. The Hague: Mouton, pp. 67–83.

Osanloo, A. (2009) *The Politics of Women's Rights in Iran*. Princeton, NJ: Princeton University Press.

Pamuk, O. (2004) *Snow* (transl. M. Freeley). London: Faber & Faber.

Pamuk, O. (2005) *Istanbul: Memories of a City* (transl. M. Freeley). London: Faber & Faber.

Parsons, T. (1937) *Structure of Social Action*. New York: McGraw-Hill.

Parsons, T. (1951) *The Social System*. London: Routledge & Kegan Paul.

Pearce, W. B. (2005) The coordinated management of meaning (CMM). In W. B. Gudykunst (ed.), *Theorizing about Intercultural Communication*. Thousand Oaks, CA: Sage, pp. 35–54.

Pennycook, A. (1998) *English and the Discourses of Colonialism*. London: Routledge.

Pennycook, A. (2000) Development, culture and language: ethical concerns in a postcolonial world. In *Proceedings of The 4th International Conference on Language and Development*. Retrieved from http://www.languages.ait.ac.th/hanoi_proceedings/hanoi1999.htm, 30 April 2000.

Petrić, B. (2009) 'I thought I was an Easterner; it turns out I am a Westerner!': EIL migrant teacher identities. In F. Sharifian (ed.), *English as an International Language: Perspectives and Pedagogies*. Bristol: Multilingual Matters, pp. 135–50.

Philipsen, G., Coutou, L. M. and Covarrubias, P. (2005) Speech codes theory: restatement, revisions, and responses to criticism. In W. B. Gudykunst (ed.), *Theorizing about Intercultural Communication*. Thousand Oaks, CA: Sage, pp. 55–68.

Phillipson, R. (1992) *Linguistic Imperialism*. Oxford: Oxford University Press.

Popper, K. (1966) *The Open Society and its Enemies: Volume 1, Plato*. London: Routledge & Kegan Paul. (Originally published 1945.)

Quach, L. H., Jo, J.-Y. O. and Urrieta, L. (2009) Understanding the racialized identities of Asian students in predominantly white schools. In R. Kubota and A. M. Y. Lin (eds), *Race, Culture, and Identities in Second Language Education*. New York: Routledge, pp. 118–37.

Rajagopalan, K. (1999) Of EFL teachers, conscience and cowardice. *ELT Journal*, 53 (3): 200–6.

Rampton, B. (2007) Linguistic ethnography and the study of identities. Unpublished Working Papers in Urban Language and Literacies, King's College, London University, London.

Rampton, B., Harris, R., Georgakopoulou, A., Leung, C., Small, L. and Dover, C. (2008) Urban classroom culture and interaction: end-of-project report. Unpublished Working Papers in Urban Language and Literacies, King's College, London University, London.

Rastall, P. (2006) Introduction: The Chinese learner in higher education – transition and quality issues. *Language, Culture & Curriculum*, 19 (1): 1–4.

Reid, S., Spencer-Oatey, H. and Stadler, S. (2009) The global people landscaping study: intercultural effectiveness in global education partnerships. Warwick Occasional Papers in Applied Linguistics, 1. Retrieved from http://www.globalpeople.org.uk/, http://www.warwick.ac.uk/al/ July 2009.

Rich, S. and Troudi, S. (2006) Hard times: Arab TESOL students' experiences of racialization and Othering in the United Kingdom. *TESOL Quarterly*, 40 (3): 615–27.

Rostami-Povey, E. (2007) *Afghan Women: Identity and Invasion*. London: Zed Books.

Russell, K. (1962) *Pop Goes the Easel* [film], *Monitor*: BBC 4.

Said, E. (1978) *Orientalism*. London: Routledge & Kegan Paul.

Said, E. (1993) Holding nations and traditions at bay. *The Independent*, 1 July.

Said, E. (2003) Preface to *Orientalism*. *Al-Ahram Weekly Online*. Retrieved from http://weekly.ahram.org.eg/2003/650/op11.htm, 10 January 2006.

Sakamoto, R. (1996) Japan, hybridity and the creation of colonialist discourse. *Theory, Culture and Society*, 13 (3): 113–28.

Sangari, K. (1994) Relating histories: definitions of literacy, literature, gender in early nineteenth century Calcutta and

England. In S. Joshi (ed.), *Rethinking English*. Delhi: Oxford University Press.

Sarangi, S. (1994) Intercultural or not? Beyond celebration of cultural differences in miscommunication analysis. *Pragmatics*, 4 (3): 409–27.

Sarangi, S. (1995) Culture. In J. Vershueren, J. Östman and J. Blomaert (eds), *Handbook of Pragmatics*. Amsterdam: John Benjamin, pp. 1–30.

Satrapi, M. (2003) *Persepolis*. New York: Pantheon.

Sawyer, L. and Jones, P. (2008) Voices of migrants: solidarity and resistance. In G. Delanty, R. Wodak and P. Jones (eds), *Identity, Belonging and Migration*. Liverpool: Liverpool University Press, pp. 241–60.

Schudson, M. (1994) Culture and the integration of national societies. In D. Crane (ed.), *The Sociology of Culture*. Oxford: Blackwell, pp. 21–43.

Schutz, A. (1964) *Collected Papers*, Vol. 2. The Hague: Martinus Nijhoff.

Schutz, A. (1970) *On Phenomenology and Social Relations*. Chicago: University of Chicago Press.

Scollon, R., and Scollon, W. S. (2001) *Intercultural Communication: A Discourse Approach*, 2nd edition. Oxford: Blackwell.

Shuter, R. (2008) The centrality of culture. In M. K. Asante, Y. Miike, and J. Yin (eds), *The Global Intercultural Communication Reader*. New York: Routledge, pp. 37–43.

Silberstein, S. (2004) *War of Words: Language, Politics and 9/11*, 2nd edition. New York: Routledge.

Søndergaard, M. (2004) 'In my opinion' – on 'cultural differences'. Retrieved from http://geert-hofstede.international-business-center. com/Sondergaard.shtml, 21 December 2009.

Soueif, A. (1992) *In the Eye of the Sun*. London: Bloomsbury.

Spears, A. K. (1999) Race and ideology: an introduction. In A. K. Spears (ed.), *Race and Ideology: Language, Symbolism, and Popular Culture*. Detroit: Wayne State University Press, pp. 11–58.

Spencer, J. (2001) Ethnography after postmodernism. In P. Atkinson, A. Coffey, S. Delamont, J. Lofland and L. Lofland (eds), *Handbook of Ethnography*. London: Sage, pp. 443–52.

Spencer-Oatey, H. and P. Franklin (2009) *Intercultural Interaction: A Multidisciplinary Approach to Intercultural Communication*. London: Palgrave Macmillan.

Spencer-Oatey, H. and Stadler, S. (2009) The global people competency framework: competencies for effective intercultural interaction. Warwick Occasional Papers in Applied Linguistics, 3. Retrieved from http://www.globalpeople.org.uk/, http://www. warwick.ac.uk/al/, July 2009.

Spencer-Oatey, H. and J. Xing (2000) A problematic Chinese business visit to Britain: issues of face. In H. Spencer-Oatey (ed.), *Culturally Speaking: Managing Rapport through Talk across Culture*. London: Continuum, pp. 272–88.

Spradley, J. P. (1980) *Participant Observation*. New York: Holt, Rinehart & Winston.

Stake, R. E. (2005) Qualitative case studies. In N. K. Denzin and Y. S. Lincoln (eds), *Handbook of Qualitative Research*, 3rd edition. Thousand Oaks, CA: Sage, pp. 443–66.

Stenhouse, L. (1985a) The case-study tradition and how case studies apply to practice. In J. Ruddock, and D. Hopkins (eds), *Research as a Basis for Teaching: Readings from the Work of Lawrence Stenhouse*. Oxford: Heinemann, pp. 52–5.

Stenhouse, L. (1985b) The illuminative research tradition. In J. Ruddock and D. Hopkins (eds), *Research as a Basis for Teaching: Readings from the Work of Lawrence Stenhouse*. Oxford: Heinemann, pp. 31–2.

Stevenson, N. (2003) *Cultural Citizenship: Cosmopolitan Questions*. Maidenhead: Open University Press.

Stone, O. (2004) *Alexander* [film]. (Producer M. Borman). Warner Brothers Pictures.

Stråth, B. (2008) Belonging and European identity. In G. Delanty, R. Wodak and P. Jones (eds), *Identity, Belonging and Migration*. Liverpool: Liverpool University Press, pp. 21–37.

Street, B. V. (1984) *Literacy in Theory and Practice*. Cambridge: Cambridge University Press.

Tan, A. (1989) *The Joy Luck Club*. New York: Putnam's.

Tomlinson, J. (1991) *Cultural Imperialism*. London: Pinter Publications.

Tong, W. M. (2002) 'Filial piety': a barrier or a resource? A qualitative case study of English classroom culture in Hong Kong secondary schools. Unpublished PhD thesis, Department of English and Language Studies, Canterbury Christ Church University, Canterbury.

Triandis, H. C. (1995) *Individualism and Collectivism*. Boulder, CO: Westview Press.

Triandis, H. C. (2004) Foreword. In D. Landis, J. M. Bennett and M. J. Bennett (eds), *Handbook of Intercultural Training*, 3rd edition. Thousand Oaks, CA: Sage, pp. ix–xii.

Triandis, H. C. (2006) Culture and conflict. In L. A. Samovar and R. E. Porter (eds), *Intercultural Communication: A Reader*. Belmont, CA: Wadsworth, pp. 22–31.

Tromans, T. (2008) Genre and gender in Cairo and Constantinople. In Tromans (ed.) *The Lure of the East: British Orientalist Painting*. London: Tate Publishing, pp. 76–101.

Trompenaars, F. (2007) *Riding the Whirlwind: Connecting People and Organisations in a Culture of Innovation.* Oxford: Infinite Ideas.

Urry, J. (2002) *The Tourist Gaze*, 2nd edition. London: Sage.

Usher, R. and Edwards, R. (1994) *Postmodernism and Education: Different Voices, Different Worlds.* London: Routledge.

Wallace, C. (1992) Critical literacy awareness in the EFL classroom. In N. Fairclough (ed.), *Critical Language Awareness.* London: Addison Wesley Longman, pp. 59–81.

Wallace, C. (2003) *Critical Reading in Language Education.* Basingstoke: Palgrave Macmillan.

Wang, W. (1994) *The Joy Luck Club* [film] (Producer, O. Stone). Hollywood Pictures.

Waters, A. (2007a) 'ELT and "the spirit of the times"'. *ELT Journal,* 61 (4): 353–9.

Waters, A. (2007b) Ideology, reality, and false consciousness in ELT. *ELT Journal,* 61(4): 367–8.

Waters, A. (2007c) Native-speakerism in ELT: Plus ça change ...? *System,* 35: 281–92.

Weber, M. (1968a) Ideal types and theory construction. In M. Brodbeck (ed.), *Readings in the Philosophy of the Social Sciences.* London: Macmillan, pp. 496–507. (Originally published 1949, *The Methodology of the Social Sciences,* Glencoe, IL: Free Press.)

Weber, M. (1968b) The interpretive understanding of social action. In M. Brodbeck (ed.), *Readings in the Philosophy of the Social Sciences.* London: Macmillan, pp. 19–33. (Originally published 1947, *The Theory of Social and Economic Organizations,* New York: Oxford University Press.)

Wenger, E. (2000) Communities of practice and social learning systems. *Organization,* 7 (2): 225–46.

Wodak, R. (2008) 'Us and them': inclusion and exclusion. In G. Delanty, R. Wodak and P. Jones (eds), *Identity, Belonging and Migration.* Liverpool: Liverpool University Press, pp. 54–77.

Yeğenoğlu, M. (2008) 'Comment' posted alongside the painting, 'The Seraff – a doubtful coin'. On *Lure of the East* exhibition, 4 June to 31 August London: Tate Britain,

Yin, J. (2008) Constructing the Other: a critical reading of *The Joy Luck Club.* In M. K. Asante, Y. Miike, and J. Yin (eds), *The Global Intercultural Communication Reader.* New York: Routledge, pp. 123–41.

Young, R. (2006) The cultural politics of hybridity. In B. Ashcroft, G. Griffiths, and H. Tifflin (eds), *The Post-Colonial Studies Reader.* London: Routledge, pp. 158–62. (First published 1995, *Colonial Desire,* Routledge.)

Zhu, H. (2008) Duelling languages, duelling values: codeswitching in bilingual intergenerational conflict talk in diasporic families. *Journal of Pragmatics*, 40 (10): 1799–816.

Zimmerman, A. L. (2006) *Innocents Abroad*. Cambridge, MA: Harvard University Press.

Index